#15

3

KENNETH McNALLY

Olly McGilloway was born in the Waterside, Derry, in 1936. He was educated at Waterside Boys' School and the Christian Brothers' 'Brow of the Hill' School. After considering entering the priesthood, he studied at London University, University College Dublin and the New University of Ulster. He established the first degree course for nurses in Ireland at the New University of Ulster, where he was a senior lecturer and director of studies; he retired from teaching in 1991. His broadcasting career began with Radio Foyle in 1980, when he presented a weekly ten-minute piece on angling and nature for the *Afternoon Show*; this eventually expanded into the *Nature's Way* series, based on the people, wildlife and countryside of Derry, Donegal and Tyrone. In the years that followed he presented numerous natural history programmes for Radio Foyle and Radio Ulster, including *Final Frontiers* and *Along the Faughanside*. He achieved huge critical and popular success with the television series *McGilloway's Way*, produced by Derry's Northland Film Productions, and broadcast on both UTV and RTE; it won a *Belfast Telegraph* EMA Award in 1994 for most entertaining television programme. He also produced and presented the Channel 4 educational series *A Sense of Tradition*. He regularly contributed articles and features on both nursing and wildlife issues for a broad range of newspapers and journals, including a weekly column for the *Irish News*. His published books include *Along the Faughanside* (1985), *Nursing and Spiritual Care* (editor, 1986), and *Greyhood: The Year of the Mink* (1988); *Gaston's Glynnes,* a collaboration with wildlife artist Roy Gaston, will be published in 1994.

Olly McGilloway had just finalised his script for *McGilloway's Ireland* when he died suddenly in May 1994. He is survived by his wife Elizabeth and five children.

OLLY McGILLOWAY

McGilloway's Ireland

Olly McGilloway

PHOTOGRAPHS

Richard T. Mills
Éamon de Buitléar
Dermot Donohue
Paul Kay
Kenneth McNally

To - Alison, Vince + Julia

From - Elizabeth McGilloway   Best Wishes

THE
BLACKSTAFF
PRESS
BELFAST

ACKNOWLEDGEMENTS

Blackstaff Press is grateful to the Ulster Bank
for its financial assistance with this book.

First published in 1994 by
The Blackstaff Press Limited
3 Galway Park, Dundonald, Belfast BT16 0AN, Northern Ireland

© Text, Olly McGilloway, 1994
© Photographs, the photographers, 1994
Typeset by Textflow Services Limited

Printed in Northern Ireland by W & G Baird Limited

A CIP catalogue record for this book
is available from the British Library

ISBN 0-85640-540-X

in memory of
Olly McGilloway
1936–1994

to Elizabeth

CONTENTS

Dunfanaghy seen from Horn Head,
County Donegal

INTRODUCTION

For a time every wild plant and creature has its place in the world. A butterfly may live for a few hours, a tree may live for a few hundred years. For all plants, insects, fishes, amphibians, birds and mammals, life is part of a continuum, so smooth and easy-going that we have to watch closely to begin to understand nature's way. This book tells the story of the lives of a number of wild plants and creatures which are commonly found in Ireland. Many of these wildlife species are easily seen in gardens, nearby laneways, along roadsides, on waste ground, and about the local countryside. It is a book for everyone interested in nature. It is for the person who likes to explore out of the way places, or for the person who is quite satisfied with a stroll through the park. Although careful walking is the best way to get to know the countryside, driving is now the usual means of getting from one place to another and, in reality, most people have neither the freedom nor time to ramble. For the overworked, the elderly and the disabled, the car has become the only means of escape from the endless noise and busyness of towns and places of work. But once there, out in rural landscape, the motorists can stretch their legs, relax, and watch and listen to their hearts' content.

I grew up beside the River Foyle, which runs through the city of Derry. In those days a few minutes' walk brought me into lovely open country. And through all the seasons for over fifty years I have walked the countryside learning nature's way. At first stimulated by my father's knowledge and love of wildlife, and then encouraged by Irish and British writers, poets, artists, ministers of religion and naturalists, who helped me to achieve a broad view of nature, I have looked at sea, land and sky, all the time getting to know the ways of wild plants and creatures, and taking in the moods of the seasons and many wonderful places.

When I was five years old I began learning to flyfish, and I caught many brown trout. I was also interested in sticklebacks and minnows, stone loaches and elvers – I caught them too. I caught the tiny fish with a home-made net and put them in a jam jar. Trying to catch butterflies, bees, wasps and their mimics, I also learned about the stinging nettle, the dog rose, and the bramble. I learned

DERMOT DONOHUE

more about the bramble when I gathered blackberries for jam. When I wanted
to give my mother a present, I gathered bluebells, cuckoo flowers and primroses; and I showed my young sister how to make daisy chains. When I was
old enought to watch birds nesting, I would lie still and observe the behaviour
of parent birds – that was how I discovered the very hard-to-find nests, in holes
in the ground or at the end of a long tunnel through tough grass. At ten years
old my father showed me badger setts, otter holts, the dens of stoats, rabbit
warrens, foxes out of earth, hares, pipistrelles, and taught me many other
things: the looks, flights, and sounds of birds; and the kinds of leaves and seeds
to bring home to the canaries, and how goldfinches, greenfinches, and linnets
could be crossbred with canaries – an illegal practice nowadays. By the time I
was twelve, I was using all my free time noticing new plants and searching for
insects, birds, wild mammals, frogs and fishes. I had a beginning notion of how
all of these things needed each other, and I knew the best times to find them,
and where they were likely to be.

Knockfola, Bunbeg, County Donegal

This compelling interest has remained with me throughout life, and I make
no excuses for spending so much of my time wandering the countryside
looking at newts, daisies, lichens, and other wildlife which many people take
for granted, and sometimes abuse. Their importance and beauty apart, our
wild plants and creatures are very good company. With them, I never feel
alone. I can spend hours full of pleasure and interest studying them. Throughout Ireland and Britain countless other lovers and students of nature know
similar feelings.

For the past ten years I have lived between the mountains and the Atlantic
Ocean, on the outskirts of the delightful, tiny village of Dunfanaghy. The back
of the house is slightly more than two hundred metres away from an inlet of
Sheephaven Bay, a truly beautiful place. A rough pasture and a narrow fair-
way of Dunfanaghy Golf Club lie between the back of the house and the inlet:
a long beach, with good dunes and high rocky headlands. When the tide ebbs,
I can easily walk across the inlet and stroll up braes of heather and gorse,
where foxes live, and then climb steep, tiny meadows, where sheep graze, to

the top of Horn Head, one of Ireland's most spectacular sea cliffs. The front of the house faces the big, broad mountain of Muckish, or Mucais, which means 'hogback'. As a raven flies, Muckish stands about five kilometres away, and between the house and Muckish there is typical Irish countryside. A ten minute walk in any direction brings me to many different wildlife habitats; a ten minute drive brings me to remote wilderness places. All the time, I see and hear wildlife.

With clean, fresh air, and beautiful scenery, and so many wild things nearby, I am very fortunate to live in the countryside of Donegal. However, I have enjoyed similar conditions in Britain. It is interesting to note that despite two hundred years of progressive industrial change, with towns, factories, power stations, coal mines, motorways and railways seemingly all over the place, and an increasing human population, some 85 per cent of the island of Britain remains rural. For the most part, the rural landscapes and the wildlife of Ireland and Britain are similar: our fauna and flora are of woodland ancestry, and the wildlife of our inland waters, coastlines, and the sea are the same. I sit here writing in a room in the north of Ireland. Even so, with its ancient hills, and basaltic plateau, drumlins, eskars, lakes, rivers, woodlands, raised and blanket bogs, shores, headlands, sea loughs, the north of Ireland gives us a composition of everything rural that the British Isles has to offer. There are

Gartan Lake, County Donegal

many places where cloud, hill and valley, forest, lake, stream, meadow, copse, scrub, rock, bog and sea are so close together that every kilometre of road always opens the eye to something different and beautiful; and the view from every hilltop of the closeness of water, land and sky is humbling. These features are common throughout Ireland, Scotland, Wales, and most of England. But before all else, there is the enduring nature of the most exposed places of both islands: living with the moods of the Atlantic. Hundreds of kilometres of our coastlines front the ocean and cope with furious gales and heavy rains, yet benefit from the warmth of the Gulf Stream, with inland places soon experiencing similar conditions. Unlike most of mainland Europe, our close relationship with the ocean affords us that most pleasing sight of ever-changing cloudy skies, and purple, orange, and deep red curtains before the setting sun.

Returning to our cliffs and their shores, we find countless birds, many of them nesting – gulls, terns, cormorants, divers, rock doves, dunlins, eider, fulmars, gannets, and so on. We find common seals and grey seals breeding, and competing with fishermen, who demand culls because they claim that the seals not only take salmon out of nets but that they actually herd runs of fish into the nets. The inshore waters also host sea trout and many different finned fishes, sharks and whales; and these waters hide wrecks of ships that are very old. Still numerous are crabs, barnacles, and shelled molluscs such as cockle, mussel, oyster; and empty shells – banded, nut, necklace, Faroe sunset. We find marine worms like the ragworm and lugworm. There are sandhoppers, bristletails, isopods, springtails and other small seashore creatures. Also, urchins and starfish. There are jellyfish, and the beadlet and tube anemones, dead man's fingers, sponges, sea squirt, and other plant-like sea animals. Also found are carrageen, dulse, laver, kelp, eelgrass, marram. And, of course, the estuaries have swans, herons, ducks, and waders; and the sand dunes keep snails and many moths, including the cinnabar and six-spot burnet; also

DERMOT DONOHUE

Muckish, County Donegal

lapwings, pipits, larks, rabbits, hares, and a wide range of flora.

Just a few miles inland are the ancient folds of the mountains and the high ground, some 500 million years old, and their rock debris. Together these provide different soils, calcareous and acidic, and a splendid variety of plant life in the valleys and glens. And from the rains down mountain and hillside, rivers start: some running very fast to the ocean, others dallying inland. There are deep lakes and good woodland, marsh, drystone walls, and meadows competing with bogland and heath. About such places there are many aquatic and non-aquatic insects or invertebrates, birds, and at least twenty-eight different wild mammals.

This book has twelve chapters, representing the months of the year. Opening each chapter I give a very brief, but general, description of natural events especially characteristic of the month. Simply named January, February, and so on, the chapters comprise accounts of wildlife individuals, selected from the worlds of flora and fauna. Weights and measures are in metric, except when fish are described: here I give the still popular imperial measure of pound weight. Throughout I use the most up-to-date taxonomy or classification and, at the same time, make use of well-known local names, such as 'bacon-and-eggs', as well as its English name, common bird's-foot trefoil, and Latin name, *Lotus corniculatus.*

Bearing in mind the effects of the Atlantic seaboard with its maximum rainfall, exposure, range of temperature, and the fact that the island of Ireland does not extend through a sufficient range of latitude to show any marked difference between north and south, but with a greater divergence between the west and east of the country, I carefully describe the behaviours of wildlife individuals in time and place. I give the usual month for plants coming into leaf, flower and fruit, for eggs hatching, for birds migrating, and for mammals giving birth, moulting, and leading their own lives.

JANUARY

After Christmas Day, while hill farmers fear for their ewes, and hooded crows look on, foxes hunt rabbits across the moorland. With January, snow falls and Suffolk lambs are born indoors; and the threatening crows are trapped in fixed cages and killed. The foxes are killed too. Many have come down from the hillside to mate in earths in woodland. Eyes glowing in the dark, lamped with orange or red filters and squealed at – fetched across meadow, from hillside and woodland, by contrivances that make sounds like hurt rabbits – the foxes are easily shot dead. Ferrets chase rabbits into poachers' nets. Feral mink are trapped and illegally drowned in cages.

Heavy floodwater cleans river beds. Trout and salmon complete spawning; spent or kelt hen fish shelter in lodges, or lies; the kelt cock fish are washed down river and drowned in spate water. Sometimes hooking spent fish, salmon anglers use large lures called spinners, plugs, and tube flies, in heavy, cold water. And while salmon struggle, deadly pike freely hunt slow-moving waters.

Still and solitary, the heron seems reluctant to leave the river's edge. Migratory thrushes, swans, geese, and ducks continue to arrive for food and shelter. The thrushes arrive to feed on berries; the other birds visit to feed on the mudflats rich in worms, shellfish, eelgrass, algae, and nutrients from entire river systems. When the tide comes in, the birds fly off to nearby higher ground; then it is the turn of fishes and shore creatures to search the rich mud. Still the ducks fly in; and on windy days at dawn and just before twilight wildfowlers kill the ducks.

On waste ground and roadsides, heliotropes fade, their vanilla-like fragrance gone. Woodland birds visit gardens for shelter, and helpful people feed them. Red squirrels and grey squirrels are welcomed into gardens as well. In the woodland, while the last showing of orange-peel fungus keeps parts of the floor colourful and the thin leathery brackets of the young many-zoned fungus are alive and glowing on a fallen branch, the hard black cramp ball looks unpleasant attacking a dead ash. Still, nearby, in pale sunshine, the smooth trunk of the healthy wild cherry tree gleams chestnut-brown; its branches showing grey-brown twigs with attractive clusters of bright, brown pointed buds on very short sideshoots. And then pretty snowdrops begin to grow stronger in January's hour of return light.

The Ulster Way at Drumbeg,
County Down
NORTHERN IRELAND TOURIST BOARD

BIRDS IN THE GARDEN

The north wind doth blow,
And we shall have snow,
And what will poor Robin do then,
Poor thing?

While the cold and damp threats of January keep us warm and comfortable indoors, perhaps looking out our windows, many wild birds will benefit from our interest and help. Out and about – without any shelter, and food very hard to find – our loveliest creatures, still wearing the warm colours of spring, summer and autumn, visit our gardens and back yards seeking our help. We can get to know and admire them. And we can save their lives. Most wild birds, including soft-bills like robins, can find food during November and most of December; but the New Year brings disaster. A period of crisis follows snow and ice, covering natural food. Woodland birds like the friendly robin, handsome chaffinch, canary-like greenfinch, the agile tits – even town birds like the cheeky house sparrow – become wet and hungry and very cold, and will collapse and die during harsh weather. This is to be expected, I suppose. Yet I'm sure we should try to help them.

Years ago I lived beside a man who replaced his front lawn, and plants in good soil, with concrete. It was a strange thing to do. Anyway, he soon wished he had kept his old garden. That following winter, when he ruefully commented on the surprising numbers and varieties of woodland birds using soil beds and shrubs in neighbours' gardens – while he could only entice starlings, pigeons, rooks, and a few sparrows – he concluded that his garden was too artificial. Yet all gardens are artificially created places. They vary with location, and the taste and skill of their owners. Well-tended or uncultivated, all gardens should provide food and shelter for birds. For example, soil beds provide worms and insects; trees and shrubs offer shelter from rain, wind and snow, small trees also supply fruit and insects – but much more can be made available during January and the damp, chilly days ahead.

Erect a bird table, a simple structure: open or roofed, a platform on a sturdy post will do nicely. This is the usual and safe way of offering food to many of our birds. If possible, place the table near a high bush or a tree branch. Wild birds are very careful, cautious creatures, so – to help them to watch out for the cat – a bush or a branch will allow them to perch and look about before approaching the food. In a small back yard a number of the birds will perch on the clothesline, away from the wall. Because birds feed differently, it is helpful to use a range of feeding devices. The blackbird and chaffinch seem to be happy either on the bird table or on the ground. The dunnock and the thrush like to feed on the food spilled from the table. Some birds love to test their agility while eating. Suet on a string, or peanuts in a hanging feeder, will very quickly attract the tits, house sparrows, and greenfinches. Sensibly located, inconvenient for mice, rats, squirrels, cats and dogs, use simple shelves and trays as well; and use the window. It is possible to buy bird feeders that can be fixed to the windowsill, glass, or frame. And, if you're fortunate enough to have flowerbeds, turn the soil every day – especially during frosty weather.

About food: breadcrumbs will entice house sparrows, starlings, jackdaws, and street (feral) pigeons, and slices of bread will attract gulls and rooks; but an assortment of morsels will fetch many colourful and very interesting companions. Do not give the birds salted peanuts or any kind of salty food: it is very harmful. Do not give them peel of orange and lemon or banana skin, and dried foods should always be thoroughly soaked. Still, the birds may be given a great range of foodstuffs. To mention a few: they enjoy ordinary peanuts, suet, fats, and dairy products such as cheese will appeal to most of them. Other items include meat scraps, seeds, boiled potatoes, finely chopped hard-boiled eggs, raw or boiled rice, crumbled biscuits, oatmeal, peanut butter, pears, raisins, chopped apples, figs, the white of coconut. Watch what the birds are eating, make them a cake; give them fresh water as well. Many birds eat both fats and seeds. Most of them like suet: it is very nourishing, and is not liable to freeze; it is cheap, and can be tied to a post or a branch in such a way that cats and mice have difficulty stealing it. And, to keep squirrels from taking it, suet can be melted or cut into small pieces and put in tiny holes and fine cracks in walls and trees; it can also be put in coconut shells.

Put the food out early in the morning and, again, in the mid-afternoon. The breakfast is very welcome and necessary after a cold night's roost, while the afternoon meal prepares the birds for another cold night. Once you decide to feed the birds, feed them regularly and try not to let them down. They quickly learn to depend on you and many are likely to abandon seeking food in other distant places. Suddenly to disappoint the birds, especially during very cold weather, will cause many of them to perish. Keep restocking your supplies and you will enjoy plenty of colourful and delightful company during January and remaining winter. From mid-March into beginning April, let them find their own food.

Here, I write a few words about our most common visitors to the garden – the robin, tits, chaffinch, greenfinch, thrush, and wren. I describe the other birds when they begin nesting.

ROBIN
Erithacus rubecula

No matter what garden or dark woodland I visit during January, a robin, or ruddock, as it is sometimes known, always welcomes me. Flitting to a nearby branch, it will settle to see what I'm going to do. Trusting and familiar, with face and throat and breast warm and glowing, and with its large shiny eyes and engaging curiosity, the robin is the only wild creature that comes near me – all the others hurry away. For me, it is a most companionable little bird; it is very interesting too.

Stories about the bird predate written history and, more recently, centre on Christ's crucifixion. From pagan times, legend tells that the robin flew up to the sun and down to hell to fetch fire for man, and it singed itself red. In Christian times it plucked out the sharpest thorn that was piercing Christ's brow, and as it carried the thorn a drop of blood fell onto the robin's breast and dyed it red. Such stories have caused the bird to be admired and loved, and bad luck – even disease – will affect any person who kills or cages a robin, or disturbs its nest.

Robin

A native and resident bird and a member of the thrush family, the robin is a successful survivor. From tip of bill to tip of tail, it measures 13–15 cm. Hen robin or cock bird, both dress the same, and equally territorial, will readily chase any other robin which dares arrive in an already claimed garden or patch of woodland. In contrast to its long association with peace and good will, the robin's attitude towards its own kind is a threatening one, and the red breast is worn as a danger signal. Its seeming friendliness to humans is another example of selfish behaviour – to do with feeding. Some say that the bird sees the human being as a ground disturber: something that will make natural food readily available. Freshly turned earth will certainly fetch the robin, and other sensible birds as well. In wood, hedgerow, parkland, garden and back yard, the robin redbreast still delights us.

Other visitors to the garden include the tits. Agile and acrobatic and very active, hardly stopping still for a moment, fluttering about the bird table and hanging feeder, and often hanging upside down repeatedly glancing over shoulder while busily pecking, the great tit, bluetit, and coal tit deserve our attention.

GREAT TIT
Parus major

The biggest, brightest and noisiest of all the tits, the great tit measures 14 cm and appears black and yellow. The strong black stripe from chin to vent easily distinguishes this bird from the others. But close observation will also reveal its bluish-grey and green upperparts and various white markings, moving all together, as it feeds furiously. It loves nuts and seeds and is very skilled in finding ways to reach them. If the bird likes the garden, it might come back in late March and build its cup-shaped nest there. It likes holes in trees, walls, banks of earth, and old drainpipes, but it will also use a nest box.

RICHARD T. MILLS

Great tits

BLUETIT
Parus caeruleus

Fluttering about like a butterfly, and very clever indeed, the bluetit – often called tomtit – is the most common and familiar of these little birds. Attracted by a garden's supply of suet, fat, and nuts in feeders, it is often the first bird to find such food. Smaller than the great tit and more fidgety, the bluetit measures 11–12 cm and looks blue all over. Its crown and wings and tail are blue, the underparts and the back are yellow. It also looks bad-tempered, with white cheeks, dark eye-stripe, chin strap and bib. Away from the hanging suet and peanuts, it uses the bird table; and this was the bird clever enough to pierce milk-bottle tops. It will make good use of water baths. Like the great tit, the bluetit might come back to the garden in late March to build its cup-shaped nest in a nest box.

COAL TIT
Parus ater

A true titmouse, smaller than the others at 10.5–11 cm, the coal tit is the last in the pecking order. Dominated by the great tit and bluetit in behaviour and colour, the coal tit appears shy and appealing. It uses the table and hanging feeder, but often takes spilled seeds on the ground. With black cap, buff underparts, grey or olive-blue upperparts, and a white nape patch that distinguishes this bird from the other tits, the delightful little coal tit enjoys being about gardens; and, in late March, it will build its cup-shaped nest in a hole in a tree.

On branch, bird table or hanging food, the tits are the star performers in the garden bird show.

Greenfinch

RICHARD T. MILLS

GREENFINCH
Carduelis chloris

With the looks of a canary, and a short conical, pale bill – heavy and powerful enough to crack seeds – *Carduelis chloris* is a typical finch. Also called the green linnet, this is a lovely-looking bird, green and yellow, with a flashing forked tail. It is very busy and acrobatic – active and aggressive at the bird table, and competing with the house sparrows and tits for the most difficult-to-get peanuts.

Greenfinches flock with their own kind, and several will arrive in the garden at the same time. The male bird is 14–15 cm and very handsome with olive-green upperparts and a grey patch above the distinctive bright yellow along the edge of each wing; there is also a bright yellow patch on either side at the base of the tail. The female looks like the male, but she is smaller and browner, without the grey patch on the wing, and she shows soft streaking on her breast.

A resident bird, which normally lives in tall hedges about farmland and woodland edge – and in April–June builds cup-shaped nests in bushes – the greenfinch loves visiting gardens for peanuts and sunflower seeds.

CHAFFINCH
Fringilla coelebs

The most common of our finches, found in a wide variety of habitats, this is another attractive bird, and like the greenfinch and other finches, the chaffinch has a stout bill for cracking seeds. Measuring 14.5–16 cm, the male bird is very striking. There is no mistaking his cheerful pink front and grey head. His grey crown and nape, pink cheeks, breast and upper belly, and his obvious white wing bar and shoulder patch make the cock bird noticeable.

The female, greenish-brown above and paler below, wears the same wing and tail markings as the male. Much less striking than the male, she is, however, refined and lovely; and in April–May her neat cup-shaped nests in the forks of hawthorns are marvellous to see.

Once regarded as one of our most numerous birds, the chaffinch is now less common. Still a regular winter visitor to the garden, it makes very good use of the bird table, and also searches the ground for seeds and other food scraps.

SONG THRUSH
Turdus philomelos

An alert, brown and white bird, with a buff breast and black speckles, and usually seen searching the lawn, the song thrush is unmistakable. However, even though it is not a tiny bird – at 22–24 cm, slightly bigger than a starling and slightly smaller than a blackbird – the song thrush needs special attention. In January and through winter, thrush populations in Ireland and Britain can suffer a high level of mortality during severe weather. Surveys on British birds show the thrush to be one of the birds most adversely affected – probably due to the nature of their diet. In their normal habitats they eat snails, earthworms, a variety of insects, other invertebrates, vegetable matter as well: soft fruits such as the cherry, various berries, and seeds.

A study carried out by Dr David Snow of Oxford revealed marked seasonal changes in the diet of song thrushes, mainly associated with the seasonal changes in the abundance of various food items. Earthworms are regularly taken from December till June, when worms are particularly numerous near the surface of the soil. When caterpillars drop from plants to pupate in the soil, they are taken for periods in May and June. Through July and August, and during cold spells in winter when other foods are scarce, snails are eaten: the importance of snails in the diet seems to be connected with scarcity of usual foods rather than an abundance of snails.

The ability of song thrushes to break open snail shells at 'anvils' is their best-known habit. After cracking open the shell by repeated hammering against a stone or other hard surface, the thrush extracts the flesh; then before it is eaten the flesh is wiped on the ground to remove both slime and any pieces of shell attached to it. Zoologist Desmond Morris found that song thrushes hunt snails by systematically searching a small plot of vegetation. When a snail is found and broken open and eaten at a nearby anvil, the bird returns to continue foraging in the same area – and may partially clear the small plot of its snails. During any particular spell of feeding, the thrush returns time after time to the same anvil. When the bird moves to another plot, it will select a new anvil. Another interesting finding was that thrushes seldom break shells near their nest – probably to prevent attracting predators.

Although territories are temporarily abandoned during severe weather, when the birds have to search widely for food, resident thrushes are territorial throughout the year. Territories are established during late autumn and most of them are occupied by males, resident birds and immigrants. Yet even immigrant song thrushes temporarily vacate their new territories. Often, especially during harsh weather, they may roost together at night, and return to their territorial attitude during the day.

Through January and remaining winter, thrushes come into our gardens for shelter and food. They make good use of shrubs like holly bushes, and they search the lawns and flowerbeds. For their sake, as well as the robin's, beds of soil should be frequently turned; and although the song thrushes may appear nervous at the bird table, or taking seeds on the ground, they are sure to return for good food.

WREN
Troglodytes troglodytes

With whirring wings over short distances, flying directly from one clump of low vegetation to the next, the wren hurries mouse-like through the garden's bushes. Easily recognised by its flight, small size (9–10 cm), and cocked

tail, the wren – an insect eater – is badly affected by severe winters. Yet in fable, mythology, and folklore, this tiny bird is probably more famous than the robin redbreast.

In fable it is the 'king of all birds'. When all the birds came together to choose their king, there was much dispute as to how it should be done. But the eagle, so strong and fierce, compelled the assembly to agree to the test he proposed. 'What raises us above all other creatures?' the eagle exclaimed. 'The power of flying! We must choose as king the bird that flies highest!' The eagle soon soared above them all and went up to an amazing height before his strength was exhausted. Then a wren, which had been perching on the great bird's back, flew a little higher. So the tiny wren became king.

Wren

The wren was also the Druids' sacred bird. In Ireland it was known as Fionn's doctor, the bird representing the sleeping lord.

In reality the bird has been the object of much abuse, especially at Christmastime when wrens were hunted and killed by Wren Boys on St Stephen's Day. In places where the custom was observed – as far apart as the south of France and Dingle in southwest Ireland – men dressed up, called at houses, and asked for money to 'bury the wren', which was carried in a box – its tiny coffin – or attached to a branch of gorse. Arriving at a house, they sang:

> The wren, the wren, the king of all birds,
> On St Stephen's Day he was caught in the furze,
> Although he was little his family was great,
> Rise up young lady and give us a trate.
> Up with the kettle and down with the pan,
> A penny or tuppence to bury the wran.

In 1845 the custom of hunting the wren was forbidden by proclamation of the mayor of Cork, and it is now an illegal practice. Yet, both the origin and the purpose of the tradition remain unexplained. According to Lady Wilde in 1896, the wren was mortally hated by the Irish, for on one occasion when Irish troops were approaching to attack Cromwell's army, the wrens perched and tapped on the Irish drums. These tapping sounds wakened the English soldiers who then killed the Irish troops. For that reason, she says, the Irish people hunted the wren and taught their children to stab it to death with thorns. According to Padraic O'Farrell in 1989, the wren betrayed Saint Stephen and for that reason the bird was hunted on the day after Christmas, killed, displayed on a bush and paraded around the countryside.

Wrens hide in our gardens and will accept grated cheese sprinkled over leaf litter. Sometimes they will take seeds from the table. And, although in April–May the wren can build a beautiful dome-shaped nest in many places, it might use an ordinary nest box.

BIRDS IN THE FIELD

A field in January hosts many different birds, but the most noticeable are the redwings, fieldfares, the mistle thrush, and the rooks.

REDWING
Turdus iliacus

Three years ago I wrote: 'At 2.35 p.m., Sunday October 27, the first redwings of the year arrived in the field behind the house. I watched them coming across the golf links. With flight feathers spread slightly forward and twisting under the force of the downbeat, the birds flew fast and straight toward me; but they found difficulty keeping low. They landed together only twenty yards from the kitchen window.'

From as far away as Siberia the redwings – about thirty of them – had crossed Europe, the North Sea, passed Inishtrahull, the island of the strand of blood, hurried over Malin Head and the Fanad peninsula, then Melmore Head, before veering left to take a shortcut across Breaghy Head, to pick up speed along Sheephaven's Killyhoey strand and over the golf links to reach the field behind my house. I was excited for several reasons. From the land

Redwing

of the sable, elk and polar bear, these birds would be the first visitors to accept my berries and seeds, and they would be nearby for Christmas Day and the remaining winter as well.

The birds arrived during the very first day of our wintertime, when we put the clock back; and two hours after they arrived an easterly wind – the coldest, cutting air of the year – caused me to shiver and hurry indoors. The redwings had arrived before the cold. They obviously knew what they were doing.

From northern Europe and Iceland, the redwing has been described as the northern counterpart of the song thrush. This observation is acceptable. Both birds belong to the thrush family and they are about the same size – 20–24 cm. But the redwing's upperparts are a much darker brown, and the breast and belly are more heavily streaked than the underparts of the song thrush; and the redwing has a noticeably shorter tail. The birdwatcher will also clearly see the visitor's pale eye-stripe, the red patch on its side against the closed wing and on the underwing in flight. The song thrush doesn't require these adornments.

Looking out the window, even without much light, other differences are obvious. In the field a song thrush is usually alone, alert but confident, looking bright, upstanding, and simply hopping over familiar ground. The redwing appears dull, and its movements seem nervous. After every three or four modest hops, it stops and quickly looks about before lowering its bill to eat the same kinds of seeds as the ignored seeds now lying behind it. Unsure of itself in a strange place, the redwing likes to have friendly birds nearby. Seldom without the company of ten or twenty other redwings, it often joins fieldfares. It is a lovely bird and it will stay about the field for the rest of winter.

FIELDFARE
Turdus pilaris

During the mid-afternoon of Sunday 5 December 1993, I watched more than ten fieldfares lighting on a high wire. After a few moments they flew down into a field. These very attractive birds had just arrived from Scandinavia. Within a week snow followed them.

In movement the fieldfare is a typical thrush: it perches openly, walks, hops, quickly takes off, and has a strong and powerful flight. It is 24–27 cm and has lovely markings. The head, nape, and rump are dove-grey; the yellow bill shows a black tip, and the facial markings leave the bird looking cross; the back and wings are chestnut-brown; the tail is black; and the warm buffy-yellow breast and underparts are densely speckled. The dove-grey rump and the white underwing are conspicuous in

Fieldfare

flight. The male and female are similar and stay with us until the close of March.

Fieldfares are flocking birds, often sharing their feeding places with redwings. They like open ground, especially large fields with hedges. They take worms and grubs from soft ground, and feed on haws and other berries about hedges and copses.

MISTLE THRUSH
Turdus viscivorus

This thrush has the name 'storm cock' for its defiant singing, often in a gale, and is famous for defending its territory and nest. It is fearless with other birds, attacking larger birds, but it fears humans. It is bigger (26–28 cm) than our other resident thrush, the song thrush. Both birds are brownish above and speckled underneath, but the mistle thrush has paler and greyer upperparts, the tail is relatively long and it shows white margins – overall it has a greyish look. When it flies the underwings seem white, not buffish as in the song thrush, and the flight is undulating rather than direct. Its flight call is a harsh chatter.

The mistle thrush eats a variety of berries. The name 'mistle' derives from a belief that in the mistletoe area of France mistletoe berries formed a part of the bird's winter diet. It will also eat snails, worms and insects. It lives about woodland edges and in open countryside with scattered trees. It is also found in wild and remote areas with little cover, and about parkland, orchards, and large gardens. Since its first appearance in Ireland in 1800, the mistle thrush has become a fairly common resident; and curiously there is a heavy winter immigration from Britain.

ROOK
Corvus frugilegus
With a bare white face patch, thinnish bill, all black plumage with a purple gloss, and long thigh feathers with a 'trousered' look, the rook is easily identified. It is a common bird (size, 45 cm), and is gregarious at all times, but it is very difficult to understand. At this time of year rooks crowd the field outside my window, and they are certainly not feeding on wireworms and leather-jackets. Sometimes the field is black with rooks, many of them stabbing the earth, obliquely, with beaks slightly open; others just stand looking at each other; a number strut about, and on occasions hitherto stationary birds start hopping, using half-opened wings. Then like large black leaves, they all rise into the air to tumble, dive, and roll spectacularly with the strong Atlantic breezes. And they all land again and resume their stabbing, strutting and hopping.

Rook

Down through the years people have recalled observing a circle of rooks – on the ground – with a single rook standing in the centre. After much cawing, a number of the rooks from the circle set upon the solitary rook in the centre and kill it. The numbers of rooks in such a circle may be tens to hundreds. This kind of assembly has been called a 'rook parliament' and is explained in human terms: the rook community is holding court and, having found the defendant guilty, they execute the bird; or it may be a compassionate killing, a ritualised slaughter of a sick bird, to protect the community against infection or contamination – and to spare the bird misery. These are human notions. In truth, nobody knows why rooks behave in such ways. I have yet to see such an event, so I keep watching the rooks in the field outside my window.

Nobody really knows why so many rooks flock together. Many of us have seen fields black with rooks and every nearby tree holding rows of them. 'Safety in numbers' is an expression often used to explain their gregarious behaviour. Finding a fledgling rook on the ground and being threatened by scores of adult birds, I am inclined to accept that protection against predators is one reason for their communal behaviour. However, humans are the birds' worst enemies: despite the superstition 'kill a crow and the devil will know', people still hold rook shoots to control numbers. I once heard that all members of the crow family grow alarmed and fly off when anything resembling a gun is pointed at them – this is nonsense.

BIRDS ON THE MUDFLATS

During January there is plently of birdlife about the mudflats of our estuaries and loughs. These muddy and marshy places are very rich, containing worms, shellfish, plant life and the nutrients drained from river systems and returned with the tide. Because of this, every autumn into spring, great flocks of water birds – among them, migrants from breeding grounds in cold, faraway places – visit us for shelter and food. About the mudflats thousands of waders and wildfowl use bills of different shapes and sizes: the very long downward curved, or straight plunging bills of the curlew and godwit; the stout bill of the oystercatcher, able to catch worms and open a shell; the medium-sized bill of the redshank searching for shallowly burrowing spionids, tellins, amphipods; the small-billed waders like the plover picking up surface fauna; the migrant swans and geese grazing in nearby fields.

Here is a selection of birds on the mudflats.

WIGEON
Anas penelope
From Iceland and northeast Europe, very gregarious birds, at times gathering into huge flocks, they feed on grass, eelgrass and aquatic vegetation. The drake has a chestnut head, yellow crown, grey underparts, with a white wing patch; female rufous and barred above and below. 43–48 cm.

TEAL
Anas crecca
A resident, but there is a huge immigration through autumn from mainland Europe. They feed on aquatic vegetation and at high tide they move to nearby fields to feed on seeds. The drake has a distinctive chestnut and green head; female mottled brown and buff. 34–38 cm.

MUTE SWAN
Cygnus olor
Resident, weighing up to 18 kg, one of the world's heaviest birds, easily identified by the characteristic serpentine curve of the neck, and orange bill with black base. It feeds on aquatic vegetation. 145–160 cm.

WHOOPER SWAN
Cygnus cygnus
From Iceland, it forms medium-sized flocks with other swans. In flight it makes loud trumpeting 'whoops!' It feeds on aquatic vegetation, grass, grain, and roots. It usually holds its neck straight, and has a black bill with yellow base. 145–160 cm.

BEWICK'S SWAN
Cygnus bewickii
From Siberian tundra, and Holland, this is the smallest of our three swans. Noisy calls are honk-like. It forms huge flocks and feeds on

RICHARD T. MILLS

Oystercatchers

aquatic vegetation, grass, grain, and roots. Shorter, curved neck, with
black bill and truncated yellow base. 116–128 cm.

PINK-FOOTED GOOSE
Anser brachyrhynchus
From Iceland, a small 'grey' goose with strong flight; very vocal in
flight with a high-pitched 'unk unk!' Feeds on grass and grain.
Reddish brown head, pink legs, and pink band on black beak.
61–76 cm.

WHITE-FRONTED GOOSE
Anser albifrons
From Greenland, this is the most widespread though not the most
numerous of the 'grey' geese. Its flight is strong, powerful and direct.
Flight calls are more musical than those of other geese. It feeds on
grass, cereals, and potatoes. White forehead, orange legs and barred
belly. 65–76 cm.

GREYLAG GOOSE
Anser anser
From Iceland, and the ancestor of the domesticated farmyard goose,
the greylag is the largest and most frequently seen 'grey' goose. Very
vocal – 'aahng-ung-ung!' – with strong and powerful flight, it feeds
on grass, grain, and roots. Large head and orange bill, with pink legs.
76–89 cm.

BARNACLE GOOSE
Branta leucopsis
From northeast Greenland, a very attractive 'black' goose. Some say
the bird was given this name because seafarers once thought that it
hatched from the clinging barnacle shell. Its flight is strong and
powerful and the calls are a mixture of dog-like barks, yaps and
growls. It feeds on grass. Neck and breast are black, wings and back
are grey, face is white with black crown. 58–69 cm.

PALE-BELLIED BRENT GOOSE
Branta bernicla hrota
From Greenland, this is the smallest of the 'black' geese. It is gregarious; the flight is strong and powerful and its voice makes a grumbling sound. It feeds on eelgrass, cereals, and grass. Pale belly, black breast and neck, with small white neck flash. 56–61 cm.

CURLEW
Numenius arquata
Resident large shore bird with long legs and very long, decurved bill. Upperparts buff and brown, underparts heavily streaked, in flight it shows a white V extending up its back. It has a long, mournful, 'coorlu!' call, and eats worms, molluscs and crabs. 51–61 cm.

BAR-TAILED GODWIT
Limosa lapponica
From Lapland and Siberia, a large wader with long legs and a long, thin, upturned bill. It feeds on worms and molluscs. In winter, upperparts are buffy grey, streaked black, with white underparts. 36–40 cm.

RINGED PLOVER
Charadrius hiaticula
Resident breeder on sandy and shingly shores, and is found on mudflats all year round. Easily identified by its black breastband. It feeds on worms and other invertebrates. 18–20 cm.

TURNSTONE
Arenaria interpres
From Greenland and northern and Arctic Europe, is often seen turning stones and shells searching for food. Mottled brown and white, with orange legs, it feeds on invertebrates. 22–24 cm.

OYSTERCATCHER
Haematopus ostralegus
A very attractive resident, strikingly black and white with long orange bill and long pink legs. Its low flight along the shoreline is also striking, with a noticeable white wing bar and loud piping calls. It feeds on molluscs and worms. 41–45 cm.

REDSHANK
Tringa totanus
Resident, but many of the winter visitors are from Iceland. The bird's most noticeable features are its red legs and base of bill; and in flight it shows a white rump and white trailing edges to the wings. It feeds on worms, molluscs and crustaceans. 26–30 cm.

KNOT
Calidris canutus
Huge flocks arrive from northern Greenland and Arctic Canada. The flocks perform amazing aerobatics in unison. The knot is grey above, with pale feather margins. It feeds on molluscs, worms and crustaceans. 24–27 cm.

RICHARD T. MILLS

Feral goats

THE FERAL GOAT
Caprahirens

In the late autumn at Barnes Gap, between the villages of Creeslough and Kilmacrenan in Donegal, I notice wild (feral) goats silhouetted against the skyline. Shaggy and crowned with scimitar-shaped horns, the goats added a biblical quality to the rugged nature of the hills.

At the beginning of January, fifteen minutes after an old nanny led them down to browse, and chew the cud, I watched the goats. Near the roadside, nanny goats and billy goats stood on hind legs to eat shoots from willow trees; other adults, with bucklings and goatlings, fed on tough fibrous heather, gorse, and rushes. Away from the roadside, leaning against a rock, a white billy looked fast asleep. But goats do not sleep; they merely have periods of drowsiness. I counted twenty-one goats of different shape, size, and colour: white, black, brown, black and white, brown and white. A few goats were hornless, at least four were too big, four had neck tassels and several wore noticeably short coats: all of these features are clues to impurity in a feral herd. For generations, the wild goats of Barnes Gap had interbred with modern milk stock. All together, the most delightful raggle-taggle herd of wild goats a person could wish to see.

On the island of Inishfausy, Upper Lough Erne, the wild goats are proper: they look near perfect descendants of the domestic animals of four thousand years ago. These goats have real pedigree and they are very similar in physical detail. Standing 75 cm at the shoulder and weighing less than 22 kg – smaller and lighter than the modern domestic breed – Inishfausy's wild goats wear long shaggy coats, dark brown through white; and both billy and nanny carry magnificent horns, sweeping backwards and outwards, some nearly 60 cm long. Still, the goats of Barnes Gap have far greater agility than the islanders of Lough Erne. The Donegal goats nimbly

Feral goats

climb rocky hillsides that are too steep and hazardous for sheep.

Wild goats usually live in rocky, hilly country, where they move sure-footedly among difficult scree. Led by an old nanny, they usually move about in herds of five to twenty. During autumn and winter they come down to the valleys, and then return in late spring to their favourite pastures. Like sheep, goats chew cud; but while sheep graze and take mainly grass, goats browse on leaves, shoots and tree bark. The goats have usually mated by mid-autumn and, dropped between January and late March, healthy kids will run and begin to climb when ten days old. Most wild goats give birth to a single kid, and they carefully feed and protect their young. Even so, a severe or late winter could kill a whole new generation.

Vixen

RICHARD T. MILLS

THE FOX AND THE RABBIT

Going down the road to the shop, I met a middle-aged man with a large supermarket bag in one hand and a bait fishing rod in the other. The bag was bulging and stains of blood showed through. 'You've had a bit of luck!' I said. Then, looking into the bag, expecting to see early-run salmon, I saw a dead fox and a rabbit lying together.

FOX
Vulpes vulpes
A fox is a lovely-looking animal and it can be charming as well. Stories tell of how it will roll about on the ground, chase its tail, jump in the air, and do all sorts of peculiar things to attract and 'charm' other animals. The spectators, rabbits and the like, become spellbound by the performance – until a foxy flop secures one of them.

A dog fox stands about 36 cm at the shoulder and is almost 104 cm long, including a tail 38 cm long. The vixen is slightly smaller, has a narrower forehead and lacks the cheek ruffs of the dog. The male and female wear similar fur: fiery brown above and greyish underneath. On the front of the ankles and behind the pointed ears, the fur is a burnt-toast colour. In about 15 per cent of Irish foxes the tail presents a white tip. The triangular-shaped face, erect ears, and the elliptical pupils combine to give the fox a cunning expression.

For hundreds of years, because of its killing of domestic and game stocks, the fox has been persecuted. Yet its very acute senses of smell, sight, and hearing, together with its adaptability, have enabled the animal to survive. Even today the fox is hunted, snared, poisoned, gassed, and shot. During the late 1970s, into the early 1980s, a mange-free fur could fetch twenty pounds or more; but I have recently been told that the pelts 'aren't worth the bother these days'.

Foxes are seen during the day and heard at night. The dog barks and the vixen screams; their calls are especially noticeable during the breeding season. Mating usually happens during late January and the single litter for the year is delivered about April. For their first month, the cubs – usually four or five – remain in the earth with their mother, and the dog supplies most of the food, which includes frogs, rats, rabbits, squirrels, snails and insects, as well as grouse, pheasant, and chickens. Foxes will kill poultry and newborn lambs, but among healthy animals this is not typical behaviour. A crippled or maimed fox will go for easy prey. Other reasons for this un-wanted behaviour might have to do with overpopulation and scarcity of the usual kinds of food; but a mother who has taken to killing domestic stock will teach cubs to do the same. The cubs stay with the parents until they learn to fend for themselves. They become physically and sexually mature in their first winter.

Except when breeding and rearing their young, the male and female lead solitary lives. They will lie out on a hill on a warm, dry night; at other times they reside in an earth. They mostly use the sett of a badger or a big rabbit burrow, and will use several of these fox holes on their wanderings. Foxes are found about lowland, hillside and moorland, in places that afford plenty of cover, such as gorse. I hope you never find one in a supermarket bag.

RABBIT
Oryctolagus cuniculus
A rabbit is recognised by its grey-brown fur, long ears, prominent eyes, white bob of a tail and hopping movements and it usually has the company of other rabbits. A closer look will reveal that the short tail is black above and white below and that the grey-brown fur has an orangey nape. The buck, up to 48 cm long, is slightly larger than the doe. The doe's head is more slender than the buck's, and her face has finer features.

A rabbit can move its ears together, or one at a time, to pick up very faint sounds from any direction. Because its eyes are prominent and set in the side of the head, the rabbit can see objects behind or to the side better than in front. It depends on a keen sense of smell to alert it to danger. I have yet to see a rabbit whose nose isn't twitching. The chin has scent-secreting glands, and the territory is marked by chin-rubbing the ground. Longer than the front legs, the hind legs allow the hopping movements

Rabbit

Rabbits

RICHARD T. MILLS

and provide the power in running. A frightened rabbit can leap two metres and travel 29 k.p.h. over short distances. For protection, the soles of the feet are covered with hair instead of pads. The three-layered coat is grizzle-brown on the upperparts and whitish underneath. Black rabbits and, rarely, other colour mutants are seen. During the summer of 1975 twenty white rabbits appeared in fields in County Derry. Probably released by a breeder, the white rabbits soon disappeared.

Rabbits live mainly in meadows, open woodland, dunes, and sandy heath, where they burrow extensively. The burrows are close together and the warren may cover a wide area. The living quarters are like tiny rooms leading from the main passages. Adults rest on the bare soil.

A rabbit will rob vegetable gardens and eat crops, and cultured greenery of many kinds, but its main items of food are grass, the tender shoots of gorse and the juicy toothy leaves of dandelion. In winter, when nutritious herbage is scarce, it will eat the bark of saplings. Sometimes it eats snails and earthworms. It eats its own soft droppings to double-digest the food: the rabbit voids two types of droppings – one kind is eaten again, the other is discarded at a latrine away from the burrow.

Rabbits have a reputation for full-time breeding, but the almost continuous appearance of cubs is more the result of polygamy than promiscuity. Bucks cross warren territories to mate with several does and, for the first six months of the year, successive litters arrive at monthly intervals. The gestation period is twenty-eight days. Sexual maturity is reached after three months. Litters continue less frequently between June and December.

The pregnant doe makes her nest in a short, blind-ended burrow called a stab, or stop. The stab lies just under the ground, and to protect the cubs from bucks, it is located away from the main warren. The nest is built with hay-like material and lined with fur from the doe's belly. Litters vary from two or three cubs – born during the winter months – to eight or nine in the warmer months. The mother does not stay with her young. In any day she visits the stab and suckles them for about five minutes. After each visit she closes the entrance to the stab with earth.

Newborn rabbits are blind, deaf, almost naked, and weigh just under an ounce. They have no power of movement until ten days old, and they open their eyes the next day. At sixteen days, when they can run and take short journeys from the nest, they start solid food but need the doe's milk as well. They are completely weaned and independent at a month old. Until then, using her powerful hind legs, the mother protects them.

Introduced into Ireland from France and England in the twelfth century for its meat and skin, the rabbit soon made itself at home. For hundreds of years it robbed vegetable gardens, ate the bark of saplings, and dug up the countryside. Yet, until 1840, there were relatively few rabbits outside carefully guarded warrens where they were kept in a state of semi-domestication. By the 1950s the rabbit had become a serious pest, and it was severely punished. In 1954–5 the introduction of the flea-borne viral disease myxomatosis killed millions of rabbits: 95 per cent of infected animals died in misery. Fortunately, a number of rabbits avoided or resisted the virus, and because a doe can produce about twenty cubs a year, healthy rabbits are becoming plentiful again.

Myxomatosis affected only rabbits. However, both pet and wild rabbits can suffer tularaemia, or rabbit fever, an infectious disease which can affect humans. Anyone who handles an infected rabbit can become very ill with high fever, headaches, swollen glands, and sores on the body. Do not touch a rabbit which seems ill.

This apart, despite the many and varied accusations against rabbits, the animals are pleasant to see and they help keep the countryside tidy. The effects of rabbits feeding on the countryside were highlighted by the changes that followed the first wave of myxomatosis. In the year or two following the drastic reduction in numbers of rabbits, green laneways became choked with long grass, seedling trees and briars; and the edges of cultivated fields were very overgrown. On downlands the grass grew taller. At the same time many wild flowers became more obvious: in particular, wild orchids seemed more abundant. And there was an increase in brambles, gorse and heather. In some parts of the countryside, the vegetation and scenery had reverted to conditions found before 1840.

The rabbit has many enemies: humans, fox, stoat, mink, cat, dog, kestrel, owl, buzzard. Its communal behaviour makes it easy prey. The burrows are numerous, very obvious, close together, and they cover a wide area. Stabs are easily found and badgers dig them out and devour the cubs. Yet the rabbit remains a familiar and welcome sight.

THE PIKE
Esox lucius

Every month has its dominant fish: March is the time when eggs ripen in roach; the stickleback is busy in July; the blue shark comes in from the horizon during August; the trout grows excited in September; silver eels set off for the Sargasso Sea in October; salmon spawns in December; and hungry and ferocious pike hunt slow-moving waters in January.

Aptly named the freshwater shark, an adult pike will attack and kill most water dwellers. Almost exclusively a fish-eater, preferring trout, it also takes roach, rudd, and bream; and it will not refuse mallard, coot, moorhen, frogs and rats. In any year, to keep itself in peak condition, a pike will eat five times

Pike

ÉAMON DE BUITLÉAR

its own weight, and can grow to 107 cm in length. It is the fiercest predatory fish in the freshwaters of the northern hemisphere.

Here, before anything else, I must repeat a story that a very good fly-tier told me a few years ago in Garrison, County Fermanagh.

Near Garrison there is a lake that had a mallard which hatched white ducklings, not unknown in other places but still quite wonderful. For good reason, local anglers and wildfowlers were very pleased and proud to have white mallard in their lake. But the ducklings began to disappear. With feathered hooks, the fly-tiers of Garrison dressed a tennis ball to look like a white mallard duckling and they soon caught the culprit pike which was transferred to another lake – and the remaining white ducklings survived to fly away.

With its long body and large shovel-shaped head, a pike is easily recognised. For reasons of camouflage, the body colour ranges from dark green to olive with golden flecks. The eyes are well developed, and set in the top of the head, they look mainly forwards and upwards. The dorsal fin is sited directly above the anal fin and both lie immediately in front of the tail. Placed so far back on the body, these fins allow the pike powerful thrust and rapid acceleration. The pike's ferocious mouth has a very wide gape and the large jaws house a bristling arrangement of needle-sharp teeth. The teeth on the lower jaw are strong and stick upwards; those on the upper jaw are equally strong and curve backwards. The roof of the mouth also holds numerous backward-pointing teeth; these prevent the victim from wriggling free. The mouth is designed for grabbing and holding, no matter how much the victim struggles.

Lying in wait beside an object on the river bed, or in among water plants with which their colours blend, pike spend most of their time in still and slow-moving water. They usually remain motionless in one place and then suddenly appear to seize the ambushed prey. By sight, rather than by smell, they wait for potential victims fifteen metres away. As well, they probably use vibrations in the water to detect approaching prey. Amazing hunters, adult pike are deadly accurate and are in peak condition during the month of January.

Pike spawn from late winter through spring. During February the younger fish breed first; their seniors then continue the breeding season into May. Despite this, there is no closed season in Ireland for pike fishing – pike are caught at all times of the year. The parents abandon the eggs, but the young soon fend for themselves. Tiny pike feed on water fleas, worms, and the fry of other fishes. As they grow, they take larger prey; but they continue to snap up the tiny fishes – including younger pike. They will also eat small mammals and amphibians. The size of the prey will depend upon the size of the pike itself. With maturity, a pike's gastric juices grow exceedingly strong: even hooks are eaten away by the stomach juices. Except when very young, pike have few enemies and most of them live for about seven years. The specimen weight for pike caught in a river is 20 lb; specimen weight for lake is 30 lb. The Irish record for river is 42 lb; Irish record for lake is just over 38 lb.

THE SNOWDROP
Galanthus nivalis

Throughout the year, about all sorts of places – meadow, river bank, sand dune, woodland, moorland – I see many beautiful and familiar plants and I sometimes stop and admire them. But the plant that delights me far more than the others is the hardy little snowdrop. No matter my frame of mind or the need to be somewhere else, I always dally to admire these lovely flowers.

While heliotropes defy their name and die in the growing light, and ferns make-ready spores like prehistoric organisms, and fungi grow colourful on dying and dead things, the snowdrop is always new and pure, green and white. And regardless of the freak actions of the weather, the snowdrop always appears in January. From a small bulb and to a height of 15–25 cm, two green leaves and a leafless flower stem appear out of damp soil. A small leaf-like sheath covers the top of the flower stem. The leaves become long and narrow, and a nodding bell-shaped flower grows alone on its stem. The flower has three outer spreading petals – which are very white – and three shorter inner petals, which show tiny notches. The white inner petals are tipped with green. The snowdrops continue until late March and are pollinated by bees. Meanwhile, the swollen bases of the leaves and flowering stem form the fleshy scales of a new bulb.

Probably introduced into Britain and then Ireland from central Europe in medieval times, and cultivated in gardens since the sixteenth century, the snowdrop was not re-corded growing in the countryside of Britain until the 1770s. And though it is still not recognised as a wild plant in Ireland, it continues to appear and spread in forgotten places, where it was planted many years before. Walking the countryside I find considerable patches of snowdrops in old damp woodland with a ruined cottage nearby, or inside a derelict walled enclosure, and along stretches of river banks that once belonged to grand estates. The plant takes its name from the delicate white blossoms which look like snow, and appearing out of wintry dampness in response to new light and heat, it is the plant of January. In folklore the snowdrop symbolises hope, the anticipation of brighter times ahead.

Snowdrops

FEBRUARY

February brings another hour of daylight, and a tiny light-sensing structure called the pineal body – situated in the base of the brain – causes many animals to become sexually excited with the lengthening days. More foxes mate; dog mink visit bitches in dens; rats and rabbits rear young. With the returning heat, while the eggs of trout and salmon show signs of life in the gravel beds of rivers and mountain streams, and cormorants watch lamprey moving up tidal reaches of brackish water, frogs return to their own place of birth and spawn.

Many badgers start changing their bedding. Along the broad-humped banks of streams, and in sandy knolls, and deep in woodland, also adjoining meadows, setts show evidence of spring-cleaning. Ravens court and begin nesting. Also linked with pair-forming, robins threaten and chase each other, and issue melodious songs; on bare branches, high in the trees, pairs of rooks touch each other and look down at other rooks crowding open fields; charming greenfinches use sheltered meadows; and linnets – grey and auburn-coloured – cause the flowers of gorse to tremble.

Now grey wagtails, fast and dipping across broad streams, are landing on slippery stones and dancing delightfully; still and solitary, the heron remains at the water's edge; beautiful kingfishers and dippers are busy, hurrying and searching; magpies wait to steal and chatter; and thrushes, blackbirds, wrens, and even the shy bullfinch all wait to sing. And the stoat and the feral cat watch all the goings-on and hunt to kill.

THE BADGER
Meles meles

It is many years since my father and I watched badgers about the townland of Ardnabrocky, County Derry. Ard na Brocaí means 'the height of the badger's burrow'. My father is gone now, and the badgers of Ardnabrocky are gone too, but I still spend many hours watching these marvellous animals.

During the evening of Monday 26 June 1993, in a remote glen in northwest Donegal, I lay on a rock and looked down at a sett, about twenty metres below me. The evening had a broken sky, and a stiff breeze came in my direction. The Saturday before, during the evening of the year's longest day, I lay on the same rock but, from behind me, the breeze was carrying the smell of me straight into the sett. On my return visit, after waiting for an hour and growing very cold, I feared another disappointing watch. It was 8.20 p.m. and a narrow shaft of sunlight focused on one tiny field away across the valley. It was a lovely sight. Then the field darkened again, and the sun went away – and stayed away. At 8.30 p.m. the sow badger appeared. Without any doubt, before leaving her sett, the sow had waited for the evening to dull down. Now, still at the entrance tunnel, she looked about and then quickly moved into a spread of tall rushes about five metres from the entrance. I watched the rushes moving – with all her limbs, the sow was tugging at them. Moments later, using her front limbs like arms, she held a clump of pulled rushes and shuffled backwards to the sett and carefully backed down into the tunnel. The sow continued to gather rushes for about twenty minutes – then she stayed inside the sett.

Shortly after 9 p.m. she appeared again – out of another tunnel. While she sat near a tussock of grass and started cleaning herself, I saw a head stretching up from the tunnel, and then another head; and within a few minutes, four cubs were out beside their mother. Almost as big as their mother, but childish in behaviour, and with patches of brownish hair, as well as grey, on their flanks, and wearing noticeable tails, the cubs spent minutes cleaning and stretching themselves. They nipped and scratched themselves, and nipped and scratched each other. At times the mother inspected their backs and seemed to be picking and removing things. While she attended to one cub, another cub was nudging her and nipping her legs, impatiently demanding similar attention.

The grooming completed, their mother went into the sett, and the cubs started tugging at each other, and mouthing at each other, and on occasions they appeared to be biting each other. Soon they were quickly running and chasing, rolling and tumbling, playing, falling backwards down into the sett and scrambling out again to get up to all sorts of devilment. Sometimes they would purposefully go into the sett for a few minutes, and then come out and play again. I spent about three-quarters of an hour watching the badgers

Badger

enjoying themselves, and not once did they make a vocal sound. When the cubs went into the sett and stayed in, and their mother started collecting rushes again, I went home.

The badger is a stocky, well-built animal: slightly less than a metre long and weighing up to 18 kg. The shaggy coat almost conceals the tail – about 15 cm long. The legs are short but powerful, so a badger can run very quickly. The feet have five toes, and the front feet have strong claws. The badger's evening and nocturnal habits make it an elusive animal. The best time to see it is during summer, especially later June when we have only about four hours of darkness. During the long nights of autumn, it usually appears 'between the lights', or during the first hour of darkness.

Taking its time, the badger appears to shuffle along, and at a distance it looks a greyish colour. But the individual coarse hairs are black and white, or blackish-brown and white. Another interesting thing about its colouring is that the badger has black on the belly and legs: most wild animals are lighter in

colour on the underparts. But the coloration of its head is the most obvious feature of the badger. It has a white head with two very conspicuous broad black stripes of hair running along each side, round the eyes, from the muzzle to behind the ears. It may be that the animal gets its name from the 'badge' or markings on its head.

Some say that the colour pattern of the badger is for reason of camouflage, with the stripes on the head simulating shafts of moonlight through the trees. I find this difficult to accept. In the shadows a badger is easily seen. A more likely argument is that the stripes serve to warn off other animals, to protect the cubs. However, the badger has little to fear from other animals; its only enemy is human – the baiter, the car driver, and those who

Badgers

act on the dubious assumption that the animal is the cause, indeed the only cause, of tuberculosis in cattle.

Normally a placid animal, not easily made angry, when it is startled or annoyed, the badger can become a frightening thing: it emits a stink from glands at the base of its tail; the back hairs stand on end, making the animal appear twice its size; it gives out a string of violent grunts and its stance is forward and deliberate looking. Any sensible intruder will quickly leave the scene when a badger is angry.

The badger's sight is weak, but it has a strong sense of smell; it survives in a world of scents. An omnivore, it eats both animal and vegetable food. Its wide, powerful jaws and strong teeth make it capable of attacking and ingesting large prey. Its strong claws can quickly and easily dig out cub rabbits from stabs; and robbing a wasp nest, its thick coat and skin protect it against stings. It will even eat hedgehogs, but the major item in the badger's diet is the earthworm, especially when it is suckling. Other food includes mice, frogs, and an assortment of insects; it will take wild and domestic birds when there is a scarcity of meat, but this is not typical. As well as animal flesh, the badger will eat bulbs, fungi, grasses, apples and other fruit. The forms of food intake vary with the seasons and the kinds of plants about the neighbourhood of the sett.

A sett is usually found in a wooded area bordered by fields, and sandy soil seems to be preferred. In truth, however, some of the best setts I know are miles away from woodland, very much out in the open, sometimes in old quarries, and often deep in pure clay. More importantly, successful setts survive for a very long time. I still watch the setts that I watched fifty years ago. The setts I mentioned earlier, in Ardnabrocky, are gone because they were replaced by the founds of houses. The usual sett comprises an underground arrangement of tunnels and chambers, which may accommodate a dozen badgers – including in-laws – and the entrance to the system is often found in a slope or a bank. By its large size, and the heap of earth and stones or gravel that lies outside it, a sett entrance is easily distinguished from the openings into rabbit, stoat, and mink dwellings. The sett is located near a small stream, or burn, and regular well-worn paths lead from the stream to the sett.

Other signs of badger are footprints: the badger leaves a heavy heelprint and five toe marks. The print of a fox or a dog shows a light heelprint and four toe marks. Strands of vegetation strewn along narrow animal paths also point to badger activity. The badger uses its forelegs to trail material such as rushes, bracken and bluebell leaves to the sett for bedding, which is frequently changed and piles of used vegetation are found some twenty metres from the sett. The used bedding is found near scrapes in the ground and shallow pits or latrines, which contain badger dung. Other signs include wisps of hair on barbed wire and gorse and thorn bushes, also evidence of scratching – where the animal has stood on hind legs and scratched the trunk of a tree. Scratching frees claws that are clogged with mud and keeps them sharp and in good condition.

Badgers mate by early August, but because of delayed implantation when embryonic growth is arrested, the three to five young are not born until February. The young stay underground for eight to ten weeks before following their mother out of the sett. When the cubs are ready to emerge, the behaviour of the sow is noticeably cautious. She wanders about the locality, and stops, and sniffs the air from all directions, before leading her young into the outside world. At first the cubs appear reluctant to leave the sett, and they have to be coaxed to move a few metres away from it. Surprisingly fearful, they remain outside the tunnel for short periods and keep returning to it. It takes a week or so before they investigate further afield and, even then, they are always ready to hurry back to the sett. After a few weeks the cubs are more courageous and play their rough-and-tumble games. From mid-summer they are seen digging the softer earth and finding food for themselves. Then their mother mates again, and the cycle continues.

THE FERAL CAT
Felis catus

A feral cat is a household cat that has left home to live in the wild. Cats are independent animals and will readily go wild or feral, and it is usually the larger cats that leave home. Surprisingly numerous, most of them form communities of a dozen or so in the grounds of hospitals, factories, or even in town centres. However, individuals often reject the urban way of life and hunt the countryside. All tame cats have the potential to be very good hunters, especially at night, hunting by sound and sight, stalking with infinite patience or lying in wait. All feral cats become marvellous hunters; and not only achieve a size and ferocity unusual in big household toms but their young often revert to the tabby, whatever the colours of their forebears.

In feral cats the tail is more pointed and the coloration is usually tabby,

Feral cat

black, or ginger. Although many tame cats are taken into the countryside and abandoned, the number of feral cats suggests large-scale breeding in the wild. With interbreeding, tabby is dominant over black, and short hair is dominant over long hair. In Scotland feral cats have interbred with wild cats. Why tame cats – turned feral – grow so big is not fully understood; it may be the result of a more active life style, as well as a diet of natural food. The recorded maximum length of a feral cat is 105 cm overall, but eyewitness reports suggest that feral cats might attain the maximum size of a wild cat: length 120 cm overall; weight about 14 kg. The size of feral cats was underlined by the story of the Surrey puma: between August 1964 and November 1967, over three hundred people reported seeing a puma hunting that area. In different districts animals were killed and measured and feral cats were found to be the culprits.

A few years ago in February while searching scrubby ground for a good blackthorn stick, I came across a farmer shouting curses and throwing stones at a big tabby. The cat had attacked the farmer's Labrador pup. Many times, in the depth of woodland, or out on moorland, or along river banks, or about dunes, miles from human dwellings, I have met a lone cat hunting.

Cats are majestic, clever, and mysterious animals. About four thousand years ago the Egyptians carved wooden figures of cats, and they believed that the goddess Bast, or Bubastis, who represented the life-giving heat of the sun, had the head of a cat. Anyone who harmed a cat was punished; if a person

Feral cat

killed a cat, the punishment was death. When a pet cat died, its master shaved off his eyebrows as a sign of mourning. The Egyptians mummified cats and buried them in cat cemeteries; they also put mummified rats and mice in each cat's grave. It is likely that Phoenician traders, who carried Egyptian cats in their ships, brought the first tame cats to Europe around 900 BC. The interbreeding of the Egyptian cat and the European wild cat produced the forebears of our domestic cat.

The curiosity and powers of observation of cats are remarkable. They carefully examine any unusual object they hear or see and, in a very short time, appear to know all about it. According to tradition, cats are exceedingly clever: nothing should be held improbable or impossible to their intelligence. Tradition also holds that cats are decidedly bad: selfish, revengeful, treacherous, cunning, and generally very dangerous. A cat can see in the dark and, if black, cannot itself be seen – except for its green eyes – hence creating a ghostly illusion. In superstition the devil often assumes the form of a black cat. Black cats are supposed to have powers and faculties different from all other felines – some believe they are endowed with superior reasoning and can fully understand human conversations, some claim that they bring good fortune, others believe they are unlucky. If on a journey you meet a black cat which looks at your face, you are advised to turn back – for a witch or a devil is in your path.

THE BROWN RAT
Rattus norvegicus

A native of central Asia, the common rat, officially known as the brown rat and often miscalled the water rat, arrived by boat from Russia at the beginning of the eighteenth century. The rat lives where it can find safe, undisturbed shelter in farms, warehouses, slaughterhouses, dumps, sewers, ordinary houses, and along overgrown river banks. Although an elusive and mostly a nocturnal creature, it is a familiar sight in the town and countryside. It can run, climb, burrow, gnaw, and is a very good swimmer. An adult male is about 28 cm long from whiskered snout to base of thick scaly tail, which is 23 cm long. The female is rather smaller. The rat has coarse, shaggy, greyish-brown fur, with paler underparts.

Brown rat

RICHARD T. MILLS

The face is long and narrow, with bright eyes and short, finely haired ears. The front feet have four toes, the hind feet have five toes. But the rat's most interesting and damaging structures are its teeth.

A rat is a rodent, a word derived from the Latin *rodere*, meaning 'to gnaw'. Like fingernails, rodent's teeth continually grow and can become very blunt, cumbersome and useless. The teeth have to be kept short and sharp. Also rodents, squirrels gnaw on the barks of trees to keep their teeth in good condition; rats gnaw on objects such as lead pipes and electric cables. The rat's incisors are long and curved; and while gnawing keeps the teeth short, it also causes the top and the bottom teeth to rub together, keeping them very sharp.

Despite all sorts of measures to control the animal, remarkably millions of rats survive by breeding themselves out of danger. Mating occurs without any form of courtship or pairing. A doe can start breeding at three months old, and she will produce up to fifty young in a year. In a burrow or some hidden place, the female makes her nest comfortable and warm with leaves, grass, bracken, straw, rags. She usually has three to five litters in a year; then she dies. The buck or male might live for eighteen months. And although 95 per cent of offspring die, counting litters from children and so on, a pair of rats is capable of generating two thousand offspring in any year. For rat survival, such breeding promotes growing resistance to standard poisons.

Rats have a short life span, and a rat which comes into a house during winter might be there to die. However, as well as death due to natural causes and the efforts of humans – with poisons, traps, terriers, ferrets – the rat has many wildlife enemies: owl, stoat, mink, fox and feral cat.

Out in the countryside rats run a very well-organised settlement. However, about a dump or 'sanitary landfill site' they run wild. On an overgrown river bank, which sheltered maybe three hundred adults, I watched rats swimming across the river. Always they seemed to adhere to a kind of schedule. Taking one example: for a fortnight I watched a rat crossing the tail of Hessie's stream near the River Faughan at exactly the same light times every evening. Before dusk the rat left the vicinity of its nest and crossed the stream at the same place each evening; it always left at the same time and crossed at the same place. The rat, a nursing mother, then returned to her nest – using the same crossing place – just before the sea trout began showing. This happened with unerring consistency over a period of fourteen days.

A small community of rats has a strict extended family structure of dominance and privilege. Beyond a certain number of members, however, the community loses structure and control. One February night when my two sons and myself were required to go to a dump with a tractor load of waste, we saw thousands of rats. The place was crawling with them. They touched the sides of our boots. At times we stood on them. While during the day these rats pretend to fear man, in the darkness they pay us very little heed. For them, darkness belongs to rats.

Along a river bank, or out in the wild, rats have a home range, or territory, for the family group, and strangers are chased. There is a strict structure of ranking. The territory comprises a complex arrangement of connecting tunnels with many different entrances, and passages through undergrowth and along the water's edge. The senior rat lives in the best locale, the best burrow within range of easy food, and will produce the most and better offspring. The territory is concentric-like: with the senior rat in the middle, important rats near the centre, and the lesser and younger rats in the periphery. The territory is secure, everybody is watched and stranger rats are chased. In the dumps there are too many subordinates, inferiors, and strangers to control.

Rats in the town will eat what humans eat. Rats in the countryside eat grain, seeds, worms, snails, eggs, young birds, dead fish. Always, rats are destructive and dangerous, attacking crops and likely to cause fatal harm to humans, causing the condition leptospirosis, or Weil's disease, contracted by handling clay or materials in ditches, or other places where rats expel urine. Still, through careless and wasteful behaviour, humans are the rat's best friends.

RICHARD T. MILLS

Stoat

THE STOAT
Mustela erminea

What is a whiteret? This word or something similar is often heard in Ireland and Scotland: 'He's just a wee whiteret!' – meaning a tricky, evasive person or animal. According to one observer in County Derry, 'It's the half-sister of a she rat. They're as wicked as you'll get!' How do you spell it? I failed to find the word in Irish dictionaries. However, in *Chambers Scots Dictionary* (1911) the weasel is listed as whatrick, whiteret, whitrack, whitreck, whitterock, and fifteen other similar names. Years ago a health visitor told me that she was advised not to go up a certain lane because it was 'full of whiterets'. A farmer told me, 'There's a family of them in a stone wall up the back field. They bite the cows' tits off.' None of his cows had teats missing.

Another farmer explained: 'They're weasels. Wee brown articles with white chests and wee black tails. You'll see them darting across the road into a hedge or ditch.' And others agreed. But there are no wild weasels in Ireland; and weasels do not have black on the tail. Translated, 'Whiteret', is *Mustela erminea hibernica* – the Irish stoat, which is very handsome and interesting.

It has a long, lithe body, which is about 35 cm long, including the tail. The male is larger than the female. The fur is a beautiful fiery brown colour on the upperparts and whitish underneath. Its bushy tail, about 10 cm long, displays a noticeable black tip. Like the Irish hare, the stoat does not turn white (ermine) in the winter any more. The stoat is very agile, alert, elusive, and curious. It bounds along over short distances always seeking cover. When it finds a tussock of heavy grass, rush, or a fallen tree, it conceals itself and then in a delightful way it quickly raises its head upright and appears to look all about the place; sometimes it stands on hind legs on a stone, or another platform, as if to get a better view. When it does this, the stoat is using senses of smell and hearing, for its sight is very poor.

Very active during February, the stoat swims and searches river banks to kill rats and to rob their nests, and it climbs bushes to drink eggs and eat birds – nestlings and parents. Flyfishing between the lights I have seen the stoat at work. I've watched a stoat searching a bank and, a while later, I would hear rats squealing in the undergrowth, or the frantic chattering of a blackbird, followed by a sudden deathly silence. On one occasion, after a noisy row, I saw a stoat pulling a rat along a river bank.

A carnivore, the stoat is well known for its bloodthirstiness. As well as rats and birds, including poultry and game bird, the stoat eats fish and their eggs. Its main food is rabbit; and an adult rabbit – a hare as well – will scream pitifully and become paralysed with fear, and stay still and wait to die, even when a stoat is a safe distance away. Apart from farmers and gamekeepers, and mink, the adult stoat has few enemies but the kits or cubs are taken by owls and kestrels. Stoats mate during late summer, but due to delayed implantation, the six to twelve kits are not born until the following spring, usually late April or beginning May. During the autumn, family parties get together and terrorise the countryside.

Although mostly a nocturnal animal, car drivers will often see the stoat during a February day. Usually it is hurrying across the road, into the safety of hedge, ditch, or drystone wall. It's seldom run over.

THE RAVEN
Corvus corax

During early February ravens indulge in courtship aerobatics. All black, with heavy bills and wedge-shaped tail, seen soaring, nose-diving with wings closed, sometimes gliding upside down in a corkscrew roll, somersaulting, turning and twisting and tumbling with necks outstretched and pointed throat feathers standing out, pairs of ravens 'kronk' and get very excited. On the ground, after he makes musical vibrating sounds and caresses her beak with his, and touches her under the chin, the male persuades the hen to touch his beak with hers.

Raven

By mid-February both birds combine to build a solid nest of sticks and twigs mixed with clay and fibrous roots, and lined with moss, grass, wool and hair. The raven is our first bird to brood and its nest is built on a ledge or crevice in a steep cliff overlooking the sea or a lake; sometimes it is built inland on a mountain overlooking moorland; sometimes it's built in a tree. In late February four to seven pale, greenish-blue eggs are laid. The eggs show light and dark olive-brown blotches, sometimes with greyish shell marks. And while the hen incubates, the cock feeds her. The eggs hatch in twenty-one days; and fed by both parents, the young remain in the nest for forty days.

There is an old notion that ravens neglect their young. In Psalm 146 – 'Praise God from whom all blessings flow' – we read:

> who giveth their food to the cattle,
> and to the young ravens who cry for it.

In German a cruel mother is *Rabenmutter*. In literature and in folklore parent ravens are noted for neglecting their young – probably because they roost away from the nest soon after the eggs hatch.

The largest member of the crow family, the raven (64 cm) has been regarded as a coward down through the centuries, and a murderer of lambs, poultry, and game – yet it will defend its own nest against a peregrine or a group of robbing gulls. It will kill weak lambs but its varied diet comprises carrion, rabbit, rat, mouse, hedgehog, bird, egg, snail, insect, and will scavenge anything edible: plant or animal of moorland, woodland, meadow, shore. Above all, the raven has been seen as a harbinger of ill tidings. The all black plumage, its high intelligence, habit of feeding on carrion, following sick animals and association with corpses, all together, probably led to the notion of the raven as a prophet of doom. However, there have been beliefs in the raven's beneficence: the raven that pecked out people's eyes would give sight to a blind man who had been kind to it; and a bowman could become an unerring shot by eating the hearts of three ravens reduced to ashes.

THE MAGPIE
Pica pica

One of the easiest birds to identify is the magpie. At 42–45 cm, it is the only large black and white bird in the countryside. It is also quite colourful, with black head, breast and back; wings black with a blue wash and bold, white oval patches; belly white; and the distinctive long, narrow, wedge-shaped glossy green tail, tinted with purple and blue. The magpie nests in late March into April. But on February mornings we see it on the roadways picking at carrion; and, being a crow, it has many interesting behaviour patterns. It is impudent, cunning, a thief, a mimic, and it is quite elegant. With the jay and the chough, the magpie is one of our most handsome crows. It is difficult to

RICHARD T. MILLS

Magpie

accept that such a well-known bird is a comparatively recent arrival. Now resident and increasingly common, with large domed nests of sticks a familiar feature of the countryside, our first magpies – about a dozen of them – arrived in Wexford in 1676.

The bird's name derives from its harsh 'chacka-chacka-chak!' call and its bold coloration: 'Mag', the diminutive of Margaret, formerly a pejorative name for a chatterbox; and 'pie', from 'pied', or black and white. Like jackdaws, magpies will imitate human voices and other sounds, and thieve bright and colourful objects. But the magpie's notoriety as a thief is associated with its stealing eggs and killing the nestlings of other birds. In robbing nests a magpie shows much cunning: quietly and systematically moving through hedgerows, or from bush to bush, hungrily searching; or watching from a distance as parent birds take turns incubating eggs or carrying food to the nest. However, when a cat, or stoat, or mink or some other enemy goes anywhere near a magpie's nest, its alarm chatter can be heard two hundred metres away.

In superstition the magpie is famous. It is not only unlucky to meet a magpie when going on a journey, but if a magpie comes chattering to the door and looks at you, pray earnestly – for nothing else can avert the doom that that bird brings. However, two magpies at the door will bring you prosperity; in fact, meeting more than one bird usually signals good fortune or pleasant times ahead:

One for sorrow,
Two for joy,
Three for a wedding,
Four for a boy,
Five for silver,
Six for gold,
Seven for a secret
Never to be told.

Varied throughout the land, this rhyme contradicts many superstitions concerning the magpie. Position is important: while two magpies seen on your right-hand side brings good luck for a year, three seen to the left of you is an ill omen. Irrespective of time or position, seeing one magpie is always a sign of bad luck.

With magpie numbers growing every year, and with their scavenging habits and grisly reputation, they are fast becoming unpopular. Still, they are always around, eager and ready to keep our roadsides and motorways clean.

THE CORMORANT
Phalacrocorax carbo

Walking the rocky shoreline during February, one of the few creatures I meet is the cormorant: with yellow bill, straight and thick; dark bronze back, white cheeks and thigh patches; and, when perched, holding its wings outstretched to dry. It is a bird of true pedigree. There were cormorants nearly 30 million years ago, when less than half today's animals had evolved.

For years I have listened to anglers and professional fishers complaining about the cormorant taking young trout and salmon. However, while the bird will take easy fish, its main diet consists of flat fish and eels. No matter, the cormorant is an awful glutton. It eats even when it can hold no more. It eats until the meal is returned, impossible to digest because the bird's insides are stuffed with food; this is when we observe the cormorant ashore, on a rock, looking quite listless and not its elegant self.

Even with plenty of room inside for more food, it is a feat of strength for this large bird (84–89 cm) to get into the air, but once launched, it is one of our most graceful, strong and unwearying birds. And down in the water, a cormorant's skills are truly 'submarine': it can swim with its back awash; it can swim under the water; it can lower its long head and neck beneath the surface, and it can catch fish as it travels.

Cormorants were once trained to fish and fill the creels of human masters. A learner bird had a ring – a kind of necklace – slipped over its head to keep it from swallowing the catch; but trained birds needed no collar – they retrieved for their masters like well-taught water spaniels. Still, in natural ability, a cormorant is superior to any spaniel, or any mammal, for it can walk on land, swim the waves and strong currents, and sail the air with much power and endurance.

Cormorants

THE WINTER HELIOTROPE
Petasites fragrans

You can find beauty in the most unpleasant places. Recently on a wet and windy February day, on a trip to a rubbish tip, I found a heliotrope growing out of sand and gravel near a chain-link fence. With tiny clusters of fragrant lilac flowers, each shaped like a slender tube broadening into a five-pointed star, and facing towards the strongest light, the heliotrope was a very welcome sight.

A native of the central Mediterranean, and called helio-trope because its flowers turn to follow the sun, the plant was brought to these western islands in 1806. Since then, it has become naturalised throughout most of Ireland and Britain, except for Scotland where it is very local. It grows to 45 cm along hedge banks, roadside verges, stream sides, and on waste ground. The flowers have a characteristic vanilla-like fragrance and, pollinated by early insects, they appear from December to March – at the same time as the wrinkled oval leaves. Because the winter heliotrope flowers and comes into leaf at the same time, it differs from other species.

Winter heliotropes

RICHARD T. MILLS

GORSE
Ulex europaeus

A member of the pea family, the furze or gorse or whin bush is one of my favourite plants. In fact, I have hundreds of plants of gorse hedging my garden. It is so well known that a detailed description is unnecessary, except to say that it is one of our most taken for granted yet loveliest flowering shrubs. It grows to a height of two metres over a good deal of the countryside and is characteristic of our landscape and climate – thriving under temperate conditions. The many short branches end up in stout thorns. The flowers are golden and in form are very much like those of the pea. Borne on the shoots of last year's growth, the flowers appear in February and continue until mid-June.

In folklore the gorse is the symbol of enduring affection.

Lamprey

RICHARD T. MILLS

THE RIVER LAMPREY
Lampetra fluviatilis

It is said that Henry I died of eating a surfeit of them; and that his great-grandson, King John, fined the men of Gloucester forty marks because they did not pay him 'sufficient respect in the matter of them'. At this time of year they are seen moving about streams of brackish water in tidal reaches. I refer to river lamprey.

Lamprey, lampern, or sucker eels as they are known by local anglers, are special creatures. They look like eels, and have sometimes been called lamprey eels or lamper eels, but they are not eels and they are not any kind of modern fish. They are very primitive: survivors of fish-like animals called the agnatha, the dominant fish group during the Devonian period, 350–400 million years ago. Most of the species of agnatha, which means 'without jaws', became extinct; however, from some of them modern fishes have evolved. Yet the lampreys – river and sea lamprey – and hagfishes have retained characteristics which it is thought were possessed by all the agnatha. The fact that they have managed to survive is quite amazing.

As well as being jawless, lamprey have no bony structures, no scales to protect them, no paired fins, and their internal arrangement of systems and organs seems simple. However, as if compensating for their primitive characteristics, the lamprey have highly specialised methods of feeding and breeding, and their mouth parts are very efficient.

The snake-like, scaleless body of a mature river lamprey is about 50 cm long and about 4 cm thick. The upperparts are dull, slaty-brown or olive-green and the lamprey is not easily seen in the stream. The underparts are a yellowish-white or creamy colour. The dorsal fins are found along the centre line of the back. Usually well-spaced, the dorsal fins are joined together during the breeding season. In the middle of the head, a single nostril opens into a blind sac. The eyes are noticeable, but the mouth is the prominent feature of the head.

The mouth is a large, funnel-like protuberance, with horny teeth lining the funnel. A strong projection of muscular tongue stems from the base of the funnel, and teeth – similar to those lining the mouth – protrude from the tongue. Designed for securing and taking in food, the mouth is also a respiratory passage, and the lamprey can breathe by sucking in water, to pass across the gills, for oxygen extraction.

A lamprey is parasitic on fish, and finds its host by sight. By pressing the circular edge of its mouth against the body of the host, it attaches itself to fish such as haddock, salmon, perhaps a basking shark. When the mouth is fixed in

Common frog

position, the protruding tongue punctures the host's skin by rasping the teeth on it. This causes bleeding and the lamprey sucks the blood. It may take in the torn fragments of fleshy tissue as well, but blood is preferred to flesh.

River lamprey spend about one and a half years at sea feeding on fish, molluscs, crustaceans and worms. With physical and sexual maturity, they stop feeding and migrate into the brackish water of a river to spawn, coming into the tidal reaches of a river during winter and spawning in April and May. They are strong swimmers and have been known to make their way over rocks, weirs, and up vertical walls – hauling themselves up with their sucker mouths. However, upstream progress is usually impeded by weirs and similar obstructions.

Each pair of lamprey constructs a nest by lifting pebbles with their mouths. The nest is a depression in the bed of a hurry or stream. After the eggs are laid, the exhausted parents drift away with the tide and die. The eggs hatch after two weeks, and the tiny, worm-like lamprey wriggle into the rich mud or silt downstream of the spawning bed. Blind and toothless, the baby lamprey survive by feeding on particles of plant and animal tissue. After four or five years, depending on good feeding and suitable water conditions, the young lamprey begin to look like their parents; then, silvery coloured and about 12 cm long, they migrate to the sea to start their parasitic life.

THE FROG
Rana temporaria

At the close of February frogs are on the move, making their way back to familiar breeding grounds. They return to ponds, even puddles which might dry up before the eggs hatch. Like salmon, frogs return to their own place of birth, sometimes arriving to find their ponds filled in. The belief that any pond will do for spawning frogs is wrong. Every year, since I first began searching for frogs, I have found tiny pools heavy with spawn and – a few metres away – what looked like really good places without any spawn. Why some places are preferred to others remains a mystery.

During later February frogs are seen hopping across roads, going home, eager to mate. The smaller males arrive first and the females keep them waiting, usually a couple of days, sometimes a week. Then, sounding like motorbikes scrambling, thousands of males croak continuously. Not appearing disturbed with males climbing all over her, the female lays up to two thousand eggs in a matter of seconds, and the males spray the eggs with milt. Less than a fortnight later the eggs hatch tadpoles.

It normally takes about four months for the egg to develop into a frog. The period of remarkable structural development will vary according to availability of food and suitable water conditions. At six weeks the buds of the hind limbs start to develop. At eight weeks the hind legs appear. By twelve weeks the front legs have grown, and the head is frog-like. At fourteen weeks the tadpole is absorbing its tail. Usually by sixteen weeks the metamorphosis is complete and the tiny frog moves away from its pond into damp rushy ground. When three years old, a mature adult, 7.5 cm in size, the frog will return to its place of birth and continue the cycle.

MARCH

M arch brings the end of winter and the start of spring, with just as many cold, blustery days as mild sunny ones. There is a saying that 'March comes in like a lion and goes out like a lamb'. Country folk once believed that if any rain fell during the first days of the month there would be a poor harvest, so seeds were not planted until the end of the first week. Superstition apart, by 21 March the sun rises directly in the east and sets in the west, making the length of our days and nights the same. Then the wild geese and other winter visitors go home.

Meanwhile, the frogs have spawned and tadpoles are swimming. The hedgehog is waking up from hibernation. The robin, song thrush, mistle thrush, heron, and other birds start nesting. And while the eggs of trout and salmon are hatching alevins, eggs are ripening in roach. The shamrock is picked for St Patrick's Day and the last of the snowdrops begin to die down. Now the wood anemone, lesser celandine, primrose, dandelion, and many wild flowers are growing. Sap flows in the trees and bushes, and buds begin to appear. The willows are most noticeable, with growth buds spirally set on twigs of different colours: the white willow with brown twigs shows buds with silky white hairs; the golden to brownish-green twigs of the crack willow carry appressed yellowish-brown growths with long tapering points; with olive-green, or red, or purple twigs, the goat willow supports single-scaled, shiny brown buds and catkins. The large and shiny brown sticky buds of the horse chestnut wait to open. The dark alders are showing new life, and last year's fruit – woody and cone-like – have delivered their seeds to low muddy banks to germinate. The hazels and thorn bushes are ready to grow. And the birches are ready too. Soon most of the plants will grow with the light. All the while, the hare and the otter are busy.

THE OTTER
Lutra lutra

T he otter is a shy and likeable animal. It is my favourite wild mammal: it is difficult not to be fond of a wild creature that makes a smooth slide on a steep river bank and keeps using it, for fun, like a child in a playground. The

Loop Head, County Clare
RICHARD T. MILLS

otter is remarkable in other ways: it can lope along a bank like a cocker spaniel and then swim underwater for two hundred metres without coming up for air. Carefully designed, its streamlined, flexible body, waterproof undercoat, long tapering tail and webbed feet allow the otter to make good use of water. It swims the way it runs, mainly by undulations of the body, but the broad surface of the webbed toes – which offers much greater resistance to water than would ordinary separate toes – affords an additional thrust and allows the animal to rapidly twist and turn after fish. Many times an otter has zigzagged past me, only a metre away, and I always enjoy recalling the times I had the otter for company during the hours of darkness. From my fishing diaries, here are a few examples of such occasions.

25 JUNE 1974

An otter came into the lower end of Biggar's Stream tonight again. It zigzagged past me, a few feet from my legs, at 1.30 a.m.

12 AUGUST 1976

In the throat of the Lower Rock Hole. Not so misty tonight. About 10.45 p.m. (very dark) I heard the distinctive 'yinny' call of an otter. The call came from upstream. Within a few minutes I heard very heavy splashing and the call was much louder. I crept along the bank on my hands and knees – very quietly. Then I saw them: a mother and three cubs playing about the stream. As soon as I arrived they scattered and the 'yinny' ceased. What a great pleasure to see them.

RICHARD T. MILLS

Otter

13 JULY 1978

A small school of trout are lying at the tail of the Rock. Saw an otter leaving the pool at 11.30 p.m. with a good trout in its mouth. Water still very low – tonight was cloudier.

30 JUNE 1993

In the Garden Pool, far too bright without much cloud cover, not a trout turned until after 1.15 a.m. Then the trout started showing. When they started splashing I said, 'There's an otter in the pool.' Minutes later I saw him sitting on a rock, waiting. I went home. For no angler can compete with an otter.

Apart from the deer, the otter is our largest land mammal: 90 cm long from snout to base of tail, which is 40 cm long, it weighs up to 16 kg. The head is large and appears flat, and shows a broad heavily whiskered muzzle. It has noticeable nostrils, attractive eyes, strong teeth, and sharp claws; the ears are tiny and almost hidden by fur.

A typical fur bearer, the otter wears two coats. The short, soft undercoat is pale brown and waterproof. The outer coat is a covering of long stiff hairs which are grey at the body ends and rich brown at the tips. At a distance the coat has a sleek, rich brown appearance on the upperparts; the throat is a whitish colour and the underside is pale brown. On land an otter is difficult to see – it merges into a background of bushes and vegetation. The ability to hide itself is due to movements of the outer hairs causing changing shades of colour in the fur.

The otter is a carnivore. It will eat birds, frogs, snails, insects, but the main diet is fish: elvers; slow-moving fish; also salmon and trout in low water conditions. Except when breeding, it is a solitary, elusive animal and will instantly submerge or disappear into the vegetation of a bank at the first hint of danger. It can mate in the water and the two or three cubs may be born from late March into April. The holt, or den, can be in an enlarged burrow of another animal but is usually under a tree, with the entrance in the side of a river bank.

The dog otter covers miles of river but the bitch stays near the holt. They mark their territories with black tarry-looking spraints, which contain tiny fish bones and scales. The spraints are left on rocks, stones, or sandy spaces in gravel at the water's edge. Other evidence of otter can be found in its prints, or seals, of five webbed toes by the riverside. The otter is very active during the game fishing season. It will be found about pools where schools of trout and salmon gather. Go out with an experienced flyfisher during the few hours of darkness of late June and you will likely see a mother and cubs.

THE HARE
Lepus timidus and *Lepus capensis*

Just over thirty years ago, during an evening in later September, while walking a river bank in County Tyrone, I saw a reddish-brown and white hare and I didn't know what to think. I was very surprised. The animal definitely looked like a hare, but its back and flanks showed the colour markings of a fox terrier. The animal turned out to be an Irish hare, also called the mountain hare, running about with a patchy moult. Years later, during two evenings of July 1977, another hare surprised me.

11 JULY 1977

Saw the kingfisher flying between the Tumley and the Rock Hole, but the most peculiar thing I've seen was in the Rock Hole itself. At about 7 p.m. I waded the right side of the stream and into the throat of the Hole fishing wet flies beneath bushes overhanging the left bank. As I rounded the entrance to the Hole proper, I saw a hare sitting on a partly submerged rock in the left belly of the pool. It was a brown hare and seemed to be washing its face with front paws. It was definitely a brown hare – only twenty yards away – I saw it clearly. When the hare saw me, it leapt off the rock, swam to my side of the pool and scrambled up the bank. It dog-paddled, with its head raised out of the water, and crossed the pool at a surprisingly fast rate.

12 JULY 1977

The weather is sunny and dry. Saw the kingfisher this evening again. The water is still low and a scum is forming at the throat of the Rock Hole. I saw the hare in the Hole again. It swam the pool and sat on the same rock for just under twenty minutes. It's a brown hare all right. What a very strange business!

N.B. I didn't see the hare again.

Ireland hosts two kinds of hare: the Irish hare and the brown hare. A rare delight, the brown hare, *Lepus capensis* – male size to about 55 cm long, female slightly smaller – was introduced from England and seems to have survived only in counties Derry, Donegal and Tyrone. The fur is brownish-yellow with a reddish tint on the shoulders and flanks. The sides of the face and the outer surfaces of the legs show a yellow tinge. Except on the breast and legs, it is whitish underneath.

RICHARD T. MILLS

Irish brown hares

The Irish hare, *Lepus timidus* – male size to 50 cm long – is very slightly smaller than the brown hare, but its body is more thickset and the ears are shorter. The Irish hare has a longer, broader head and the tail is white. In summer through autumn the warm brown fur becomes patchy brown and white; usually there is no change with the moult. Like the Irish stoat, the Irish hare (a subspecies of the Arctic hare) does not turn white in winter any more.

Excepting the breeding season, both kinds of hare lead solitary lives. For most of the day they live in a form – a hollow in coarse grass or rushes, heather, bracken, or other low vegetation. They usually lie low and keep perfectly still until disturbed. The strong, long hind legs give them the power to run – especially uphill – at very high speed; but they also rely on sudden twisting and turning movements to escape a pursuer. And they can stop suddenly. My father had a lurcher who broke his back chasing a hare downhill. The hare ran and twisted and turned and then immediately stopped; and trying the same, the lurcher – speeding past and attempting to pull up and turn – crippled himself. On slope or hilltop, over moorland, across lowland, against any hound under normal conditions – which excludes coursing – hares are match-less movers.

Mating takes place at any time of the year but is at its height during early spring. The mating is preceded by a range of peculiar antics, when the hares leap about, buck, box and kick each other. This pre-mating behaviour has led to the saying: 'As mad as a March hare!' The motorist will see a hare running ahead of the car, along the centre of the road; the hare, slow-witted, looking every which way, taking ages to escape.

Litters of three to five leverets may be born at any time of the year, but most are born during late March into mid-April. The leverets, fully furred and open-eyed at birth, are taken by their mother to separate forms. There they stay, alone, still and quiet, waiting for their mother to feed them. She feeds her young for the first week or so. Then, after weaning, their solitary existence really begins.

Totally vegetarian, their diet includes grass, heather, rushes, gorse or whin, branches of young trees and a variety of herbage. Their enemies are humans and dogs, stoat, mink, fox and birds of prey. It's no wonder you hear hill farmers and shooting men say, 'You don't see as many hares as you used to.'

Hedgehog

RICHARD T. MILLS

THE HEDGEHOG
Erinaceus europaeus

Years ago three young boys arrived at my door. The biggest held a card-board box with a hedgehog inside. The hedgehog was motionless, curled up like a prickly ball. 'Is it dead?' he asked.

The animal was dead and the boys looked bothered. I felt a bit bothered myself. But with all the busyness and concerns of modern times, when attention to detail and small matters are made to wait, I suppose it hardly seemed grown up to bother about things like hedgehogs. It's just that hedgehogs seem such inoffensive, lonely creatures, strolling along in the twilight, leading solitary lives, making little contact with others of their kind. Apart from children, and car drivers glancing at something lying as flat as a mat on the road, or seeing magpies and greyback crows emptying a fresh cadaver, humans don't seem interested in hedgehogs. 'They're full of fleas!' people say; and what they say is true. But there is more to a hedgehog than its fleas, which aren't interested in humans, anyway.

Sometimes called the furze pig, hedge-boar and hedge-pig, the most obvious feature of the hedgehog is its top coat of modified hairs, or spines. When danger threatens, these hairs – several thousand of them, each sharply pointed and about 2 cm long – can be erected to turn the animal into a ball of prickles; its reaction to danger is to stick out its spines, curl up, and stay still. Yet foxes and badgers kill and eat the hedgehog, outwitting it by rolling or carrying it to the nearest tiny burn or drain and grabbing its soft chest or belly when the animal attempts to swim.

The spines make grooming by the normal methods of picking and scratching difficult, and perhaps because of this, the hedgehog hosts large numbers of fleas and other parasites. However, hedgehog fleas prefer hedgehogs and will leave humans and pet animals for other fleas to bite.

Hedgehogs usually mate in the later spring; some wait until the start of summer. The courtship is a straightforward affair, with the boar snorting and sniffing and walking round the sow. At first the sow ignores him and some-times butts him. After mating they stay together for a week, then the sow chases the boar. Alone, the sow makes the nest. About the size of a football, roomy enough for herself and her five to eight young, she builds a nest of leaves and grass, lined with moss or lichen or other soft material. In 1969 in an old orchard in Bangor, County Down, I saw a hedgehog's nest – and a robin's nest – lined with orange-coloured fibreglass, normally used for insulating roof spaces.

After a gestation period of six weeks, the young are born. About 6 cm long, blind and deaf, and sparsely clad with pale flexible hairs, the babies look rubbery. Within two days, however, the hairs become sharper and darker; and, although still blind and deaf, the baby hedgehogs grow active, butting and squeaking as they search their mother's belly. At a week old, weighing an ounce – twice their weight at birth – they can erect their growing spines. At eleven days old they learn to curl up; and three days later their eyes open, first one and then the other. Soon after that, they crawl out of the nest and weaning begins, though they still find their way back and take their mother's milk. At six weeks old, when they have cut their permanent teeth and their

Hedgehog and its young

baby spines have been replaced by the strong, dark, sharp coat characteristic of the adult, the young hedgehogs fend for themselves. They grow quickly and before autumn (although not sexually mature until the following year) those from early summer litters will be full grown: to 25 cm head and body; 13 mm tail. When they leave the nest, they wander off to lead solitary lives. More than half of them die before becoming a year old. Born in later summer, second-litter young seldom survive. But those that manage to survive – from first or second litters – may live to be seven years old.

Insectivores, hedgehogs have a huge appetite for almost any high protein, carbohydrate, and fatty food: beetles, caterpillars, snails, slugs, worms, grubs, carrion. Food seems to be found by sense of smell and is captured with the mouth. Sometimes they eat the eggs and the young of ground-nesting birds; and mice, young rats, frogs and newts may be eaten. They eat a small amount of fruit, drink water, and can be enticed to drink milk from a saucer. They are blamed for taking milk straight from cows' teats. According to poet John Clare,

> They say they milk the cows and when they lye
> Nibble their fleshy teats and make them dry.

This is probably untrue, yet the notion lives on. Perhaps there is still much to be learned about hedgehogs.

When the weather cools and food supplies begin to dwindle, the hedgehog prepares for hibernation. During August and September, very heavy feeding allows the animal to lay down substantial deposits of white fat under the skin; and high energy brown fat round the neck and shoulders will act like an electric blanket. For hibernating, the hedgehog makes its bed in a disused burrow, compost heap, among the roots of a well-grown tree or a similar sheltered place. The bed is lined with leaves and moss carried in the mouth.

Hibernation usually begins in late October and lasts until March or April. Individuals vary: some sleep through the whole period; others sleep intermittently. During sleep, with its body temperature matching that of the immediate surroundings, and its breathing so slight that it can hardly be detected, and its heart rate dropping from about two hundred beats to twenty per minute, the hedgehog lies curled up with spines erect. And it might stay that way until the spring.

THE ROACH
Rutilus rutilus

Over forty years ago, fishing the brackish stretch of County Tyrone's River Dennett, which runs into the upper reaches of the River Foyle, I kept hooking strange little fish. Silvery bright and about 12 cm long, the fish came towards me with little struggle; they were poor fighters. Without any play, they seemed exhausted before coming within reach. Then, before setting the fish free, I had difficulty trying to remove the tiny fly from their small protruding mouths. Looking at them, their faces wore pouty expressions.

Those little fish turned out to be roach, just two years old. Since then, through the month of March, and away from trout and salmon waters, deliberately fishing worm for adult roach, I have caught many good fighting fish, just under the specimen weight of 2 lb, which I always set free. Still, for me, it is interesting to know that the commonest takeable coarse fish in Ireland today were newcomers to the brackish stretch of the River Dennett when I was a teenager trout-fishing there.

A roach is a handsome fish. It is silvery and deep-bodied. The silvery body is grey-green to olive on the upperparts, and brassy to greenish-gold on both sides. The dorsal fin, directly above the pelvic fin, and tail fin are dark grey or brown. The pectoral fins are tinted red; the pelvic and anal fins are orange to red, and the iris is red. Roach can be confused with rudd (*Scardinius erythrophthalmus*; size to 30 cm, described by the seventeenth-century angler Izaak Walton as 'a kind of bastard roach'), but the coloration and shape of jaw are slightly different: including the tail fin, the rudd's fins are redder, and its back is brownish-olive to green and the iris is a golden colour. Another difference between the roach and the rudd is that the upper jaw of the roach overhangs the lower – the reverse of the rudd's jaws – and while roach tend to be bottom feeders, rudd feed at the surface. However, because of roach x bream hybrids and rudd x bream hybrids, it is often impossible to identify the fish in the net.

Mature roach are up to 36 cm long and the Irish record weight is 2 lb 13$\frac{1}{2}$ oz, but the usual weight is 1 lb. Growth very much depends on the availability of food and water conditions. Under the best conditions, the fish will reach 8.75 cm in one year, 12.5 cm at the end of the second year, and 25 cm in six years. Roach are mature by the end of their fourth year and the life expectancy is eight years. They live in still or slow-moving water. They avoid light but sometimes come to the surface to take insects. In winter they move into deeper water. Gregariousness is their most obvious behavioural feature. They are shoaling fish and scores of them are observed following salmon in tidal reaches. Or maybe the salmon stay with the roach. No matter; in tidal water, when I go after salmon, I always look for shoals of roach.

Small roach eat algae and water fleas. Growing roach eat the larvae and pupae of midges, flies, and water beetles. Mature roach eat water snails, worms and small fishes. Spawning may take place from the end of March into May, when the water temperature is about 15°C. The transparent, yellow, sticky eggs are deposited among water plants and hatch after a fortnight. Swimming about in dense shoals, the larvae are vulnerable to bottom feeders such as eels, fluke, and even dragonfly larvae. The fry are vulnerable to other fishes and the mature roach are eaten by pike. However, predation does very little to stem the increasing populations of roach.

According to Hugh Gough's *Coarse Fishing in Ireland*, and other sources, in 1889 the first roach were brought in cans to be used as live bait for pike in the Blackwater in County Cork. Some of the bait escaped or were released into floodwater and, before long, Munster had resident roach. After the turn of the century, anglers brought roach from Munster to the Baronscourt demesne in County Tyrone. From there the roach spread into the River Mourne, and before the close of the 1930s, a few were caught in the upper reaches of the River Foyle. In the Erne waters, Roach were caught in the 1950s, and at Belturbet and Killykeen – between Cavan and Killeshandra – during the 1960s. Since then, roach have invaded at least seven other catchments: Bann, Boyne, Fane, Corrib, Foyle, Liffey, and Shannon. Since the early 1970s, they have totally invaded the Erne catchment – infiltrating headwater streams.

The spread of roach throughout Irish rivers, canals and lakes has been phenomenal. Only occasionally caught for the table, and finding their new homes suitable, they are beginning to overtake resident trout populations. Their success is due to production of large numbers of young – more than one hundred times the number of young produced by trout and salmon; also, roach have a good resistance to pollution and they have a relatively long life span. Nowadays it is illegal to transfer roach from one water to another. And it is illegal to use live fish as bait.

RICHARD T. MILLS

Barn owl

NESTING BIRDS

During February ravens were the first to nest. During March thirty other birds nest. Here I give a brief description of the more common birds, their nests and broods. Some of the birds have already been described and these are marked with an asterisk (*).

BARN OWL
Tyto alba

This is the ghostly white owl that hovers and glides while quartering over fields and heathland at dusk, hunting rats and mice. It will perch openly. It is a lovely-looking bird (33–36 cm), with a flat, white, heart-shaped face and dark eyes. Its upperparts are golden buff, lightly mottled with grey. The underparts are white and the long legs are feathered. Its all-white appearance in flight – and its variety of shrill shrieks, hissing and snoring sounds – have given *Tyto alba* a deserved place in folklore.

It breeds in barns, old buildings, church towers, and also in natural sites, such as hollow trees and ledges on cliff faces. It does not build a nest; it simply lays eggs on a platform where unwanted pieces of carrion accumulate. The three to seven matt white, ovate eggs are incubated by their mother for thirty-two to thirty-four days. Then, at first showing sparse white down, replaced by creamy down, the young remain in the nest for sixty days. In years of abundant prey, there may be a second brood in June–August.

BLACKBIRD
Turdus merula

A well-known and very popular bird (24–27 cm), especially the cock with his black plumage, yellow bill and eye-ring, and rich, fluty, warbling song. The hen is brown, with underparts mottled grey-brown or rufous red, and her

Blackbird

bill is brown. In March, feeding on insects and worms, the blackbird nests in a bush or tree, an ivy-clad wall, sometimes inside a derelict building. Usually the nest is between one to three metres from the ground; but some nests are found in the most unusual places, even near the ground. The bowl-shaped nest of twigs, rootlets, moss and dry leaves, made smooth inside with damp clay, often has a bedding of bits of grass. The four to six greenish-blue eggs have red-brown streaks or blotches. Incubation is thirteen to fourteen days. With dark grey down and yellow gape-flanges, the young remain in the nest for thirteen to sixteen days. Usually two or three broods: March–July.

COLLARED DOVE
Streptopelia decaocto

Before the 1930s this bird was found only about the Balkans. Since then it has colonised most of Europe. The spread of the polite collared dove is baffling. It first nested in Norfolk in 1955, and is now found all over Britain and Ireland. It is an unassuming attractive bird (32 cm), with a buffish-grey body – pink underneath; dark wing tips, white tailband, and a neat black-lined half-collar on nape of neck. It glides and voices repeated 'coo-cooo-coo!' calls.

The collared dove feeds on seeds and grain; and it nests at varying heights

RICHARD T. MILLS

Collared dove

four to sixteen metres from the ground, in trees and tall bushes. It prefers conifers. The nest is a loose, fragile platform of twigs with an overlay of grass and fibrous rootlets. The two pure white, glossy eggs are incubated for fifteen to sixteen days; and, with yellowish down at first, the young remain in the nest for fifteen days. Usually two or three broods: March–October.

CORMORANT*
Phalacrocorax carbo

Nests in colonies which often number hundreds of pairs. The cormorant (90 cm) will build on sea cliffs and islands with rocky ledges. It will also nest by river and lake, and sometimes in tall trees. The usual nest is a mound of sticks and seaweed, but I have found nests with things such as blue or orange nylon cord, pieces of fishing net, and torn black polythene bags built into them. The three to four long ovate pale blue eggs are incubated for twenty-three to twenty-four days. Naked and with blackish skin at first, looking like prehistoric animals, the nestlings can fly when a month old. The cormorant usually has one brood. However, finding the bird on eggs in July suggests there may be a second brood.

DIPPER
Cinclus cinclus

This exciting bird, at 18 cm the shape of a large wren, gets its name from a dipping action when standing on a stone in a river or stream. It has a conspicuous white bib and chestnut belly. Searching for insects, it can walk on the river bed. The flight is fast and low, and the 'zit-zat!' call causes you to stop and look around. Made of moss and lined with leaves and bits of grass, and with a round entrance hole near its underside overlooking the stream, the marvellous domed nest is built under a bridge, or in a crevice behind a waterfall, or between tree roots in an overhang of river bank. Pure white, the four to six eggs are incubated for fourteen to sixteen days. Then, at first showing bluish-grey down on head and back, and yellow gape-flanges, the young remain in the nest for eighteen to twenty days. The dipper has two broods: March–July.

DUNNOCK
Prunella modularis

This little bird (14.5 cm) is also called the hedge sparrow, probably because at one time all little birds were called sparrows. The dunnock is not a true sparrow: it is more warbler or accentor than sparrow. It has a grey head, thin bill, grey throat, grey breast and belly; its brown back and wings are noticeably streaked with black. It flicks its wings almost continuously and the flight is low and undulating. It warbles like a wren, but less aggressively, and it feeds on insects and berries. In bushes, hedges, brambles, even in heavy tussocks of grass, the cup-shaped nest of moss and fine twigs – lined with hair and sometimes colourful moss – may host the cuckoo. Deep blue-green, the four to five eggs are incubated for twelve to fourteen days. With black down at first, and pinkish gape-flanges, the young remain in the nest for eleven to fourteen days. The dunnock has two or three broods: March–August.

Grey heron

GREY HERON
Ardea cinerea

Along the shore of a lough or bank of a river, especially down-stream of a weir, I expect to see a grey heron (90 cm). Its tall slender shape, white crown with black crest, long, sinuous, white neck with black stripe, and long, orange-yellow legs leave the heron unmistakable. Standing solitary and motionless in or beside shallow water, yet poised alert, the heron watches and patiently waits for small fish to come within reach of its long, dagger-like bill. Harshly calling 'snark!' and rising to fly with laboured glides and neck drawn back, the heron is found in superstition. Certain people of Strangford Lough call it Kate the Cran and warn that a heron flying over the house is an unlucky event.

The heron nests in broad-leaved woodland, sometimes in conifers, and less often in bushes such as willow or in reed beds. Colonies or heronries in trees are often in the highest branches; solitary nests are usually in the lower canopy. About 120 cm across, the nest is an untidy structure of sticks, twigs or reeds. The size of ordinary hen eggs, the heron's four to six matt greenish-blue eggs are incubated for twenty-five to twenty-six days. With grey down on upperparts and crested appearance on crown at first, the young are able to fly after eight weeks. The heron has a single brood: March–May.

HOODED CROW
Corvus corone cornix

With heavy, rounded bill, grey back, belly and rump, black wings and square-ended tail, and laboured flight, this large familiar bird (47 cm) has few friends. Its aggressive scavenging habits, loud 'kraa-kraa!', thieving of eggs and chicks, and its very nasty habit of attacking lambs and pecking out their eyes, have caused gamekeepers and farmers to trap it in fixed cages and kill it.

Hooded crow

Also called the grey crow, scald crow, greyback and corbi, the hooded crow of Scotland and Ireland is a subspecies of the carrion crow: *Corvus corone.*

The hooded crow has a solitary nest usually about ten metres up a tall tree, deciduous or coniferous. It will also nest on a cliff. Bulky and bowl-shaped, measuring 50 cm across, the nest is built with sticks and twigs mixed with clay and roots, and lined with pieces of bark and hair. Pale, greenish-blue and marked with brown blotches, the five to six eggs are incubated for seventeen to nineteen days. With pink skin and sparse down at first, and narrow yellow gape-flanges, the young remain in the nest for thirty-two to thirty-five days. The hooded crow has a single brood: March–May.

HOUSE SPARROW
Passer domesticus

Probably our most familiar bird found about houses and farm buildings permanently in use by people. The house sparrow (14.5 cm) is largely dependent on humans for its food and nesting places. It eats insects, seeds and bread. The flight is fast and direct, and the voice offers 'chirrup!' and various twitters. The male has a grey crown, chocolate nape, large black bib, whitish front, and streaked brown and black back. The female plumage is duller, without the grey crown and black bib.

Built out of straw, rootlets, wool, paper or similar waste material, and lined with feathers, the untidy nest is found in a hole in the wall of a house or under the eaves of a building. However, the house sparrow will also nest in a hedge, bush or tree. White, bluish-white or greenish and strongly marked with grey to brown spots, especially at the blunt end, the five to six eggs are incubated for thirteen days. Without any down at first, and pinkish-blue inside the mouth, the young remain in the nest for fifteen to sixteen days. The sparrow may have three broods: March–August.

LAPWING
Vanellus vanellus

Also known as the green plover because of its iridescent back plumage, or the peewit because of its distinctive 'pee-wit!' call, the lapwing (30 cm) is common throughout Ireland and Britain. Gregarious outside the breeding season, the aerial displays of broad flaps and twisting, rolling dives are a treat to see. Appearing black and white at any distance, a closer look reveals the bird's metallic-green back with a purple sheen. The head is white with attractive black markings, and holds a long wispy crest. The black of the throat widens into a noticeable black breastband. The

RICHARD T. MILLS

Lapwing

belly is white, the broad, rounded wings have white tips, the rump is white, and the tail has a black bar. In winter the throat and upper breast become white.

Mostly seen about arable fields, moors, damp pastures, and freshwater marshes, the lapwing nests on the ground. Usually in the open or where ground cover is low, the nest is a depression simply lined with bits of grass stems or nearby plants. Olive-brown with brownish-black flecks and blotches, the four eggs are incubated for twenty-four to twenty-six days. Then, with a mottling of black and brown on the upperparts and white throatband at first, the young leave the nest soon after hatching. The lapwing has a single brood, and sometimes a replacement clutch: March–June.

LITTLE GREBE
Tachybaptus ruficollis

The smallest, yet most frequently seen, and most numerous of the grebes, and known as the dabchick, this little bird (25–30 cm) is found in freshwater lakes. Not much bigger than a duckling, it is often heard before seen. The loud, high-pitched, quavering, whinnying call carries far from the bird's presence in rushes and reed beds. Then, out in the open, it is seen diving to catch small fish and insects, and bobbing up again. In flight, low over the water, its short, rounded tail looks peculiar. During summer it has a black crown and upperparts, and wears chestnut cheeks, neck and throat, and shows a noticeable pale patch near the base of the bill. In winter the cap and upperparts are brown and the chestnut colour becomes buff or yellowish-brown.

The nest is a floating platform of water plants, close to the bank or the water's edge. Usually stained, the four to seven bluish-white eggs are incubated for twenty to twenty-one days. Then, able to swim and dive after a few days, the black downy chicks are also carried on the backs of their parents. The little grebe has two, sometimes three, broods: March–August.

LONG-EARED OWL
Asio otus

Due to increased conifer planting, the number of long-eared owls is increasing. The bird's preferred habitat is coniferous woodland. Strictly nocturnal, it roosts in dense tree cover during daylight hours. It is dark brown: upperparts mottled buff and brown, underparts buffy and heavily streaked with brown. It has a distinctive flat face with bright orange eyes. The apparent ears are tufts of feathers; the actual ears are hidden by feathers on the sides of the head. It feeds on small mammals, and its flight is laboured and gliding. Its call is a low and quivering 'oo-oo-oo!'

The long-eared owl (34 cm) uses the old nests of other birds, such as the hooded crow, magpie and pigeon; it sometimes uses the old nests of the heron and sparrowhawk; occasionally it will occupy old squirrel dreys. The four to six short, ovate, white eggs are incubated for twenty-seven to twenty-eight days. Downy white at first, the young remain in the nest for twenty-one to twenty-four days. In years of abundant prey, there may be a second brood: June–August.

LONG-TAILED TIT
Aegithalos caudatus

Unlike the other tits in shape as well as plumage, this tiny bird (14 cm) has a tail longer than its body; compared to length of body, no other woodland bird has such a long tail. The bird is always on the move in woods, heaths, gardens, and hedges. It has a white crown with a black headband over the eye extending to its black back. It has a very tiny bill. The wings are black and white with a warm crimson-pink band across the upper edge. The underparts are white, with pink beneath the tail. The long black tail has white outer edges. It feeds on insects, spiders, seeds and buds. The flight is flitting, and the call is a buzzing 'zee-zee-zee!' It is found in small flocks throughout the year, especially in winter, when very many die in severe weather.

Sometimes in the fork of a broad-leaved tree, but often seeming to dangle from the distant end of a branch, as high as twenty metres above the ground, the nest of the long-tailed tit is a delight to see. In truth, it is less spectacular when found in thickets of gorse, briar, or bramble. Still, the beautiful oval nest is carefully made of moss and cobwebs, bound together with hair and lined with many feathers. A delicate and well-camouflaged structure, the

RICHARD T. MILLS

Long-tailed tit

nest has a side entrance. Dull white with fine reddish spots, the seven to eleven eggs are incubated for twelve to thirteen days. Naked at first, and with white gape-flanges, the young remain in the nest for fifteen to sixteen days. There are usually two broods: March–June.

MAGPIE*
Pica pica

The magpie builds a large globe-shaped nest of sticks and thorny twigs, lined with clay and fine rootlets, and showing an entrance hole at the side. The solitary nest is easily seen in tall trees, untrimmed hedges and thorn bushes. Densely marked with grey and brown spots, the greenish-blue, or yellowish, or greenish-grey five to seven eggs are incubated for seventeen to eighteen days. Naked at first, with yellow skin, the young remain in the nest for twenty-five to twenty-seven days. The magpie usually has a single brood, March–April; but it sometimes has a replacement clutch in May or June.

MALLARD
Anas platyrhynchos

This is our most familiar duck, widespread throughout the year, in many different habitats. The mallard (58 cm) seems as much at home on a lake in the centre of a city as it is on river or lake in the countryside, or a reservoir in the hills. The drake's yellow bill, green head, white collar, maroon breast, pale grey upperparts and belly, and short orange legs make him easily recognised. The brown female has a dark cap, dark eye-stripe and orange-yellow bill. Both adults have violet-blue wing patches. They feed on aquatic seeds, plants and invertebrates. The flight is strong and powerful. The drake whistles and makes grunting sounds; the female quacks.

The mallard nests in a variety of places: in ground cover near water or in a small bush overhanging a river; also in tree stumps and near small ponds in woodland; sometimes in old nests up trees, and on town buildings. The bulky nest is built with leaves, stems, feathers, and is lined with greyish-brown down. Usually greenish-blue with a waxy surface, the seven to eleven eggs are incubated for twenty-eight days. Olive-brown with some yellow throughout, the young leave the nest soon after hatching. The mallard has a single brood: March–May. However, nests have been recorded for February.

MISTLE THRUSH*
Turdus viscivorus
The mistle thrush builds a bulky nest in the fork of tall trees, also on ledges of cliffs, on buildings, and in small bushes. The bowl-shaped nest has a framework of twigs or stems, moss and grass, cemented with clay and lined with fine, stiff grass. Usually greenish-blue and spotted red, the three to five eggs are incubated for thirteen to fourteen days. With sparse pale down at first, and pale yellow gape-flanges, the young remain in the nest for fourteen to sixteen days. There are two broods: March–June; and sometimes a replacement clutch.

MOORHEN
Gallinula chloropus
This is a familiar bird seen about ponds, rivers, canals, and marshy places near lakes. Despite its name, the bird is not a moorland species. The name derives from the Anglo-Saxon *more*, meaning 'mere' or 'bog'. Because of its long legs and feet, the moorhen (33 cm) has a jerky walk; and it nods its head like a chicken. And because its long toes have no webbing, the swimming action is jerky. To get into the air, it runs or patters along the surface of the water, the flight is laboured with green legs trailing. It has dark brown upperparts with a white lateral line, a brown rump, dark grey breast and belly, and a black and white undertail. The tail is pointed. But the bird's most noticeable feature is its red bill with yellow tip. It eats aquatic insects, molluscs, seeds, and plants; and its voice offers a high pitched 'kik-kik-kik-kik!'

The nest is usually a woven structure of reeds and sedge on a foundation of growing tussocks, or in ground cover along a river bank; other nests are in low bushes overhanging the water. Buff-coloured and marked with reddish-brown flecks, the five to ten eggs are incubated for twenty to twenty-one days. Showing black down, a red bill and forehead, the young leave the nest soon after hatching and they start swimming; they fly after six weeks. The moorhen has two or three broods from March to mid-summer.

PEREGRINE
Falco peregrinus
The peregrine falcon (38–48 cm) is a superb bird of prey, and kills on the wing: a moment ago a tiny speck high in the sky, then, after swooping at more than 160 k.p.h., killing a pigeon or a duck in full flight. The peregrine's favourite haunts and nest sites are cliffs, coastal and inland; but during the past fifteen years, they have taken up residence in church steeples and tall buildings in towns and cities, where they prey upon feral and racing pigeons, and cause fanciers to complain. In 1989, during renovation work on a cathedral in the city of Derry, three hundred pigeon rings were found. The peregrine population is recovering from a long-term decline which put the bird's survival at serious risk, especially in the 1960s. However, like all birds

of prey, the peregrine is still vulnerable to pesticides. It is a handsome bird with slate-grey upperparts, finely barred whitish underwing and underparts, and attractively barred tail. The white neck and face show noticeable black, moustache-like markings. The call is a loud 'kek-kek-kek!'

The eggs are laid on a bare ledge or on debris of an old nest. Buff and speckled red, the three to four short, ovate eggs are incubated for twenty-nine to thirty days. Then, with white down and pink bill at first, the young remain in the nest for forty days. The peregrine has a single brood: March–April or June–July.

ROBIN*
Erithacus rubecula
The robin uses many nest sites: under ground cover; in different holes in tree stumps and banks; in ivy-clad walls; in discarded buckets and tins, and so on. Usually at or just above ground level, the nest often hosts the cuckoo. A cup-like structure on a base of dead leaves, the nest is usually lined with fine fibres and animal hair. White and marked with reddish-brown speckles, the five to six eggs are incubated for thirteen to fifteen days. Wearing blackish down on head and back and showing dark yellow gape-flanges, the young remain in the nest for twelve to fifteen days. The robin has two broods: March–July.

ROOK*
Corvus frugilegus
In clumps of tall trees, nesting in the outer branches of the crowns, with several nests in the same tree and very noticeable against a fine network of bare branches, colonies or rookeries often house hundreds of rooks. The bulky bowl-shaped nest is made out of sticks and twigs mixed with clay and rootlets, and lined with pieces of bark and animal hair. Pale blue-green, blotched brown, the three to five eggs are incubated for sixteen to eighteen days. With sparse down and yellow gape-flanges, the young remain in the nest for twenty-nine to thirty days. The rook has a single brood: March–April.

SHAG
Phalacrocorax aristotelis
Described as a smaller version of its relative the cormorant, the shag (76 cm) is more confined to predominantly rocky coasts; and although it swims, dives, and stretches its wings like a cormorant, the shag has faster wing beats and seldom flies high. It also lacks the white patches on face and flanks, and it has a glossy, green sheen and a short, tufted crest during summer.

Shags and cormorants are usually in separate colonies, and shags sometimes nest on the lower rocky ledges. Still, the bulky nest of sticks and seaweed can be built on an inaccessible ledge, and near or inside sea caves. The two to five long, ovate pale blue eggs are incubated for thirty to thirty-one days. Naked at first, followed by light brown down, the young can fly when a month old. The shag may have two broods: March–August.

SKYLARK
Alauda arvensis
As it loudly sings while hovering in the sky above open fields, heaths,

Skylark

RICHARD T. MILLS

moors, and marshes, the skylark (18 cm) is often heard before seen. However, it is a ground-dwelling bird and is easily seen as it walks, flies a short distance and lands again. It is a heavily streaked, brown bird, with a white throat, buffy streaked breast, white belly, and a long white-edged tail. It also has a noticeable crest. For distances low over the ground, the flight is undulating. However, in beginning March through late July it is frequently seen rising almost vertically in a hovering flight, often to become a tiny speck high in the sky, while continuously warbling. On the ground it voices 'chirrup!' and then searches for seeds and insects. Built with coarse grass and lined with fine grass, the cup-like nest, hidden under cover, may host the cuckoo. Greyish and blotched brown, the three to five eggs are incubated for eleven to twelve days. Showing yellow down and yellow gape-flanges, the young remain in the nest for nine to ten days. There are two or three broods: March–July.

WOODPIGEON
Columba palumbus

This is the largest of our pigeons, distinguished from the others by its white neck patch and the white wing bar. In flight, contrasting with the white wing bar, the wing is black and the tail has a terminal black band. The flight is strong, powerful, and very noisy when the bird 'claps' out of the trees. The woodpigeon (40 cm) has an overall grey plumage, with green on the neck, a pinkish breast, and short red legs and feet. It eats crops, seeds, and grain. The voice is a soft cooing which is repeated endlessly: 'coo-coo-coo-cu-coo!'

A platform of loose twigs, without any lining, the nest is placed at varying heights in the outer branches of trees – broad-leaved and coniferous – and in bushes or high hedges. Sometimes the bird uses old solitary nests, or an old squirrel drey. Pure white and glossy, the two eggs are incubated for sixteen to seventeen days. With bluish-pink patches of skin and yellowish down at first, the young leave the nest after a month. The woodpigeon has two or three broods: March–September.

THE PLANTS

During March we find shepherd's-purse, chickweed, colt's-foot, groundsel, speedwells, ground-ivy, butterbur, woodrush. But every month has its special plants, and for March I choose the anemone, celandine, dandelion, primrose and the shamrock.

WOOD ANEMONE
Anemone nemorosa

The wood anemone, or windflower, is a fascinating little plant. It takes its name from the Greek *anemos*, 'wind'. In a breeze the plant nods its head in a most agreeable fashion and it likes exposure to the sky, and because its flower does not produce nectar, it is probably greatly indebted to the wind for enabling its propagation. Still, its most responsive and pleasant attitude is to the sun. In structure the plant appears delicate and simple – yet it is a long-time survivor and it is very sensitive. It has a solitary flower of six petal-like sepals, usually white with a pink blush behind; and the flower rests on an ordinary stalk above a single ring of three deeply cut leaves. It grows to 5–30 cm with the improving light and heat of spring; and its very existensce is indicative of a fragment of wood-land that has experienced hundreds of springs. Carpets of anemone are telltale of very old woodland – no matter the nature and age of the present trees.

Wood anemones

One of the most delightful unfoldings of every year is the flowering of the wood anemone. And one of my most delightful experiences is watching its behaviour. Come spring, spend an afternoon with a broken sky – of sunshine and cloud – and sit watching the anemones in woodland. When the light becomes strong, the closed drooping flowers raise their heads and open their faces to beam back at the sun. When the light fades or weakens, the flowers' faces close and heads hang down again.

Carpets of wood anemone are found in most broad-leaved woodlands, but they seem to prefer heavy soils below or near peaty moorlands. They flourish when and where they can see the sun, and feel the sun's rays during early spring when the trees are leafless, and in coppiced woods where there is more light than shade. During early spring, when other herbage is scarce, animals sometimes have to eat the plant. Anemones dislike disturbance and, when picked, the pale flowers quickly wither.

LESSER CELANDINE
Ranunculus ficaria

Where there is a 'lesser' there is usually a 'greater' – in the case of celandine this is true in name only. While the lesser celandine and the greater celandine have a common name, they have nothing else in common – except the colour of their flowers. The lesser celandine is a relative of the buttercup and wood anemone; the greater celandine – *Chelidonium majus* – is a poppy.

Easily found throughout Ireland and Britain, lesser celandine is a most delightful, bright and busy little plant which introduces true spring. From March into May, lesser celandine is one of our first ground flowers to appear in damp broad-leaved woodland, along hedgerow, in wet pasture, and about streamside; it even covers splashed rocky ledges below steep peaty waterfalls. Growing to a height of 6–15 cm, it thrives in damp places and forms a dense carpet of rich, glossy green, heart-shaped leaves and many-petalled golden flowers. Wordsworth described the plant's burnished flowers as shining 'bright as the sun himself'. And it is a flower of the sun: its petals stay closed on a dull day and during darkness; they unfold in bright morning light and, approaching the end of a bright day, they close as the sun sets.

From the Greek *khelidon*, the name 'celandine' is taken to mean 'appearing with the arrival of the swallows'. (Greater celandine is also known as swallow-wort.) The English name 'pilewort' is less pleasant, more clinical. According to physician and herbalist Nicholas Culpeper, the rootstock of lesser celandine – a clump of small whitish, or flesh-coloured tubers – is the 'perfect image of the disease they commonly call piles'.

During beginning March the leaves appear on long, slim stalks. Rising from the tuberous roots, the stalks appear to splay under the weight of their leaves. Noticeably heart-shaped, and somewhat fleshy, the leaves are shiny, dark green and sometimes bear black marks or mottling. Taller than the leaves, the golden yellow flowers are brilliant in the sunlight. Borne singly on erect stalks and measuring 2.5 cm across, the flowers can have up to a dozen petals on a collar of three to four pale green sepals. Oval and showing pointed tips, the petals fade with age, and fall before the end of May, and the leaves wither before the end of summer.

Lesser celandine

Lesser celandine is known to have poisoned sheep and cattle. But it has helpful properties as well. A decoction of the fresh plant applied to the face will close up pores and tighten the skin to prevent wrinkles. In times past, a mixture of the leaves and roots made into an ointment or an oil was said to cure piles, and scrofula, a form of tuberculosis that caused inflammation of the joints and glands, especially glands of the neck. In England the disease was called 'king's evil' because people once believed that the disease could be cured if a king touched the sufferer. Possibly originating with the pious Anglo-Saxon king Edward the Confessor, the custom ended during the 1800s. In folklore, lesser celandine is the symbol of joy.

DANDELION
Taraxacum officinale

Viewed by many people, gardeners especially, as a nuisance and a weed, the dandelion is one of nature's examples of a good and very useful wild plant: outside the garden, for the pleasure of the countryside, it fills laneways, fields, and waste ground with a golden blaze of colour from March through to early winter; for the student of botany it makes easily known how plants survive and propagate; for the teacher of botany it is a perfect example of the family Compositae; for the beauty therapist it provides a means of keeping human skin healthy and clean; for the practitioner of herbalism it offers a very wide range of alternative treatments for conditions of ill health; for the romantic and playful it will tell whether 'She loves me. She loves me not' or 'What's o'clock?'

From its smell, shape and quality of its root and leaves – its composite nature – the appearance of the seed head and the games people play with it, the dandelion has many local dialect names; these include pee-the-bed, piss-a-bed, crow parsnip, lion's tooth, Irish daisy, priest's crown, blowball, doon-head-clock, fortune-teller, one o'clock, and so on. It is the toothed shape of its leaves that give the plant its English name 'dandelion' – from the French *dent de lion*, meaning 'lion's tooth'.

Dandelion seeds

In the ground there is the thick brown tap root, white within, containing a milky juice. A strong penetrating structure, the tap root stores the plant's nourishment. From the root the long toothed leaves radiate to form a spread, or rosette, almost flat on the ground. The leaves are arranged in a way that allows each of them equal share of the sunlight. There is an important division along the middle of each leaf, which ensures that the last drop of rain falling on the leaf runs down to the root.

Some of the leaves reach up from the ground, but they stay intact – protected from grazing animals by the release of a bitter, milky juice. From the leaves, rises a fleshy stalk to a height of 5–30 cm, which contains a similar bitter, milky juice, and atop the stalk sits the flower head, a composite arrangement of maybe two hundred florets.

Dandelions

The life of the open flower head is surprisingly short. After three or four days of sunshine or good light, the head withers into seed. Count the seeds and know the number of florets: enjoy amazement after one hundred and the thrill of arriving at two hundred. Then help the wind – blow them away.

A decoction of the plant will moisturise the skin and is said to be good for eczema and various eruptions; and, in alternative medicine, the roots and the leaves of the dandelion are widely and reliably used for conditions of the liver and gall bladder, crippling arthritis, chronic skin diseases, constipation, and as an aid to promote the flow of urine, enhance the appetite, and aid digestion. The basal leaves are used for salad and wine.

PRIMROSE
Primula vulgaris

Widespread throughout Ireland and Britain, although less frequently in some places than formerly, sometimes due to digging out, the primrose is another delight of spring. It brightens woodland clearings, coppice, hedgerows and damp, roadside banks. From March until May, the pale yellow flowers grow to a height of 15 cm from the centre of a rosette of toothed, wrinkled leaves. Hairless above and downy beneath, the fresh green, oblong leaves gradually taper towards their base. On long hairy stalks the solitary flowers have five joined, notched petals.

In spreads of primroses there are two kinds of flower, the pin-eyed and the thrum, and fertilisation is more successful when pollen is transferred from one kind to the other. This is why so many objectionable attempts to transplant the primrose from the wild to a garden end in failure. Unless very closely examined, the two kinds of flower look the same. The pin-eyed primrose has a long stigma and short stamens; the thrum primrose has a short stigma and long stamens. Pollination of a pin-eyed by thrum pollen effects a higher level of fertilisation than pollination from a flower of the same kind. The two different flowers have different sizes of pollen, with surfaces that suit the stigmas of each other.

For its beauty, hardiness, and eagerness to bloom, everybody loves the primrose, or *Primula vulgaris*, meaning the first rose of the year, and common. Sadly the plant is far less common than it used to be. I would very much like to have a spread of primroses outside my window, but I prefer seeing them where they really belong – brightening shady river banks, hedgerows, and woodland. In folklore the primrose is the symbol of youth.

Primrose

RICHARD T. MILLS

SHAMROCK

The national emblem of Ireland, the shamrock is worn on 17 March, St Patrick's Day. In legend the shamrock is the trefoiled plant that Saint Patrick used to explain the Trinity. Down the centuries, different plants have been identified as the 'true' shamrock. The problem of identification was due to the absence of flower: only early, tiny leaves are worn on St Patrick's Day, usually with roots intact. So by taking samples of leaves and roots worn for the occasion, planting them, and then waiting for the plants to flower, five 'shamrocks' were discovered: wood sorrel, black medick, white clover, red clover, and lesser trefoil. Nowadays, the lesser trefoil is regarded as the true shamrock for St Patrick's Day.

Found throughout Ireland and Britain, except for parts of the Scottish Highlands, the lesser trefoil, *Trifolium dubium*, has leaves which have three leaflets. The leaflets are oval or heart-shaped; they are finely toothed, and the terminal leaflet is shortly stalked. Slender, and spreading close to the ground, the plant is also called suckling clover and is found in short pasture, roadside verges, gardens, and heaths. It grows to 20–50 cm on well-drained soil and has tiny, yellow flower heads. The flowers continue from May to October. In folklore the lesser trefoil is the symbol of 'joy in sorrow'.

APRIL

———

The countryside continues to brighten and enliven during April. The sun shines more and the grass grows green; the air gets warmer and the last of the ice and snow disappears. The forget-me-not and the cuckoo flower appear in meadows. The cuckoo arrives. The stitchwort grows on grassy banks, and bluebells join the anemones, primroses and lesser celandine in woodland. Other plants flower and attract early bees, butterflies, and aphids; and other insects are busy. Buds open on bushes and trees, and many more birds nest. Elvers arrive from the Sargasso Sea and move into freshwater; and the feral mink hunts the banks of rivers.

THE FERAL MINK
Mustela vison

In recorded history this little animal is the first wild, carnivorous mammal from another clime to make itself at home in Ireland and Britain. It is the wild American mink, a member of the family Mustelidae – the weasel family. The badger, otter and stoat are members of this family – in fact, almost half of the wild carnivorous mammals in Europe are musteline. The American mink is our most recent member.

Originally brought to western Europe in the late 1920s, this animal was control-bred for its rich fur. During the Second World War, the fur trade declined and minks escaped from captivity. In the late 1950s and early 1960s the trade picked up, but within ten years, it dwindled again and more minks escaped into the wild. Consequently, today's feral mink populations date from the mid-1970s. In the 1980s they were the most abundant carnivores in many areas, but because of their territorial nature and their greed, the numbers of mink levelled off within five or six years from the time of colonising those areas, and now they live unnoticed along many river banks in Ireland and Britain.

No longer wearing the beautiful cultured coats of pearl, tourmaline, and topaz, all of these wild minks have reverted to the natural coloration of their forebears. The fur of most of them is the colour of burnt toast with a white patch on the lower lip and chin, and a few white marks on the breast and belly. However, some of them appear totally black.

Ballynahinch, County Galway
KENNETH McNALLY

RICHARD T. MILLS

The feral mink is an arrogant little animal. Normally quiet and purring,   Mink
when cornered – or caged – it will emit a strong musky smell and scream in a
scolding fashion. Along a river bank it can make a den among rocks, in holes in
trees, in unused pipes or in the burrows of other animals. The female has a
short-range territory. The male will travel long distances and mate with
several females as he moves through their territories. They usually mate in
February through March and delayed implantation extends the thirty-day
gestation from thirty-nine to seventy-six days. The young are born during late
April through May. The single litter of five or six kits are mature in their first
year and breed the following spring. The average mature male, 60 cm long,
including a 16–17 cm tail, is twice the size of the female.

The feral mink can run quickly and catch a rat, leap suddenly and take a
moorhen, search small burrows and kill a stoat, climb high bushes and rob a
nest, fish for fluke and eel and other slow fishes, and swim strongly with a cub
rabbit or an adult rat in its mouth. It seems to prefer hunting from mid-evening
through the night, but a young mother with hungry kits will also be seen
during the day.

Since 1980 I have closely observed the American mink in our countryside,
and I have witnessed the failure of all sorts of control by means of human
intervention. Mink control their own numbers and they soon adapt to the ways
of our countryside. They have become important members of our wildlife
society. However, these exceptionally versatile and highly skilled predators
have been much maligned. They have been accused of breeding like rats,
attacking pets, killing poultry and lambs, and threatening numbers of available native species. These kinds of accusations have caused researchers to
prove the animal's innocence rather than its guilt.

In any year, wild minks have one litter of five or six kits, most of which die
before maturity. Minks avoid cats and dogs. They do not kill lambs. Like
badgers and stoats, they will slaughter hens and pheasants in pens, but they
can survive successfully along quiet stretches of river without going anywhere
near captive and domestic stock. Nowadays, while blaming the mink for
taking a number of chickens, many farmers praise the animal for controlling
numbers of rats. Given these facts, and the almost superstitious slaughter of

mink, and their unnatural reduction in numbers, they will probably require legal protection. Regarding this, it is now illegal to drown a mink in a cage – it is exceedingly cruel to drown an animal which can swim.

In rivers they compete with otters for eels, slow fishes and diseased trout and salmon. The otters are better fishers. Moorhens, mallard, and rats disappear for a while but they soon return. Once minks colonise an area, they protect their own territories; trapping programmes fail since they only make territories available to other wandering minks. They are wild carnivores, and soon learn not to kill too much, or store too much – there is no need.

THE ELVER
Anguilla anguilla

An elver is a fish whose slipperiness is proverbial. It is a young eel, one of the most remarkable creatures to visit our inland waters – it does not have the appearance of any of our fishes nor does it behave like any of them.

An elver is a snake-shaped fish. The body is 15 cm long and cylindrical; its yellowish-grey skin is thick and slimy with tiny scales embedded in it. The dorsal fin begins well forward and continues uninterrupted along the back to join the tail and the long anal fin. There are no pelvic fins and the paired pectoral fins are very small. On each side, just beyond where the head meets the body, the gill openings are tiny ear-like slits. It is a very tough little fish and can survive more pollution and adverse living conditions than any other freshwater fish. Born in the Sargasso Sea, between Bermuda and the Leeward Islands, an elver is three years old by the time it reaches freshwater. Very little is known about the life of the young eel at sea and it is difficult to generalise about the career of young eels – even in a river – because very soon they separate and go their own way. It is possible, however, to offer some information.

Adult eels spawn three thousand miles from Ireland, in the depths of the Sargasso. The parents die after breeding, but their eggs, afterwards larvae, float in the strong currents of the North Atlantic Drift. The tiny larvae are shaped like laurel leaves but, some time later, they change shape to become worm-like and are called glass eels. At this stage the young eels are about 6 cm long and completely transparent. They then move inshore, become yellowish-grey and are called elvers, or yellow eels. (The sand eel is not related.) Now 7.5 cm long, the elvers move into freshwater during April and May. They ascend the rivers to feed, grow and mature, before setting off in their turn to the western Atlantic on their own spawning migration.

Elvers take many years to become mature eels; most spend ten to twelve years in freshwater. The males stay in the lower reaches of a river, while the females move further upstream and will cross over land to live in lakes and ponds. They are active at night and spend the day under stones, or in crevices, but they may sometimes be seen swimming just under the surface in daylight. Younger elvers can be found in shallows enjoying the warmth of a sunny day. They rest during winter and become active in late spring, early summer, when the water grows warmer. Their usual nocturnal behaviour probably protects them from fish-eating birds. They are a delicacy for the heron, otter, and adult eel. Cannibalism is common in crowded conditions.

Elvers hunt for insects and crustaceans under stones and among water weeds, but they will eat almost any animal food – alive or dead. In all mature eels, feeding stops before migration. Growing elvers must build up high-energy reserves to enable them to make the long journey back to the breeding grounds in the Sargasso Sea, without eating on the way. After nine years, when the males are about 40 cm long – and after twelve years, when the females are nearing 60 cm – the elvers' bodies undergo marked change. Their heads become pointed and the eyes grow large; they grow fatter and the pectoral fins get bigger; the skin changes from its yellowish-grey colour to blackish with silvery-white underneath – they have reached maturity and are now called silver eels. In the autumn the silver eels make their way down to the mouth of the river, then they migrate to the sea to spawn and die.

NESTING BIRDS

During April many more birds nest. Here is a brief description of a number of the more common inland birds, their nests and broods. Some of the birds have already been described and these are marked with an asterisk (*). But, first, a few words about the cuckoo.

CUCKOO
Cuculus canorus

Some seven hundred years ago, eager to forget winter's dark silence and inspired by the cuckoo's arrival, John of Fornsete, a monk at Reading Abbey, wrote a song as remarkable as the bird itself; the first stanza runs:

> Sumer is icumen in,
>   Lhude sing cuccu!
> Groweth sed, and bloweth med,
>   And springth the wude nu:
>   Sing cuccu!

Although the cuckoo is widely known, welcomed as announcing the arrival of true spring, notorious for its breeding habits – laying its eggs in the nests of small birds such as the dunnock, pipit, and robin – it is a bird which relatively few people know to see. The two-note song 'cu-cu!' is easily recognised and is the call of the male; the female generally uses a bubbling note. It is a slenderly built bird, about 33 cm from thin black bill to tip of black and white tail. The male is ash-grey above and on head and breast, with fine black barring on the lower breast and white belly. Except for a rufous tint across her breast, the female looks like the male. From any distance the coloration of a cuckoo and a male sparrowhawk appears similar, and the cuckoo and sparrowhawk are almost indistinguishable in flight; but, in every other respect, comparisons are far from apt: the hawk is a fearless predator, the cuckoo is a scheming parasite.

Since it has been well known from ancient times that the common cuckoo does not build a nest of its own but lays

Cuckoo (juvenile)

RICHARD T. MILLS

eggs in the nests of other birds, and that the cuckoo chick evicts the true nestlings and so on, these familiar facts can be set aside to make room for observations and attempts at explanations. Cuckoos appear to be polygamous, with several males following a female; the usual number of eggs laid in a season is twelve to fifteen; the female probably uses the nests of other birds because nest-building wastes time; because of possible imprinting towards foster parents, cuckoos are likely to lay eggs in familiar nests; clutches disturbed by a cuckoo egg are likely to be deserted, but carefully placed, the cuckoo egg is usually accepted; to be accepted, the egg of the cuckoo need not closely match the eggs of the foster parents; its fearsome hawk-like flight may be deliberately used to cause potential foster parents to temporarily flee from nests – which the cuckoo then exploits; the great scarlet gape of the cuckoo chick and its persistent wheezy food-begging note appear to act as general purpose signals, for not only are they responded to by foster parents but may also cause passing birds to turn aside and provide food; adult cuckoos leave Ireland and Britain around the end of July to reach Africa – probably south of the Sahara – for winter; several weeks later and alone, the young follow them, so there seems to be no doubt that young cuckoos can find their way to winter quarters unaided by adults.

And so it continues, the story of the cuckoo: how for every cuckoo we hear with delight, a nest of other little birds has been sacrificed.

PHEASANT
Phasianus colchicus

The name 'pheasant' comes from the Greek *phasianos ornis*, meaning 'Phasian bird', after the River Phasis in the country formerly known as Colchis, to the east of the Black Sea. There are two species of true pheasant: the green pheasant of Japan and the game pheasant with many subspecies. The game pheasant is found in Ireland and Britain and was probably introduced from Asia at the end of the sixteenth century. In the mid-eighteenth century the widespread rearing of pheasant for shooting encouraged estate owners to provide suitable habitats for these birds. Foxes, stoats, otters, crows, hawks, falcons, even eagles were killed to protect them, but many other wildlife species have thrived in the pheasant's habitat.

The cock pheasant, 53–89 cm, is upstanding and very colourful with large red eye-wattles, iridescent bottle-green head and neck (some have a white neck ring), red-bronze

RICHARD T. MILLS

Pheasant

body barred above and below with black, and a very long, black-barred, majestic tail. The female is smaller and delicately barred across shades of buffy brown, and compared to the male, her tail is short and dumpy. Pheasants walk, run, and take off; the flight is direct and powerful, with long glides – especially when coming down to roost. They feed on shoots, seeds and berries. The call is an attractive and far-carrying 'kok—kok-kok!'

The pheasant always nests in some kind of low ground cover in neglected hedges, rough edges of fields, and in bracken in woodlands. The nest is a scrape, lined with dead leaves or strands of nearby foliage. The glossy olive-brown to olive-grey ten to fifteen eggs are incubated for twenty-four to twenty-five days. With yellowish-buff and rufous down, wearing two long dark stripes from the head down the back, the young leave the nest soon after hatching. The pheasant has a single brood: April–May; and sometimes a replacement clutch.

GREAT TIT*
Parus major

The great tit nests in holes in trees, holes in banks of earth, in walls – holes in a variety of places – and will use nest boxes. Cup-shaped and the same as the nests of the coal tit and bluetit, the great tit's nest has a soft foundation of thick moss, topped with more moss mixed with wiry grass and rootlets, overlayed with animal hair or plant down. White, spotted reddish, the seven to thirteen eggs are incubated for thirteen to fourteen days. With yellowish-pink skin, grey down on head only, and pale yellow gape-flanges, the young remain in the nest for eighteen to twenty days. There are usually two broods: April–July.

COAL TIT*
Parus ater

The sites and structure of the nest are similar to those of the great tit. White and speckled reddish-brown, the seven to ten eggs are incubated for fourteen to eighteen days. With grey down on head only, and pale yellow gape-flanges, the young remain in the nest for sixteen to eighteen days. There may be two broods: April–June; and sometimes a replacement clutch.

BLUE TIT*
Parus caeruleus

The site and structure of the nest are similar to those of the great tit. White and spotted reddish-brown, the seven to thirteen eggs are incubated for thirteen to sixteen days. With down on head only, and pale yellow gape-flanges, the young remain in the nest for seventeen to twenty days. There may be two broods: April–July.

BULLFINCH
Pyrrhula pyrrhula

Found about hedgerows, the bullfinch (15 cm) is a handsome, shy bird. The male has blue-grey upperparts with red throat and breast; its wings, tail, and cap are black. The female shows duller colouring; but in flight, which is undulating, both sexes have clearly visible white wing bars and rumps. They feed on buds and seeds, and the call is a soft 'heu!'

Usually one to two metres from the ground, in the dense growth of bushes and trees, mostly evergreens, and in heavy ivy, the nest is a platform of dry twigs with a shallow cup of rootlets. Pale blue, sparsely marked with reddish-brown, purple and black spots, the four to five eggs are incubated for twelve to fourteen days. With blue-grey down and yellow gape-flanges, the young remain in the nest for twelve to fifteen days. The bullfinch has two broods: April–August; and sometimes a replacement clutch.

RICHARD T. MILLS

Female chaffinch

CHAFFINCH*
Fringilla coelebs

RICHARD T. MILLS

Male chaffinch

The chaffinch builds in hedges and trees, often in a fork, about two metres or higher from the ground. The cup-shaped nest is delightful: very carefully woven out of fine grass, delicate fibrous rootlets, moss, spiders' webs, decorated with lichen, and lined with animal hair and fluffy feathers. Pale blue and scrawled and spotted with dark brown and black – edged with a lovely purplish-grey – the four to six eggs are incubated for eleven to thirteen days. With greyish-yellow down, and pale yellow gape-flanges, the young remain in the nest for twelve to fifteen days. The chaffinch usually has two broods: April–June; and sometimes a replacement clutch.

GREENFINCH*
Carduelis chloris

The greenfinch nests in hedges and sometimes in trees and heavy ivy, usually about two metres from the ground. Cup-shaped, the nest is woven out of grass, moss, and fine twiglets, and lined with animal hair and plant down. Pale blue, with reddish-brown and black spots and purplish-grey markings, the four to six eggs are incubated for twelve to fourteen days. With grey down, and yellow gape-flanges, the young remain in the nest for thirteen to fifteen days. The greenfinch has two broods: April–July.

Linnet

RICHARD T. MILLS

LINNET
Acanthis cannabina

In County Derry known as 'the grey', in the Glens of Antrim called the 'whin-grey', the linnet is one of my favourite birds. Still abundant in open areas, heaths, woods, hedges, and coastal areas, this attractive little finch (13.5 cm) was caged in Victorian and Edwardian times for its song; in more recent times, when I was a teenager, the 'grey' was bred with pure canaries, and the beautiful offspring songster was called a mule, which was sterile. The name 'linnet' derives from the Old French *linotte*, meaning 'flax', and when this crop was

RICHARD T. MILLS

plentiful the bird fed on flaxseed. Now a protected bird, the linnet still faces threat from attempts to completely destroy the chickweed and dandelion, the providers of the bird's other favourite seeds.

During late spring and summer, the cock linnet has red on the forehead and breast, a grey head and chestnut back, and white edges to the wings and tail feathers seen during flight. The female lacks the red colouring and is streaked above and below. During the winter, when the male loses his red markings, the linnets are seen in flocks. Always, the flight is undulating, and the voice is a musical twittering.

Occasionally hosting the cuckoo, the nest is found low down in bushes such as gorse, also in young plantations of conifer and deciduous trees. Cup-shaped, the nest is built with twiglets mixed with grass, moss, and fibrous roots; and lined with animal hair, feathers and plant down. Pale blue and speckled red, the four to six eggs are incubated for twelve to fourteen days. With yellowish-grey down and yellow gape-flanges, the young remain in the nest for eleven to fourteen days. There are two or three broods: April–August.

REED BUNTING
Emberiza schoeniclus

A noticeable bird, the reed bunting (15 cm) shows itself by perching on the tops of reeds and rushes in marshy fields. It has a brownish, heavily streaked plumage and the male has a conspicuous black head; the white-rimmed tail is seen during the jerky flight. Reed buntings feed on seeds. The song offers several deliberate notes ending in a hurry: 'cheep-cheep-cheep-chizzup!' Built on the ground, or close to it, sometimes in a tussock of reeds, the cup-shaped nest of grass and moss is lined with animal hair. Olive-brown, marked with strong brownish-black spots and scrawls and pale grey shell marks, the four to six eggs are incubated for twelve to fourteen days. With grey down and pale yellow gape-flanges, the young remain in the nest for eleven to thirteen days. There are two broods: April–July.

YELLOWHAMMER
Emberiza citrinella

Male yellowhammer

Found about hedges bordering wooded areas, its yellow plumage makes the yellowhammer very conspicuous and a delight to see. The male is brilliant: 16.5 cm, with a very yellow head and underparts, chestnut-brown and black-streaked wings, and chestnut-brown rump. The female is similar but her yellow is duller and her head is more streaked. The male and female like to be together but, during winter, they flock with many other yellowhammers. In April they feed on seeds; later they take insects. The flight is direct; and a

RICHARD T. MILLS

'little-bit-of-bread-and-no-cheese' is the popular version of the bird's song, but, in truth, it's a hammering song – a repeated series of notes ending in 'zeee!'

Frequently hosting the cuckoo, the cup-shaped nest is found in a natural depression in tall grass, or in a low bush or hedge. The nest is built with dry grass and rootlets, and lined with animal hair and fine grass. White or bluish-white showing purple and red scribbles, the three to five eggs are incubated for twelve to fourteen days. With grey down and yellow gape-flanges, the young remain in the nest for thirteen to fifteen days. The yellow-hammer has two or three broods: April–July.

WREN*
Troglodytes troglodytes
'The king of all birds' builds a number of magnificent domed palaces, one of which the 'queen' chooses and lines with her rich brown feathers. Without this lining, nests are not used for rearing wrens. The nests are built wherever the male chooses: ivy-clad walls, trunks of short trees, hawthorn bushes, in between dangling roots on walls or eroded banks; on almost any vertical, natural rough surface or crevice imaginable, also in nest boxes, sheds and outbuildings. Many nests are only 50 cm from the ground; many more are 100 cm high. Beautifully domed with a tiny round entrance hole at the side, the nest is built with much fresh moss mixed with crisp leaves, fronds of bracken, and lined with many feathers. White with fine, red-brown speckles, the five to eight eggs are incubated for fourteen to seventeen days. With greyish-black down and pale yellow gape-flanges, the young remain in the nest for fourteen to seventeen days. There may be two broods: April–July.

GOLDCREST
Regulus regulus
Our tiniest bird – 9 cm – the goldcrest spends most of its time in the tops of conifers. Apart from a faint, moustache-like marking, the face is plain – no eyebrow or eye-stripe – the upperparts are olive-green with black margins enclosing a golden crest or cap. The black wings have white edges and wing bars. The flitting flight is tit-like. The goldcrest feeds on spiders and insects; and the voice offers a high-pitched 'zi-zi-zi-zi!'

Usually built at the end of a conifer branch about ten metres from the ground, the nest is pot-shaped: with a small entrance hole at the top. The nest is carefully made out of moss, lichen, and spiders' webs; and the inside is comfortably lined with animal hair and feathers. Yellow but mostly white and speckled brown, the seven to eleven eggs are incubated for sixteen to seventeen days. With short grey down and greenish-yellow gape-flanges, the young remain in the nest for eighteen to twenty days. There are two broods: April–July.

GREY WAGTAIL
Motacilla cinerea
This very attractive bird (18 cm) is found about freshwater streams. Its upperparts are blue-grey, the underparts bright yellow. It has a very long tail with white outer feathers, and yellow undertail. The flight is undulating, but the grey wagtail spends most of its time trotting along the water's edge or perching and twitching its long tail on a stone in the stream, while

watching for flies, midges, and water beetles. The call is a metallic 'tzitzi!'; however, it also sings 'tsee-tsee-tsee!'

Usually built in a cavity near the water, for example, between tree roots in an eroded bank, also on ledges and holes in bridges and nearby walls, the neat cup-shaped nest made out of grass, leaves, moss, fine rootlets, and lined with animal hair and feathers, sometimes hosts the cuckoo. The four to six buffy, mottled grey eggs are incubated for twelve to fourteen days. With yellow down and yellow gape-flanges, the young remain in the nest for twelve to fifteen days. There are usually two broods: April–July.

KINGFISHER
Alcedo atthis

Seen about quiet even stretches of river, usually as a blue dart in flight, the kingfisher is one of our most beautiful birds. Its identity is unmistakable – the upperparts are bright blue with white cheek and chin patches, the underparts are orange and the legs are red. The flight is very fast, direct, and usually low. The kingfisher (16.5 cm) feeds on fish; and its call is a metallic 'chee!', often rapidly repeated.

Built in steep, sandy or easily excavated banks of rivers, the nest is a chamber at the end of a tunnel. Burrowed by the bird's long bill, and about 5 cm wide, the tunnel slopes slightly upwards for a metre or so. The nest chamber has no lining, apart from the remains of fish. Short, ovate, and noticeably white, the six to seven eggs are incubated for nineteen to twenty-one days. With pink skin at first, and bluish gape-flanges, the young remain in the nest for twenty-four to twenty-eight days. There are two broods: April–June.

MEADOW PIPIT
Anthus pratensis

About rough grass on moors, damp meadows, heaths, and dunes, the meadow pipit (14.5 cm) is seen flying up from the ground. It is brown and streaked, with white-rimmed tail feathers, and spends most of its time on the ground. However, it has an impressive rising and falling 'parachute' flight. Meadow pipits feed on insects; and the high-pitched calls are 'tissip!' and 'eest!' There is also the accelerating flight song of 'pheet!' notes which get faster as the male bird rises to some thirty metres – these are replaced by slower, more liquid notes as the pipit falls to the ground.

Built on the ground in rough grass, and often hosting the cuckoo, the nest is loosely made out of wiry grass and lined with hair. Greyish or brownish-yellow and heavily mottled with dark brown, the four to six eggs are incubated for twelve to fourteen days. With scanty grey down and dark yellow gape-flanges, the young remain in the nest for twelve to fifteen days. There may be two broods: April–July; and sometimes a replacement clutch.

RICHARD T. MILLS

Kingfisher

RICHARD T. MILLS

Snipe

SNIPE
Gallinago gallinago

Found in marshy ground and heath, the snipe is rarely seen until flushed from almost underfoot, causing it to make a repeated harsh call. A brown, long-billed game bird, 27 cm, showing dark and pale stripes on head and back, its flight is zigzag and very fast. It makes a drumming or bleating sound, caused by air rushing through the outer tail feathers; this sound prompted our grandparents to call the bird the heather-bleat. The snipe feeds on worms and insects; and it calls 'chirper-chirper!'

Hidden by tussocks of grass or rushes, the nest is a shallow grass-lined scrape in the ground. Olive-brown and blotched dark brown, the three to five eggs are incubated for nineteen to twenty days. With black down, tipped white, the young leave the nest soon after hatching. The snipe usually has a single brood: April–July.

RICHARD T. MILLS

Stonechat

STONECHAT
Saxicola torquata

Found about heaths and rough pasture, the attractive male bird displays an orange breast, black head, white neck patch, white wing patches and rump, and a dark tail. The female is paler, and her head is dark rather than black. The stonechat (12.5 cm) makes itself noticeable by perching upright atop bushes such as gorse, also on posts and conspicuous places. It flicks its wings and tail, and flies low and fast. It feeds on insects, spiders and worms. The alarm call, 'wee-tac-tac!' or 'chac-chac!' – like two pebbles being knocked together – gives the bird its name.

Often on the ground at the bottom of a bush or in a hollow hidden by low vegetation, and occasionally hosting the cuckoo, the cup-shaped nest is built with moss, grass, fine rootlets, leaves, and lined with fine wiry grass and animal hair – sometimes feathers. Pale blue and lightly speckled reddish-brown, the five to six eggs are incubated for fourteen to fifteen days. With whitish grey down and yellow gape-flanges, the young remain in the nest for ten to fourteen days. There are two or three broods: April–July.

WHEATEAR
Oenanthe oenanthe

This very attractive bird is one of our earliest summer migrants. Found about heaths, and rough pasture, it is seen perching on mounds, rocks on the ground, and posts. The wheatear (15 cm) has an upright posture with a bobbing action as it flicks wings and tail. It also darts into the air after insects. The male has grey upperparts, a black mask and black wings, buff breast and white rump – the name derives from 'wheatears', wrongly taken as plural, probably from white + arse. In flight, the black and white tail displays a bold inverted T pattern. The female is browner and wears a hint of a mask. The call is a harsh 'chak-chak!', with a brief warble mingled with rattles, squeaks and whistles. The flight is flitting, but can also be powerful and direct; and the wheatear can hover.

Built in a hole at ground level, or about 60 cm above the ground in banks and drystone walls, the untidy nest is made out of dry grass, sometimes

RICHARD T. MILLS

moss, and lined with hair and feathers. Very pale blue and unmarked, the   Male wheatear
five to six eggs are incubated for fourteen days. With
whitish-grey down, and yellow gape-flanges, the
young remain in the nest for fourteen to sixteen days.
There may be two broods: April–July; and sometimes
a replacement clutch.

KESTREL
Falco tinnunculus
Our commonest bird of prey, the kestrel (34 cm) is
seen hovering over moorland and meadow. The male
is marked with a blue-grey head and tail, and its
upperparts are reddish-brown and spotted with black;
the female bird is streaky brown all over. Both sexes
have long and pointed wings and their hovering flight
is distinctive. Kestrels feed on small mammals; and
the call is a high-pitched 'kee-kee-kee!'

Female wheatear

RICHARD T. MILLS

   Usually about ten metres from the ground on ledges of cliffs, often in
disused quarries, or in old solitary nests (of crows, magpies or buzzards) in
trees, the kestrel itself does not build a nest. Apart from accumulated remains of prey, or a flattened old nest of another bird, the kestrel's nest has no
lining. Yellowish-white and heavily speckled brown, the five to six eggs are
incubated for twenty-eight to thirty days. With white down, the young stay
in the nest for about thirty-five days. The kestrel has a single brood: April–
June.

Given the very few insects which appear in April, the most noticeable, and
worthy of mention, is the queen buff-tailed bumble.

THE BUFF-TAILED BUMBLEBEE
Bombus terrestris

Usually the first queen to appear, she is very large – 18–25 mm – and is black with yellow bands on front of thorax and abdomen, with a buffy tail. She will try to nest in a hole in the ground. The life of the queen began the previous autumn, when, after mating, she left her mother's nest and went looking for a place – usually in the ground – where she could spend the winter. In spring she emerges and flies about searching for nectar and pollen and a place to start her own colony.

Young queens are often seen walking about looking for a suitable site for nesting. A queen might take over the abandoned nest of a wood mouse or hedgehog; sometimes she will nest in a thatched roof or in an old bird nest. Her favourite places are banks below hedgerows and neglected corners of fields. Once she has selected her nesting place, usually a short tunnel into a small chamber, the queen visits nearby flowers for nectar and pollen. Inside the chamber she builds a nest of fine grass and rootlets. Except for very necessary outings, she seldom leaves the nest chamber. When the nest is ready she produces wax, which is secreted from between the plates on the underside of her abdomen, and builds a honey pot. Built near the entrance to the nest chamber, the honey pot will hold surplus nectar for use during cold and rainy weather. Then she builds a wax egg cell and lays a few eggs in it. After three or four days the worm-like larvae hatch and feed on a mixture of nectar and pollen. About a week later the larvae spin cocoons and change into pupae, and after a fortnight the young bees emerge from their cocoons.

These bees are sterile female workers, produced to gather food for the nest and to tend the next brood. Some of the workers build more wax cells and enlarge the nest. The queen lays more eggs. Before long a colony of more than a hundred workers is established. Then, the queen's only duty is to lay eggs. Late in the summer, some of the eggs produce fertile females, and males or drones. Larger than female workers, the fertile females are young queens. The drones are produced from unfertilised eggs, and have larger antennae than the other bumbles. They use their antennae to locate the fertile females. Drones do not work, and have no sting; their only use is to mate with the young queens.

Once the old queen has produced the drones and the young queens, she stops laying worker eggs; then she dies. After mating, the young queens leave the nest to find places where they can hibernate over winter. The drones die shortly after mating. Gradually the whole colony dies. Only the young queens are left to survive through to spring.

On Easter Sunday, 1990, on a bank of the River Lackagh in County Donegal, I watched a long-tailed field mouse dallying near a bumblebee nest: a hole in the bank. I waited to see if the mouse would go into the hole but an angler, eager to fish the pool, unwittingly chased it away. Field mice rob bees' nests, so do badgers and pygmy shrews; but there's an interesting story centring on the bumblebee and the field mouse.

In *On the Origin of Species* Charles Darwin stated that only bumblebees successfully visit the flowers of red clover, because red clover has a long narrow flower and other bees do not have tongues long enough to reach the nectar at its base. Darwin argued that if the bumblebee became rare or extinct, the red clover would die out also; and, because cattle were fed on red clover, this would have serious economic effects. However, he went on to explain that more than two thirds of bumblebee nests in England were destroyed by mice, and claimed that these nests were more common near villages and towns, where cats were plentiful. Therefore a large number of cats would protect the red clover, because the cats would eat the mice who kill the bumblebees. Thomas Henry Huxley provided the final link. He suggested that, since spinsters were very fond of cats, the sensible way to strengthen the economy of the country would be to increase the number of old maids: less weddings, more spinsters, more cats, less mice, more bumbles, more red clover, and more cattle.

THE PLANTS

April brings many more ground flowering plants, and bushes and trees come into leaf. Looking for fresh ground flora, I find sticky mouse-ear, stitchwort, cow parsley, forget-me-not, cuckoo flower, bitter vetchling, thrift, early purple orchid, butterbur, ramsons, alexanders; but April's special flower is the bluebell.

BLUEBELL
Hyacinthoides non-scripta

The bluebell is one of our most beautiful and special plants. Of the lily family and quite different from the Scottish 'bluebell' – which is the harebell – the bluebell is also called wild hyacinth. The rich carpets of bluebell that floor our broad-leaved woodlands and thickets are found only in Ireland and Britain. Nowhere else in Europe does the plant grow in such profusion. Just as we marvel at the tulip – that other member of the lily family, that so richly grows in the nearby reaches of mainland Europe – visitors from Holland, Germany, and the countries of Scandinavia marvel at our magnificent spreads of bluebell.

Bluebells

The bluebell flourishes near the Atlantic Ocean: the mild damp winters allow it to come into leaf in early spring, when it is also seen growing in hedgebank, even heathland. It can grow in both acid and calcium-rich soils and, like the wood anemone, celandine, and primrose, the bluebell flowers most freely in open woods, where there is more light than shade.

It grows to a height of 20–50 cm from a white oval bulb and has long, narrow, strap-shaped leaves. Showing lines from bottom to top, the rather fleshy green leaves appear in early spring. A few weeks later, a single tall flower stalk droops with its opening flowers. With blue petals and similar sepals, more than a dozen bell-shaped flowers can hang – in a row – along the lower side of a single stalk. Sometimes pink or white, the bluebell flowers from April until the close of June. Then, on their single stalks, the whitish-brown fruit capsules stretch out from clumps of remaining bluebell leaves, and split into three to release black seeds.

All parts of the bluebell contain chemical substances called scillarens which, ingested, may poison both animals and humans; and the sap of the plant may cause dermatitis. In folklore the bluebell is the symbol of constancy.

RICHARD T. MILLS

BOG MYRTLE

Myrica gale

About April's bushes and trees, I start with bog myrtle. Here I share a secret – about angling and midges and the scent of bog myrtle. It's always helpful to carry a fresh branchlet of the plant in your fishing bag, or attach a tiny sprig to the peak of your cap. There is plenty of bog myrtle, or sweet gale, in Ulster and I make good use of its fragrance: for while nearby anglers are being eaten alive by midges, the bog myrtle's scent keeps the little pests away.

On a still, mild evening in late spring or during summer, when midges fill the air like clouds of smoke, and I have to cross hillside and walk down into marshy valleys to fish lakes for good brown trout, I follow the paths where the sweet gale grows – I have yet to meet many midges above a bog myrtle bush. Where the plants are too far apart, I rely on the sprig in my cap, and wave my own branch of leaves to keep the midges at bay. Nearing a lake, where the midges become really vicious, I sink in mud and splash and squelch near bog myrtles, and when the plants release their scents, the midges hurry away. At the lake, down at the water's edge, when I rub a few leaves on a nearby plant and the strong fragrance completely fills the air, the midges fly off to bite somebody else. So, while other anglers use tobacco smoke, and apply creams to their exposed parts, and even light fires to keep the midges away, I use the scent of the leaves of bog myrtle.

Growing to a height of 60–137 cm in heathland and in very damp ground, the bog myrtle is a bushy shrub with erect reddish branches, greyish-green leaves, and catkins. Usually growing on separate plants, and appearing before the leaves, the male and female catkins show in April. Then, without stalks, the leaves appear. About 3 cm long, the tapered leaves have a few, blunt-toothed edges near the tip. The fragrance is produced by a resinous substance exuded by tiny yellow glands dotted over the surface of the leaves, which, on being rubbed, freely release their eucalyptus-like aroma.

In times past the bark of bog myrtle was used in tanning; and before the introduction of the hop, the bitter and aromatic leaves were added to beer during brewing to give it a strong flavour, and the plant's tiny berries were added to increase its intoxicating effect. The berries were also used for making candles that, when burning, gave out an incense-like aroma, hence the plant's other name, 'candle-berry'.

BILBERRY

Vaccinium myrtillus

Of the heather family, this delightful little deciduous shrub has many local dialect names. Here in Ireland, I have heard it called frawn and frochan, possibly from the Gaelic *fraochan*. In Scotland it's called blaeberry and in America blueberry, because of the colour of the fruit; hurtleberry, hurts, whortleberry and whorts possibly derive from America as dialectal variants of huckleberry. The name 'wine-berry' has obvious meaning, and 'whinberry' could be a corruption, or a name the plant earned living on whinny hills.

For at least six months of the year, from beginning April until October, over hilltop and moorland, the hill farmer, rambler, and shooting person will see the bilberry: an attractive, tasty, little shrub growing to a height of 20–60 cm in poor acid soil and tolerant of both shade and exposure. Because it sheds its leaves in autumn, the bilberry escapes notice in winter. But in spring, on green angular upright stems, numerous ovate leaves reappear. Freshly green, noticeably veined and finely toothed, the egg-shaped leaves are about 2 cm long. In April the drooping delicate flowers arrive singly, sometimes in pairs. Tipped with green, and wax-like, the globe-shaped pink flowers bloom into late June. Then the fruit appear.

Green at first, from July onwards, as they ripen, the berries become purplish with a very attractive blue-grey bloom. From high summer till autumn the berries are juicy, sweet and slightly acid. Goats, sheep, and game birds eat them. They are refreshing with cream, delicious in pies, and they make a pleasant jam. A decoction of the berries is believed to ease diarrhoea. At one time the purple juice was used to dye paper and linen. In folklore the bilberry is the symbol of treachery.

RICHARD T. MILLS

Blackthorn

BLACKTHORN
Prunus spinosa

I first met the dense, almost impenetrable and painful blackthorn bush many autumns ago. During my childhood, looking for good tough 'sticks', my father and I peered and reached into every dark thorny thicket in the local countryside. On Sunday afternoons we followed miles of hedgerows looking for suitable blackthorn bushes, growing to a height of four metres, with straight, tapering branches with lumpy heads and rough faces. We waited until Midwinter Day before taking the selected branches, then we made them into attractive walking sticks; and also made strong shillelaghs. I still look closely at blackthorns – I always like to see good 'sticks', but I don't touch them any more.

The name 'blackthorn' can be confusing: the plant's many branches are covered with a blackish bark, and its twigs are sharp thorns; yet during April its branches and twigs are covered with a mass of brilliant white flowers. Some say it should be called the whitethorn, but this name has already been reserved for the hawthorn, not because the hawthorn's flowers are whiter, but because its greyish-brown bark is lighter. To avoid confusion, like the haw and the hawthorn, the blackthorn could have been called the sloethorn.

At the end of March or the beginning of April, the blackthorn's five-petalled flowers appear before the leaves. Singly or in pairs, and with very short stalks, the soft white blooms appear to cling to the thorny twigs. The green leaves arrive on the twigs during April. Oval and about 2 cm long, the finely-toothed leaves have short red-tinged stalks. The leaves look ordinary enough, but in times past to increase the bulk or quantity of compounded or adulterated tea, dried blackthorn leaves were mixed with real tea leaves, and the product was sometimes sold as Chinese tea. Nowadays used as a mouthwash, an infusion of fresh blackthorn leaves will strengthen the gums and whiten the teeth.

Blackthorn blossom

In autumn, and borne erect along the spiny twigs, the plum-like fruit or sloes are pleasant to see, but not to taste. About 1 cm across, green at first and then ripening to black with a lovely blue bloom, the fruit are extremely sour and astringent. The tiniest taste of a ripened sloe will instantly dry up the mouth and prevent swallowing. Still, sloes are used in preserves, wine, gin, and for their astringent property. A syrup made from the fruit will leave the gums firm and healthy and free the teeth from tartar. In the past unripe fruit were sometimes pickled and used as substitutes for olives. And by adding a little sulphate of iron to give permanence, sloe juice was used as an ink for marking linen. In folklore the blackthorn is the symbol of difficulty.

WILD CHERRY
Prunus avium

In Britain the wild cherry is widespread in broad-leaved woodland, especially beech woodland on clayey soil. In Ireland it is an 'occasional' plant: met once in a while. Although this book is about commonly found fauna and flora, the wild cherry is one of a few exceptions. It is one of the marvellous discoveries in spring, a handsome reward for struggling the length of an overgrown, forgotten lane, or following animal paths or distant bird songs through neglected woodland. I never set out to find a wild cherry – that pursuit would spoil the surprise and delight. However, once I come across a tree, I usually return to enjoy its elegance.

In spring its white flowers strikingly brighten the enlivening green of hedge and woodland edge. In summer its glossy red cherries are devoured by resident birds. Through autumn, the yellow, orange-red and purplish-

Wild cherry blossom

brown leaves help bring cheer to their darkening surroundings. In winter, in pale sunshine, the smooth trunk gleams chestnut-brown, and its branches show grey-brown twigs with attractive clumps of bright brown pointed buds on short sideshoots.

For me, the wild cherry is a young tree. It quickly loses its beauty and elegance with age. About ten to fifteen metres tall, with shiny bark and good clean branches, plenty of healthy foliage, bloom and fruit, the wild cherry is beautiful. Above fifteen metres it becomes less elegant. Older trees, about twenty metres, can be sorry-looking, especially when witches'-broom takes hold and the bark is rough and splitting. The old trees have tall trunks and few lively branches, and away up, overhead, the crowns are narrow and too fluffy with blossom; and the flesh of the fruit is too light.

With the alternative name 'gean', the wild cherry is called after its fruit. From the Old French *guine*, 'gean' is taken to describe the tree's heart-shaped fruit. The tree itself, pyramid-shaped and of medium build, is usually about ten metres tall.

No matter the weather, clusters of flower buds and young leaves appear in mid-April. By the end of April the lovely flowers and the tapering leaves have unfolded. With yellow-anthered centres, and white petals above magenta sepals on a long, slender stalk, each flower measures about 2.5 cm across. Before the end of July the leaves – green above, greyish-green below – surround glossy red cherries on long stalks. If permitted, the cherries can turn black, but almost before they ripen, the fruit are quickly taken by resident birds.

Fine-grained and red in colour, wild cherry wood can be used to make furniture, veneers, and musical instruments including pipes. Containing cyanide, the pits or stones of the fruit should be discarded, but the tart berry flesh can be dried and used in scones. For gardeners, the wild cherry is the ancestor of popular ornamental trees, and of the fruit trees that give us cherry brandy, cake and jam. In folklore the wild cherry is the symbol of education.

ALDER
Alnus glutinosa

Growing to a height of twenty-two metres, but more usually eleven metres tall and standing alone, the alder looks a very ordinary tree, and because of its black bark and the deep green shade of its leaves and the dark cone-like fruit, too many together can easily heighten the dreary effects of a cold drizzly afternoon. Yet during spring the tree's purplish buds and its flowers give it appeal: the female flowers are like tiny crimson buds, and the long, male catkins, yellow and deep crimson, are attractive. The buds usually burst into leaf during the last week of April.

Alder catkins

Properly spaced along a river bank, a row of alders can be delightful and useful – the best trout and salmon will reach for a suitably dressed fly under an alder – in fact, a water's edge lacks charm without the alder. And for farmers, river workers, and commercial growers, the tree is valuable. Also called whistlewood, it provides an effective windbreak for animals, it prevents bank subsidence, and it can grow in conditions too damp for most trees or shrubs, including willows.

Concerning its commercial value, I paraphrase an account of the importance of the alder in *Our Woodlands, Heaths and Hedges* (1859), which describes the past uses of the tree. While the tree is standing the wood is white but, once cut, it takes on a pale flesh-coloured hue which remains. The wood's texture is even and soft for the turner and wood-carver to make various household items; as well as shafts of rakes, and broom handles, clogs, and soles for shoes. When dyed black,

Alder

Alder

artificially, or by long submersion in a damp place – such as a peat bog – and despite its lack of lustre and hardness, the wood was commonly substituted for ebony. It provides excellent charcoal; and if kept under water, it is almost imperishable and invaluable for piles, stake-nets and similar structures – 'it is said that on alder-piles the beautiful arch of the famous Rialto of Venice is supported'.

SYCAMORE
Acer pseudoplatanus

I have heard people describing the sycamore as the 'weed of trees'; they frown upon it. I disagree. This is a marvellous, handsome, and reliable tree. Since its introduction from France in the late Middle Ages, it has brightened our countryside and proved itself hardy in a wide range of places. Under adverse conditions, it has very successfully propagated with winged fruits. Regarding its identity, confusion exists. For many, it is the 'sycamore' in the Bible – the tree on which Zacchaeus climbed to see Christ as He passed on His way to Jerusalem; however, while the sycamore in the Bible was really a kind of fig tree – *Ficus sycomorus* – the sycamore in my garden is *Acer pseudoplatanus*, of the maple family.

When fully grown the sycamore is a massive tree, growing to a height of thirty-five metres with a contour almost resembling that of the oak. Yet,

Sycamore winged fruit

compared to the oak, the broader shape of the individual leaves of the sycamore gives it a far more substantial presence. When mature and in full foliage, the sycamore has a more dense, impenetrable shade than almost any other deciduous tree. For the sake of coolness, sycamores have been planted close to the sunny side of dairies.

At the close of April the young leaves are beautiful: when held up to the light, they show delicate transparent tints of red, amber and olive-green. As the season advances the leaves become opaque, and devouring insects cause some of them to look ragged and perforated. The sticky honeydew from aphids turns the leaves into dust traps, and they look dirty, especially near factories and roads; then fungi or bacteria mark the

RICHARD T. MILLS

Sycamore

leaves with black spot. Still, the sycamore pleases nature lovers and poets.
William Cowper well describes the tree's ever-varying hues:

> The sycamore, capricious in attire,
> Now green, now tawny, and ere autumn yet
> Has changed the woods, in scarlet honours bright.

The sycamore has other uses: the wood is a yellowish colour, compact and firm, but not very hard; it is easily worked and can offer a high polish; it is popular with turners, cabinet-makers, and musical instrument makers – it is a favourite material for violins. As a fuel, the sycamore is accepted as a very good wood, both for the amount of heat it gives out and for the length of time it burns. Medicinally, a decoction of the early leaves and bark was said to strengthen a damaged liver and spleen, and ease their pains. Disregarding damaged livers and their chief cause, the sap of the tree can be made into a tolerable sweet wine. In folklore the sycamore is the symbol of curiosity.

MAY

May is the prime month of the year. For most of our own wildlife, and for visitors from other climes, May offers a final opportunity to produce new life and growth – with the full heat of summer not yet begun, it is exciting, fresh and exuberant. Our most verdant month, its birthstone is the emerald; our most gracious month, its flower is the hawthorn; and, despite its constant pleasing humming about blossoms, and many beautiful extended songs from the sky and high trees, jingles from hedgerows, and warbles from thickets, piping and metallic sounds from lakes and rivers, whistles and wails and crackles and cackles from the shoreline, the most welcome sound is the 'crek-crek!' of the corncrake hiding in a meadow.

There are different stories about the origin of the name of the month. One claims that May was sacred to older men: that 'may' is an abbreviation of the Latin *majores*, meaning older men. Another tells how it is the month of Maia, a daughter of Atlas and the Roman goddess of spring and growth. In truth, it is the month of fresh grass, beautiful flowers like the buttercup, bugle and the herb Robert; the hawthorn and crab apple tree, the majestic ash tree and beech, the meek silver birch; tiny insects, greenfly on roses, butterflies and bees, and beetles on woodland floors; birds and fishes and mammals. It is the month of the rare corncrake and chough, of the visiting swallow-type birds, and the marvellous birds of the shoreline and the sea. And, while young pike and roach grow in slow-moving waters, and salmon and trout smolts make their first trip to the sea, and adult lamprey drift away with the tide to die, tiny fluke come into our rivers to feed. It is also the month of the pine marten, the long-tailed field mouse and the pygmy shrew.

THE PINE MARTEN
Martes martes

On Friday 13 May 1994 I received quite astonishing news. The conservation officer of the Ballinderry River Enhancement Association, County Tyrone, phoned to tell me that within the same week two pine martens had been killed by cars on the outskirts of Cookstown. Found by the chairman of the Lough Neagh and Lough Beag Wildfowlers' Association, the first pine

Foxglove, Twelve Bens,
County Galway
KENNETH McNALLY

marten killed was run over on a minor road between the townlands of Dunnamore and Tulnacross, County Tyrone. Some sixteen kilometres from the scene of that accident the second marten was killed on the road between Cookstown and Coagh, near what local people call the Dundering Rocks in the townland of Littlebridge, County Derry. From my own notes, the account of the second accident and its location is worth repeating:

> At 1 a.m., May 13, 1994, when rain was falling, a pine marten dropped from a roadside silver birch tree and landed on the bonnet of a car. The car was travelling at 65 k.p.h. One of the marten's hind paws was trapped by a windscreen wiper. The driver saw the animal twisting its body and staring in at him. When the driver instinctively brought the car to a halt, the struggling marten fell off the bonnet and died on the road.
>
> The place of the accident, Littlebridge, borders mossy ground and rich deciduous woodland where there is much ground flora, insect life, and many small birds; also red squirrel, fox, badger, mink, stoat, wood mouse, and many rabbits. The mossy ground hosts snipe, woodcock and pheasant, and the watery places keep mallard.

'I know it's hard to believe. Two of them being killed in the one week,' the conservation officer said. In truth, it was a strange coincidence, but even stranger was the news that pine martens were in the counties Derry and Tyrone. According to some sources, pine martens were found only in the west of the country, about the Burren. When I was told that both animals were in freezers and awaiting taxidermy, I went to Cookstown to see the martens for myself and to know their features.

Both were very handsome animals. Adult and male, they had broad triangular heads with pointed muzzles, and small pointed cream-coloured ears. The teeth were gleaming white and cat-like, with strong fangs and the incisors

Pine marten

evenly set. Their bodies were long, slender, and lithe with bushy tails; long strands of tail-fur extended 7.5 cm beyond the tail proper. The coats were honey-coloured, tipped with brown; the layer of underfur was dark grey; the muzzles and limbs were dark brown. One animal had a prominent cream patch on his throat; the other had a similar cream patch, but with a bright orange centre. Both animals were in beginning moult. Their shoulders and hips were very muscular and their short legs looked sturdy. Each foot had five toes with very sharp, curved claws which glistened. The remarkably large footpads were well protected by dark thick fur.

A member of the Mustelidae family, the pine marten is about the size of a cat – up to 45 cm, head and body; 23 cm tail – and is one of Ireland's rarest mammals. Once widespread in Ireland, the number of martens was greatly reduced during the late 1700s and through the 1800s. The decline continued and was probably due to the loss of suitable woodland habitat and persecution by gamekeepers. During the twentieth century, the populations were mainly found in the wilder parts of Ireland, especially the West. This discovery in mid-Ulster has caused much surprise, and also brought the heartening belief that these rare and beautiful animals were beginning to colonise the area.

Solitary and nocturnal, pine martens are rarely seen. The usual habitat is coniferous forest and other woodland, where they successfully hide. In some places they live on open ground, where they still keep out of sight. The den is among rocks or in a hollow tree; and like the other members of the Mustelidae family, martens have scent glands under the base of the tail. The secretions from these scent glands are used to mark the home range or territory.

Excellent climbers, they use the claws of all four feet to move up and down tree trunks, and they leap from one branch to another with the ease of a squirrel. The bushy tail gives balance, and if they fall with a broken branch, they can twist in mid-air and land like a cat on all four feet. Martens spend most of their time in trees but, following their acute sense of smell, they will travel many miles over ground to catch prey. They run quickly, and secure their prey by leaping and trapping the victim beneath heavy forepaws.

Pine martens are voracious hunters and take a wide range of food. They chase squirrels through the trees – indeed, the return of the pine marten would probably halt the steady increase of grey squirrel. They also feed on rabbits, rats, mice; small birds such as wrens, tits, treecreepers – and game birds and poultry. Martens also eat various caterpillars, beetles, slugs and bees; and they like blackberries, bilberries and cherries.

The pine marten sheds its fur in late spring and, again, in mid-autumn. Mating takes place in high summer – July and August – between the moults. Because of delayed implantation, the young are not born until the following spring – late March into April. There are usually three to four in a litter, but there may be two to seven young. Born in a nest of grass among rocks, or in a hollow tree, the infant pine martens have a sparse coat of cream-coloured fur. But at two months old, when they leave the nest, the young have thick adult-like coats. They are weaned at this time and then, during high summer when food is plentiful, they begin to fend for themselves.

The mother may stay with the cubs during autumn and beginning winter. The young then find their own territories, and many probably make use of the new conifer plantations. They are mature when a year old. Slightly smaller than the males, the females usually produce their first litter when two years old; and the cubs might live for seventeen years.

THE PYGMY SHREW
Sorex minutus

In Britain a rambler will sometimes hear and see squeaking common shrews angrily claiming some territory in a hedgerow, field, or woodland edge. Also in Britain, an angler will see a water shrew paddling to catch a spider. In the Isle of Scilly and the Channel Islands, observant holiday-makers will see white-toothed shrews hunting the seashores. But nobody will see any of these shrews in Ireland, for the only shrew found in Ireland is the pygmy shrew, a very special creature.

Pygmy shrews are our tiniest and mightiest mammals. Usually about 9 cm long, including the 40 mm long, thick tail, the biggest of these little creatures weighs less than an old florin. For good reason they usually try to avoid any conflict, but they will try to protect their young against rats – three times the size of any pygmy shrew. Their heads are bulbous, the eyes and ears are very tiny, and their bodies are covered with fine, dark, brownish-grey fur. They could be mistaken for mice but the relatively long, narrow nose is telltale. Pygmy shrews use their noses to explore small cracks and holes for food.

RICHARD T. MILLS

Pygmy shrew

The maximum life span of a pygmy shrew is about eighteen months, and it spends most of its life eating. They use up so much energy that, every day, they must eat the equivalent of their own weight to survive. If deprived of food for more than three hours, they will become seriously emaciated and quickly die. Their diet comprises spiders, small worms, wood lice, and insects. Their enemies are the fox, mink, stoat, feral cat, rat, owl, kestrel.

Pygmy shrews are solitary little beings and they are seldom seen. They survive in or on the ground, usually in tunnels in grass and among leaf litter. From late May through to autumn they have at least two broods of up to ten young. Most of the young die.

THE WOOD MOUSE
Apodemus sylvaticus

Also known as the long-tailed field mouse, the wood mouse measures 9.5 cm from its whiskered snout to the base of its long tail, which is longer than the body. Except that it looks cleaner, the wood mouse could be mistaken for the house mouse. Its fur is a striking fawn colour with white underparts and white feet. It has large eyes and prominent translucent ears, and its hind legs are much longer than its forelegs. It seldom goes into a building occupied by humans; it prefers a field, hedgerow, garden, graveyard, woodland edge, river bank, even lake edge.

Using runs through grass and leaf litter, and underground tunnels with entrance holes about the circumference of a golf ball, the wood mouse is active at night; but on numerous occasions I have watched it during the day. Earlier I

RICHARD T. MILLS

Wood mouse

mentioned watching a wood mouse at a bumblebee nest on a bank of the River Lackagh in County Donegal. Since then, one afternoon, in the summer of 1993, while making a television programme on coarse angling, I watched a pair of wood mice taking ants from a mossy stone on a bank of a lake in the Baronscourt estate in County Tyrone. Those mice were living in a hole about three metres from the edge of the lake.

Sometimes, without blocking the opening, a cairn of tiny pebbles – about 5 cm high, and the same across – is found close to the entrance to the long-tail's burrow. The purpose of the cairn is unknown.

After some time the cairn is dismantled and the tiny pebbles are found scattered over an area of a few metres. However, if a human dismantles the cairn and scatters the pebbles, the mouse will retrieve the same pebbles and rebuild the cairn in the same place.

Mostly underground and built with fine grass, the nests are used for breeding and sleeping. Breeding begins in early spring and continues until mid-autumn. The gestation period is twenty-five to twenty-six days. Born blind, the young leave the nest when two weeks old; they are weaned at three weeks. From five months old, a wood mouse might have up to six litters a year. She may have five to six young in May, but the warmer weather and greater amount of food supplies in June and July allow litters of eight to nine.

The diet comprises seeds, bulbs, grain, acorns, fruit, nuts, buds, seedlings, fungi, insects and snails; and the wood mouse hoards whenever a crop is available – whether acorns, hazel nuts, holly berries. Dozens of food items are commonplace in such caches; and where the contents are nuts, it's usual for people finding them to look about for squirrels. However, squirrels living in the same area as long-tails bury nuts and acorns singly. If the mouse's hoard is taken and scattered about, all will be collected and rehoarded in a few hours.

Although most are lucky to survive their first winter, wood mice can live for two years. Their keen senses, speed and agility help them to survive, but an inconsistent supply of food and the superior wit and skill of the predatory carnivores – the owl, kestrel, stoat, mink, feral cat, fox and rat – prevent wood mice from becoming pests.

THE HOUSE MOUSE
Mus musculus

Agile, but shy and easily frightened, the house mouse is about 8 cm from whiskered snout to base of long, scaly tail, which is also about 8 cm. It has a pointed face, big eyes and round-shaped ears. The fur is greasy and greyish-brown on the upperparts, and whitish-yellow beneath. Wherever humans are, the house mouse is seldom far away. It will eat almost anything humans eat, and usually lives in buildings but, if living in a hedge, field or woodland, it will feed on insects and the seeds, leaves, roots and stems of plants. It is exceptionally adaptable, and colonies have thrived even in frozen

House mouse

stores, growing longer fur to keep out the cold. Like the wood mouse, the house mouse prefers to move about in the dark, but is often seen during daylight hours. Males fight to establish dominance and defend territories.

The house mouse breeds throughout the year and may have five litters of between six to ten each time. There is a high mortality during infancy. Their foes include the owl, rat, and usual predatory carnivores. Their chief enemy is the domestic cat.

THE FLUKE
Platichthys flesus

Fluke, or flounder, breed in the sea but enter brackish estuaries and fresh-water rivers to feed and grow. Spawning always takes place in the sea, and shaped like the young of typical fish, the fluke larvae live in the surface water, slowly drift inshore, and then sink to the bottom. At the same time, their shape changes. The body becomes flattened and both eyes appear on the right side of the head. In the fluke's development, what was the right side of the fish becomes its top or upper side, and what was formerly the left side becomes the underside. The young fluke has become a flatfish with a diamond-shaped, spiny body.

Fluke grow to 50 cm and have three rows of backward-pointing spines or prickles. Two rows are found on the outer margins of the fish – at the base of the dorsal and anal fins; the other row of spines is along the lateral line, now running along the centre of the fluke's coloured uppermost side. The body colour is usually brownish olive-green on the upper side with dark and light blotches giving a speckled effect. The lower side is white with a tinge of blue. But fluke can change colour to blend into a background of mud, sand and gravel.

Tiny fluke move into estuaries and then into rivers to reach freshwater. The adult fish seem to prefer the brackish water, where reduced salinity is accept-able. Although swarms of tiny fluke frequent tidal stretches, they often fail to reach freshwater because of weirs. While elvers are able to climb waterfalls and even move over damp ground, fluke can only move up streams free from any obstruction: weirs, and sills of any sort, impede their progress. They feed on molluscs, crustaceans, and anglers' bait. The type of food taken suits the animal's small mouth and the arrangement of crushing teeth in the throat. In late winter the fluke migrate offshore and travel about five kilometres a day to well-defined spawning grounds. Using up fat reserves, they take no food on their migration. The spawning happens during February into April, and they arrive back in our estuaries and rivers during May.

NESTING BIRDS

More birds nest during May. Here I consider a number of birds observed about the shoreline and I give a brief description of the more common birds, their nests and broods. A few of the birds have already been described and these are marked with an asterisk (*). But first, a few words about the corncrake, the chough, and the visiting swallow-type birds.

CORNCRAKE
Crex crex
The corncrake, or land rail, used to be our most-heard and least-seen bird, always hiding in rushy pasture or nettle beds or the tall vegetation of disused meadows, and hay meadows and cornfields. Seeing it was always a rare occurrence, but the bird was frequently heard. Sadly few people hear the corncrake any more. The bird has become decidedly scarce – seriously 'at risk' – and is mainly confined to north Donegal, County Fermanagh, and the Shannon callows. Living in northwest Donegal, I still hear the corncrake, but I hear fewer every year, and have a strong notion that if I live for another ten years I will outlive this bird. Through making radio and television programmes on wildlife species, and working with field officers of the Irish Wildbird Conservancy and the Royal Society for the Protection of Birds, I am very much aware of dwindling corncrake populations, and the considerable amounts of expertise, time, effort, and money employed to keep the corncrake from being a thing of the past; but I fear my own grandchildren will never experience one of the challenges of my childhood:

> I have followed it for hours and all to no purpose. It seemed like a spirit that mocked my folly in running after it . . . the noise it makes is a low craking.
>
> JOHN CLARE, 1820

According to the Irish Wildbird Conservancy, a decline in corncrake numbers was first noted in the east of Ireland around 1900. By 1970, although calling birds could still be heard in every county, the birds were rare in the east and the south of Ireland. A census in 1978 showed a serious decline in both the numbers and range of corncrakes – the population of calling birds was estimated to be 1,200–1,500. A further survey in 1988 showed a continued contraction in range; and estimated a maximum of

Corncrake

RICHARD T. MILLS

1,000 calling birds. Since 1988 further surveys have reported a further de-cline in numbers. This small Irish population is very important because it represents 20 per cent of the western European total.

According to the Royal Society for the Protection of Birds, as smaller fields were amalgamated, hedgerows, hedgebanks, and rough field margins were lost, leaving corncrakes with few suitable areas for breeding. Earlier mow-ing dates for hay, and especially silage, have prevented corncrakes from raising their young in grass fields. The society desires more sympathetic mowing methods to reduce the destruction of nests and chicks, and seek the continuance of traditional methods of farming. Looking at a 1970 angling diary, I found an entry concerning a corncrake nest and its occupants, 'living articles threshed into mincemeat and snippets of feather' in a meadow in Legahory in County Derry. But farmers are only a part of the story. The drought-stricken wintering places of these birds in Africa – and the age-old practice of netting them on the way here – and the huge industrial com-plexes and housing estates built on corncrake territories have further re-duced the bird's chances of survival.

Arriving from Africa in later April, corncrakes quickly hide in available ground cover, such as rushy pasture. By the middle of May the birds are innocently nesting in meadows. The use of fertilisers to promote early growth of grass, and increased cutting for silage rather than hay means that meadows are cut earlier and more often, and this endangers ground-nesters. Meadows are now cut before the first corncrake clutch hatches, and modern machinery cuts so close to the ground that the nest, eggs, and sometimes the hen bird are cut to pieces. If the mother survives, she will lay a replacement clutch, but these young birds also risk being destroyed: they are reluctant to cross already cut grass because of the dangers from predators such as hooded crows – which also rob the nests of corncrakes. Because meadows are normally cut from the edges inwards, the birds meet death in the middle of the field. For this reason, field work officers of both protection groups try to persuade farmers to cut their pastures from the centre out and, perhaps, leave a patch of cover in the centre of the field or around the edges, allowing the birds a chance of escape. At present, grants are available to farmers who have breeding corncrakes on their land. The grants are offered to encourage farmers to delay cutting hay and silage, giving the birds a chance to raise broods.

Voicing a low rasping 'crek-crek!' call throughout the night and some-times during the day, the bird (27 cm) spends most of its time in the undergrowth, but when disturbed it flies away in a laboured manner with long, pink legs trailing. It has a narrow body, and bold chestnut wings. The upperparts have dark feather-centres edged with light brown; the under-parts are buffy with a chestnut barring. Corncrakes feed on plants and invertebrates. For nesting they prefer comparatively dry ground with veg-etation tall enough to hide the nest: on the ground, a shallow depression lined with bits of grass and leaves. A long time ago, in Ardmore, County Derry, I found a corncrake's nest in a pat of hardened cow dung. Yellowish-white or green blotched with reddish-brown, the eight to twelve eggs are incubated for fourteen to eighteen days. With blackish-bronze down and black bill and long, dark toes, the young leave the nest soon after hatching. The corncrake has a single brood: May–June; and usually a replacement clutch.

Corncrake

RICHARD T. MILLS

Chough

RICHARD T. MILLS

CHOUGH
Pyrrhocorax pyrrhocorax

In July 1990 I went to south Donegal's Sliabh Liag, Europe's highest sea cliff, looking for choughs, and I found them. The previous August I had arrived too late, the birds had flown. But on Sunday 22 July, at Doon Point, near Glencolmcille, I watched two pairs – late nesters – gathering food for nestlings, ready to fly. In 1992, I followed a flock of choughs on the outskirts of Clifden, County Galway; and, in 1993, in a place called Lag, on the Inishowen peninsula, County Donegal, I watched about thirty choughs crowding the sky. These are exciting and rare birds.

Both on the ground and in flight, the adult birds' calls give them away. Their far-carrying 'kwee-ow!' calls – higher, more prolonged and more musical than the best similar 'caws' of jackdaws – ripple louder than the sea below. The old pronunciation of the bird's name, 'chow', is an imitation of the chough's call. In 1908 Richard J. Ussher, author of *A List of Irish Birds*, described the chough as 'a decreasing species, which needs protection'. Ussher's fears were well founded. The decline in our chough population continued until the mid-1920s, but since then there has been an increase in some areas. Yet in 1990, only about six hundred pairs nested in Ireland, mainly on the west coast between counties Donegal and Cork, on our wildest, undisturbed cliffs and islands. They are very rare along the north and south coasts, and are almost entirely absent from our eastern seaboard. Told that choughs were nesting on Rathlin, I visited the island in 1993 to discover that the last pair had gone. Still, even though the bird is the rarest crow found in Ireland, we have more choughs than Britain and mainland Europe. The chough is absent from England, not known to breed anywhere in the wild since 1952. Formerly common enough in Scotland, occurring inland and on craggy coasts and islands, only a few birds remain on islands in the southwest. They continue to survive in Wales, with about a hundred pairs nesting mainly in Pembrokeshire and Caernarvon; also several pairs in other counties. On the Isle of Man about twenty pairs use the sea cliffs.

The cause of the decreasing numbers of choughs is unknown. The severe winter of 1962–3 was considered and dismissed as a cause. The decline was also attributed to the birds' need to compete with the increasing numbers of jackdaws; but in areas where there are no jackdaws the choughs still vanish.

The peregrine falcon is also blamed. The peregrine kills and frightens choughs – one of the last choughs in Cornwall was probably killed by a peregrine. Yet the bird's greatest enemy is probably human, and their decline in Ulster is thought to be due to farming 'improvement' of cliff top pastures. Although the chough is protected by law, nests are still robbed.

Once you see a chough, you will know it. About the size of a jackdaw, 39 cm, its flight is graceful and the primary feathers are well separated to form 'fingers', noticeable when the bird glides and soars. The plumage is glossy blue-black, sometimes with a greenish tinge on the wings and tail. From a safe distance, using binoculars, the long, thin, red, slightly downcurved bill and red legs make the chough unmistakable. It is a shy bird, easily frightened – two hundred metres away is near enough for any watcher. The bird feeds on insects, worms, and seeds.

Built on ledges of sea cliffs, also on rock faces in quarries, and in old ruins, the bowl-shaped nest is made out of sticks, twigs, and stems of nearby plants, and is lined with grass and animal hair. Creamy, or greenish with brown marking, the three to five eggs are incubated for about twenty-one days. With greyish-brown down and yellow gape-flanges, the young remain in the nest for thirty-eight days. The chough has a single brood: April–June.

SWALLOW
Hirundo rustica

At the close of March swallows (19 cm) arrive from Africa in ones and twos, but most of them appear in late April, early May. They return to Ireland to build nests and rear young in the barns and outbuildings they were born in themselves. Yet, after such a long journey, they rarely land on the ground, except briefly to gather mud and grassy materials for the nest. Their legs and feet, short and small, well-adapted for clinging to build the nest or to enter it, are not designed for walking on level ground.

Swallow at nest

RICHARD T. MILLS

They land on buildings, perch on telephone wires, and then take off to glide and flit in the air. They fly fast and acrobatically, searching for insects over field, moor, garden, marsh and fresh-water. They drink on the wing, dipping and skimming over the surface of water, and most of their insect food is taken at low level. The strong, long, angled wings and the deeply forked tail – with noticeable long streamers in the adult bird, especially the male – are unmistakable. The upperparts are a gleaming blue-black and the face and throat are russet, bordered by a dark band above the pale cream to rich pink of the breast and belly.

Swallows are modest singers, the voice offering only 'vit-vit-vit!', a pleas-ant twittering trill. The song is often heard as the birds perch on telephone wires or when flying low over water in the company of house martins. Swallows nest in solitary pairs but enjoy the company of other swallow-type birds when feeding. In August, when breeding and parent duties have ceased, they will join the company of their own kind, as if for a get-together before migration.

The nest is a shallow cup of mud and grass or straw, built on a high ledge

(vertical left margin text) RICHARD T. MILLS

or rafter in a barn, shed, garage or other outbuilding. The four to five white eggs with reddish spots take a fortnight to hatch. After another three weeks the young take to the air to learn to fly and feed like their parents, before the long journey to Africa in late August, beginning September. The swallow has two or three broods: May–June.

HOUSE MARTIN
Delichon urbica

Arriving from Africa during late April into May, house martins start breeding almost immediately. A compact body with a short tail, and a flashing white rump in flight, distinguish the house martin (12.5 cm) from the swallow. The tail is only slightly forked and lacks the adult swallows' streamers. The blue-black on crown and back, black wings and tail, noticeable white rump, and pure white breast and belly, clearly identify the house martin. Other telltale signs include the bird's harsh 'chirrup!' call, quite unlike the voice of the swallow; and although it spectacularly wheels and swoops to compete with swallows for insects low over water, the most marvellous flying house martin can never match the length of glide, acrobatic flit, or speed of the swallow. During September, house martins leave to return to Africa, to spend the winter south of the Sahara.

House martin

Traditionally cliff-nesting birds, house martins have adapted to building their nests under the eaves of houses in suburbs, small towns and villages, with a river or pond nearby. The nest is the familiar upside-down 'mud hut', built under high overhanging structures such as eaves. Colonies of nests are common. The outer shell of the nest is hardened mud, so a nearby source of soft mud is needed. The small entrance hole is at the top of the nest; the interior is lined with soft material like wool and grass. The four to five white eggs take about a fortnight to hatch. The young usually leave the nest after three weeks. The house martin has two to three broods: May–July.

House martins gathering mud

SAND MARTIN
Riparia riparia

The smallest of the swallow-type birds, 12 cm with sharply angled wings but a shallow fanned tail, sand martins are brown rather than blue-black. The upperparts are sandy brown and the underparts are white, with a distinctive brown breastband. Like house martins, the sand martins are gregarious; they feed, breed, and migrate together. Frequently seen feeding over water in twittering flocks, they tend to flit in an erratic fashion and only occasion-

Sand martin

ally glide. The call is a continuous harsh 'chirrup!' Sand martins also arrive from Africa at the end of April, but sadly fewer of them arrive with every year. They are a species 'at risk'. The population has declined alarmingly and is now less than 10 per cent of the mid-1960s figure. A sharp reduction in numbers in the mid-1980s was associated with the droughts in Africa, which dried up many of the non-flowing and stagnant waters that were the breeding places of the aerial insects on which the overwintering birds feed.

Like the house martin, the sand martin takes its name from its nesting habits. The nests are at the end of bird-made tunnels in sand banks, cliff faces, quarries, railway cuttings. Colonies of nests are usual.

With bill and feet, the bird digs a horizontal tunnel into the bank. The width of the tunnel is about five centimetres, the length about one metre. The tunnel leads to a nesting chamber lined with feathers and bits of straw. The four to five white eggs take a fortnight to hatch, and the young remain in the nest for three weeks. From the end of August until mid-September, the sand martins leave to return to Africa, south of the Sahara. The sand martin has two broods: May–June.

Swift nestlings

SWIFT
Apus apus

Of all our visiting species of bird, the swift is the most fascinating. It is the most aerial of birds, only ever touching solid material with its feet when nest-building, laying, incubating the eggs, and feeding its young. It only comes down to earth accidentally – it collects the nesting material and its food in the air, and drinks and bathes while skimming over water; it preens and mates in the air, and sleeps in the air after darkness. Out of the breeding season it remains airborne for months at a time, and flies very high in the night sky.

Like swallows and martins, swifts are gregarious; but watchers will never see lines of them on telephone wires. Swifts cannot perch, their legs are far too short and the feet are too weak. The claws are able to support them as they briefly cling to a wall before going into the nest; but the birds cannot walk on the ground. If accidentally grounded, they need to be lifted into the air. Flying with swallows and martins but easily distinguished by the torpedo-shaped body, long and narrow, sickle-shaped wings, short forked tail and black coloration – except for the grey breast – swifts (16.5 cm) clearly belong to a different order of birds. Well-named, they fly very fast with furious wing beats, then glide for long distances, and they scream loudly. The shrill screams of parties of swifts over streams in summer evenings cause anglers to go elsewhere. The significance of these 'screaming parties' is unknown. The swifts suddenly arrive in Ireland from Africa during May, they soon breed and then begin to leave again shortly after July.

The pieces of nesting material – wisps of animal hair, feathers, leaves, strands of straw, all collected in flight, are flattened, and glued together with saliva. The nest material is shaped like a shallow saucer in a hole in a cliff or building. Sometimes swifts nest in gaps in stonework under roofs; sometimes they take over old nests of other species, or build over old nests. Occasionally they use nest boxes; but colonies of nests are more usual. Taking food in the air, the insects are guided into the bird's large gape with the help of stiff bristles around the mouth. Food for the nestlings is stored in the parent's throat pouch, often seen distended. The three white eggs hatch after a fortnight to three weeks. The young stay in the nest for up to eight weeks. The swift has a single brood: May–June.

Swift

KITTIWAKE
Rissa tridactyla

With its soft grey plumage and black wing tips, a white graceful head, yellow bill and black legs, the kittiwake (40 cm) is unmistakable. Forming large nesting colonies on inaccessible sea cliff edges, and repeatedly calling

RICHARD T. MILLS

Kittiwake

'kitti-wa-a-k!', the bird perches openly, and soars and glides and swims. Kittiwakes feed on small fish, molluscs and shrimps. Compared with other gulls, the cup-shaped nest is deep and neatly made out of seaweed and moss. Creamy and speckled brown, the one to three eggs are incubated for about twenty-eight days. With greyish-brown down and creamy white on the head and throat, the young remain in the nest for four weeks. The kittiwake has a single brood: May–July; and sometimes a replacement clutch.

COMMON GULL
Larus canus

RICHARD T. MILLS

Common gull

Except in northwest Ireland and Scotland, this gull is not as common as its name suggests. It has a small round head and a yellow bill and legs. The upperparts are grey with black wing tips showing white spots called mirrors. The call is a high-pitched 'kee-aa!'; the flight is strong with soars and glides. Like other gulls, it swims, wades, and perches openly. It eats worms, insects, and molluscs.

The common gull (40 cm) nests in small colonies on rocks, islands, marsh, and moorland. It avoids exposed parts of the shoreline and usually nests on the ground. The nest is a hollow, lined with a variety of nearby plant material and a few feathers. Pale blue, or green, or olive-brown, marked with dark grey and black streaks, the two to four eggs are incubated for twenty-one to twenty-five days. With pale grey and black down, the young leave the nest after a few days but remain in the colony. The common gull has a single brood: May–June; and sometimes a replacement clutch.

HERRING GULL

Larus argentatus

A common and familiar gull, its loud 'kyowk-kyowk!' call rings across seashore and harbour. The adult bird (60 cm) has grey upperparts with black wing tips and white mirrors, and the legs are pink. The bill is yellow with a red spot on the lower mandible. Young birds peck at the parent's red spot to stimulate the regurgitation of food. The young remain speckled brown for several years before they grow their adult plumage. Although the herring gull eats herring, it will eat virtually anything, including small mammals and birds; and it frequently visits rubbish tips. The flight is powerful, with soars and glides.

Herring gull colonies vary in size, with individual nests well spaced out. Sited on sea cliffs, on seaside buildings, and sometimes on shingle and dunes, the nest varies from a sparsely lined scrape to a bulky structure made out of seaweed and moss. Pale-brown to stone-grey, or brown, with black markings, the two to three eggs are incubated for about twenty-eight days. With grey and black down, the young leave the nest after a few days but stay in the colony. The herring gull has a single brood: May–June; and sometimes a replacement clutch.

LESSER BLACK-BACKED GULL

Larus fuscus

A very handsome bird (55 cm) with dark, slate-grey back, black wing tips and white mirrors; white head, breast and underparts; yellow bill with red spot, and yellow legs. The flight is powerful, with soars and glides. Like the herring gull, the lesser black-backed gull will eat virtually anything. The voice offers a variety of calls such as 'kyowk-kyowk! kee-aa!' Often sited on grassy slopes overlooking the sea, there are also nesting colonies on moors, bogs and near inland waters. Built in a shallow scrape or hollow on flat ground, the nest is made out of bits of nearby vegetation: grass, seaweed, rushes, heather. Greenish-grey to dark brown with black blotches, the two to four eggs are incubated for about twenty-eight days. With grey and black down, and running about the colony, the young look very like herring gull chicks. The lesser black-backed gull has a single brood: May–June; and sometimes a replacement clutch.

GREAT BLACK-BACKED GULL

Larus marinus

A massive bird, 70 cm, and outstanding in any mixed gull flock. The adult has a large white head and hooked bill – yellow with a red spot. It has a black back, black wing tips with white mirrors, white underparts and flesh-coloured legs. The flight is very powerful, with soars and glides; the calls are 'owk!' and 'uk-uk-uk!' The great black-backed gull is a threat to any colony, it eats chicks and mature sea birds, also carrion, crabs, fish, and offal. It nests in isolation or in small colonies, usually on steep sea cliffs. The nest is a bulky structure of sticks and seaweed. Stone-grey to olive-brown with brown speckles, the two to four eggs are incubated for about twenty-eight days. With pale grey and brown down, and noticeable black markings on the head, back and throat, the young leave the nest after a few days, but they stay nearby. The great black-backed gull has a single brood: May–June; and sometimes a replacement clutch.

BLACK-HEADED GULL

Larus ridibundus

Probably our most common and widespread gull (35 cm), found about shoreline but also frequenting gravel pits, reservoirs, lakes, boggy areas. Flocks can also be seen following tractors ploughing, and frantically and noisily competing to grab freshly turned worms, grubs and insects. The name 'black-headed' is misleading: reduced to a spot behind the eye during the winter, the hood is chocolate-coloured, not black, during the summer. The upperparts are pale grey; the throat, breast, and belly are white; the bill and legs are red. The flight is powerful with soars and glides; and the calls are a repeated 'kuk-kuk!' and a rasping, angry 'kee-arr!'

Nest sites include marshes, dunes, tiny islands, crannogs; and colonies vary in size. In a scrape, the bowl-shaped nest is made out of pieces of nearby vegetation. Buffy or pale blue, olive-green or deep brown, marked with purplish and black blotches, the three eggs are incubated for about twenty-four days. With red and blackish-brown down on upperparts, the young leave the nest after a few days but remain in the colony. The black-headed gull has a single brood: May–June; and sometimes a replacement clutch.

Common tern

COMMON TERN

Sterna hirundo

A summer visitor mostly found about the west and north-west coastal areas and lakes, the common tern (35 cm) has a light grey back, white breast and underparts, black cap, orange-red bill with a black tip, and red legs. Called the swallow of the sea, its white tail is noticeably long and forked. The flight is very graceful, with glides and steady hovers – to watch the sea or water below – and then marvellous aerial dives and vertical plunges into the water to take small fish. The call is a harsh 'kee-arr! kirri-kirri!'

Sited on coastal beaches, dunes, islets, crannogs, the common tern nests in colonies and often near black-headed gulls. The nest is usually an unlined scrape or hollow on the ground. Creamy and blotched black or brown, the two to three eggs are incubated for twenty-three to twenty-four days. Wearing yellowish-grey down with black mottling, the young remain about the nest and are able to fly after three weeks. The common tern has a single brood: May–June; and sometimes a replacement clutch.

FULMAR

Fulmarus glacialis

With long narrow wings held slightly outstretched, occasionally flapping, this gull-like bird glides and skims the sea, and then rises to soar in the updraughts along cliff faces. It is a common bird. The population of fulmars has increased dramatically since the first birds arrived in the Shetlands in 1878. The increase was possibly aided by the growth in the fishing industry and the new abundance of fish waste.

The fulmar (47 cm) is a strong handsome bird with grey upperparts, a thick neck, large white head, and a short, heavy, yellow 'tube-nosed' bill. The underparts are white, the tail is grey, short and square; and the legs are yellow

and short. The bird is ungainly on land and seldom leaves the vicinity of the nest. With the parent bird at home, any person who gets too close to the nest will be sprayed with a stinking oil. From the fulmar's stomach, and strongly squirted out of the bird's nostrils, the fluid can easily hit a target a metre away. I watched a camera getting drenched with it on Inishtrahull, eleven kilometres off the north Donegal coast. The bird feeds on fish and crustaceans; and from the nesting colony, its loud clear voice offers a variety of crackling, cackling and chuckling sounds.

Fulmar

The nesting colonies are usually sited on inaccessible ledges on cliffs overlooking the sea or coastal lakes. Sometimes decorated with small pebbles, the nest on a very narrow platform has no lining or any other nest-building material. The single white egg is incubated for fifty-three to fifty-seven days. With upperparts grey, and white down on head and underparts, the young remain in the nest for forty-eight days. The fulmar has a single chick: May–July.

GANNET
Sula bassana

This is a truly marvellous-looking bird, 90 cm, with a gleaming white body and pointed tail; long, straight and pointed black-tipped wings; buffy head and neck; thick straight grey dagger-like bill, and black legs. And in flight it is magnificent. When eleven or twelve kilometres out in the Atlantic, with a northerly breeze making boat-handling difficult, and the company feeling a bit upset, gannets always make things better. Whether skimming the ocean or flying overhead, like white and black torpedoes in the sky, everybody watches them and discomfort goes away. The flight of the bird is unmistakable and its vertical dives are unforgettable, breathtaking to watch. Suddenly, from forty metres up, the gannet nose-dives into the sea to take fish. Then two or three, maybe half a dozen, circle the boat again, and cross the bow, before heading off into the horizon.

Gannet and young

At their breeding colonies on cliff faces, the gannets grunt and cackle. Close together, the nests are mounds of seaweed. The single blue-green egg is incubated for forty-three to forty-five days. Then, after about eleven weeks, the young bird makes its own way to sea. The gannet has a single chick: May–June.

OYSTERCATCHER*
Haematopus ostralegus

The oystercatcher nests on the ground, on the seashore on sand, rock or shingle; sometimes in coastal fields. The nest is a shallow scrape or hollow, usually without lining. Buff-grey to light brown, marked with dark brown and grey blotches, the two to four eggs are incubated for twenty-four to twenty-eight days. With greyish-buff down on upperparts and white underparts, the young leave the nest after a day or two. The oystercatcher has a single brood: mid-April–May.

RICHARD T. MILLS

Gannets

RINGED PLOVER*
Charadrius hiaticula
This delightful little bird nests along the seashore on sand and shingle beaches, or on sand dunes. The nest is a bare scrape, sometimes decorated with small pebbles or shells. Greenish-grey and spotted brown, the three to five eggs are incubated for twenty-four to twenty-seven days. Wearing grey-buff down with dark markings, the young leave the nest soon after hatching. The ringed plover may have two broods: May–July; and sometimes a replacement clutch.

CURLEW*
Numenius arquata
A hollow on the ground, well hidden by low cover, in damp meadow, and marshy field, the curlew's nest is scantily lined with pieces of nearby vegetation. Olive-green and blotched brown, the four eggs are incubated for about twenty-eight days. With light and dark brown on the upperparts, and pale brown below, the young leave the nest soon after hatching. The curlew has a single brood: May–June; and sometimes a replacement clutch.

THE SLUG
Arionidae and *Limacidae*

Thirty years ago at the close of May, night-flyfishing for sea trout along the tidal reach of the River Faughan in County Derry, I stood for a while talking with a man, who quickly stooped, pulled and bit through a stem of grass. He spluttered an oath and spat out a piece of *Arion hortensis*, the garden slug. Recently, I met the same man fishing a lake in County Donegal. He looked well and healthy – and why wouldn't he?

For at least two thousand years, in legend, slugs have been regarded as a cure for most ailments. In his thirty-seven-volume *Natural History*, Pliny the Elder (A.D. 23–79) recorded that quick relief from toothache could be obtained if grains of a slug's internal vestigial shell were placed in a hollow tooth. More recently, others believed that, eaten alive or boiled in milk, slugs were the remedy for tuberculosis; and taken in the form of ashes they would relieve gastro-intestinal problems such as ulcers and dysentry, and the neurological condition hydrocephalus. Many still believe that warts rubbed with slugs will wither and disappear.

One damp evening I followed a glistening track from the back door, across the kitchen, into the sitting room, where I moved an armchair to find a very plump slug with its mouth full of carpet fibre. I felt disgust; but slugs will eat most things containing organic matter, including sand. A slug's slime is produced to enable sliding and to protect the creature – if the keenest razor blade were placed edge up in a slug's path, the slime would allow that slug to crawl over the edge of the blade without suffering injury. I have never had much respect for slugs, and they seem an unnecessary nuisance in the garden. Still, relatively little of the food taken by slugs consists of cultivated matter. Some slugs feed almost entirely on fungi and rotting leaves. Many are omniverous: eating fungi, rotting meat, green leaves, tubers, dung, and kitchen waste. *Arion*

RICHARD T. MILLS

ater – called the large black even though its colour is variable – will feed on earthworms, centipedes, greenfly, and other slugs, swallowing them whole. Carrying organs of smell in their tentacles, and attracted to food over a metre away, most garden slugs will easily find and swallow the pellets thinly sprinkled to poison them.

Slugs are much sought-after. Easily tracked, slow moving and without any shell for protection, they are eaten by a variety of predators including the wood

Large black slug

mouse, rabbit, badger, fox, hedgehog, duck, thrush, and other birds. Sheep accidentally swallowing slugs while grazing can develop lungworm, caused by a parasite whose larvae have formed cysts in the foot of the slug.

RICHARD T. MILLS

Aphids on a rose

THE GREENFLY
Macrosiphum rosae

Staying on the subject of wildlife in the garden, every May and June I watch female greenfly attacking my roses. I closely watch these rose aphids (3 mm long), wriggling before sinking their greedy mouths into the soft, juicy, young stems. They keep on wriggling and piercing and sucking, swelling themselves pregnant, for during later May through June, greenfly can have young without mating. They take in an excessive amount of liquid and sugar – far more than they need – and although much is excreted as honeydew, sticky and sweet for hungry ants, moths and hoverflies, the greenfly use the energy gained from excessive feeding for excessive breeding. The greenfly on our roses during the growing warmth of later May are females, and with the plants juicy and freely budding, a female greenfly can deliver two or three baby females any day of the week. And just three days later, after feeding and expressing their own honeydew, the young start having babies themselves. During late May into June their numbers become astronomical. Insecticides apart – bearing in mind that spraying, even with soapy water, kills many helpful insects as well as pests – without the bluetit, meadow pipit, house sparrow, hoverfly larvae and ladybirds, which eat greenfly, many of our roses would quickly shrivel and die.

Ladybirds in particular are very effective. Two-spot, seven-spot, ten-spot, eleven-spot, fourteen-spot, and eyed species, famous for killing greenfly – and the blackfly, *Aphis fabae*, which have much the same life cycle as greenfly – these ladybirds do not require educating. They know what to do. Eggs are laid on roses and any other plants infested with aphids, and the slate-blue ladybird larvae eat every aphid they meet. Despite their colourful and popular image, ladybirds are gluttonous creatures. Still, if you wish to introduce ladybirds to your roses, placing a handful of them on the bushes is a complete waste of time. You will need to know when the ladybirds breed, so that their larvae are present when the aphids are growing in numbers. (The 22-spot ladybird feeds on mildew.)

At the close of May and during the first weeks of June, when neglected plants host colonies of greenfly tightly packed round stems and buds, winged females emerge to colonise other roses; and these winged females carry diseases with them to cross-infect the garden. From mid-August on, the winged females leave our gardens and fly off to wild rose bushes. There they deliver wingless, egg-laying females. Males join the females on the wild bushes and eggs follow. The eggs survive the winter and hatch more wingless females in the spring. These females, in turn, produce baby females and numbers grow and densely colonise the wild roses. Then winged females emerge and fly off to find the roses in our gardens, and produce more pear-shaped, stubby greenfly so important in food chains: without them, the animal life in our gardens would be less diverse.

THE PLANTS

May brings many more ground-flowering plants, and more bushes and trees come into leaf. The ground flora include sweet cicely, the sorrels, hemlock, scurvy grass, ground elder, cotton grass, daisy, charlock, thyme, ragwort, dog violet, tormentil, yellow rattle, yellow iris, silverweed, clovers, vetches, ragged robin, red campion, lords-and-ladies, stinging nettle; but, as ground flowers of the month, I choose the buttercups, bugle and herb Robert.

BUTTERCUPS
Growing throughout Ireland and Britain there are three common species of buttercup: bulbous, creeping, meadow. Before describing these species as individuals, there are interesting things to say about buttercups in general – starting with the name. For all species the name 'buttercup' is only about two hundred years old. In the 1700s the plants were called crowfoot, a name still officially used for water-dwelling relatives. 'Crowfoot' was chosen

because the plants' leaves are shaped rather like a crow's foot. There were many local dialect names, as well – for example, baffiners, butter-cop, butter-head, button-head, frog's foot, king's knobs, locket goulions, polts, troilflowers. Even today, the name 'crowfoot' is used to describe the meadow buttercup, and 'St Anthony's turnip' is used for the bulbous species.

The origin of the name 'buttercup' remains uncertain. Some say that this name was used because the flowers are the same colour as butter and are shaped like a cup. Others say that the flowers are more saucer-shaped than cup-shaped, and that 'cup' is a corruption of the Old English *copp*, meaning 'top'; and that the 'butter' part of the name came about because people believed that cows which ate the plant gave the best milk for making butter. Since then, most people know that cows avoid eating buttercups; that the leaves of the plant have a sharp, bitter, stinging taste and can be poisonous. Still the name survives – probably because it's too colourful and pleasing to discard. In folklore the buttercup is the symbol of childhood.

In times past, in spring, summer and autumn, it was unusual to find a meadow without masses of these attractive plants in flower. However, because most meadows have been resown with grass and clover, spreads of bright buttercups have become a less common sight. Still, in underused meadows, reaching down from hillside to damp ground, it is possible to find all three common buttercups near to each other – growing in their own places and coming into flower in their own time. From the close of March, on the upper, drier and better-drained soil, especially limy or calcium-rich soil, the bulbous buttercup blooms first; from the end of May onwards, down in the damper places, the creeping buttercup flowers last. Between the habitats of the bulbous and creeping species, on the less damp soil, covering those places that are most grazed, the meadow buttercup blooms from mid-spring through

Creeping buttercups

summer – the blooms appear soon after the flowers of the bulbous plant, and only a week or so before the flowers of the creeping species.

It is lovely to see spreads of these plants. However, they can be harmful and costly from a farming point of view. Buttercups, especially the bulbous and meadow species, have caused animal and human poisoning; and with determined overground runners, the creeping buttercup can rapidly take over fields. For the farmer working pasture, the creeping buttercup is particularly bothersome – cows avoid the plant and eat the grass about it, and this allows the buttercup to spread. Ploughing only promotes the buttercup's ambitions – cutting and chopping up the plant's runners into smaller pieces simply creates countless, potential new plants.

BULBOUS BUTTERCUP
Ranunculus bulbosus
The bulbous buttercup has a bulb-like or turnip-like swelling at the base of its stem – thus the name 'St Anthony's turnip'. It grows to a height of 40 cm and likes dry, well-drained, and preferably, calcium-rich soil. The hairy leaves have three leaflets, deeply lobed, and the flower stalks are grooved or furrowed. It is the first of the three buttercups to bloom and its green sepals

are telltale: the sepals bend back, downwards, below the five-petalled, bright yellow flowers.

MEADOW BUTTERCUP
Ranunculus acris
Growing in occasionally used or attended pasture to a height of 60 cm, the tallest and the most graceful of buttercups, the meadow, has hairy leaves of three to seven deeply lobed segments. With smooth and unfurrowed flower stalks, and properly attached sepals, the five-petalled, bright yellow flowers of the meadow buttercup open soon after the bulbous. The meadow buttercup is also called common buttercup, crowfoot, field buttercup, and tall buttercup.

CREEPING BUTTERCUP
Ranunculus repens
In low down and very damp ground the last of our three buttercups to come into flower is the creeping buttercup. Like the others, it has hairy, deeply lobed leaves of three segments, and the stalks of the flowers are furrowed. On closer examination, the middle segment of the leaf of this plant is held on a stalk. With proper, closely attached sepals, the five-petalled flower is a deep yellow colour. Growing to 50 cm and named because of its creeping along the ground before lifting itself to face the sun – and because of its marvellous runners that move where they can – this buttercup is very attractive but exceedingly bothersome.

Bugle

BUGLE
Ajuga reptans
From mid-May, when the leaves on the trees are plentiful and keep the sunlight from touching the woodland floor, and the flowers of anemone and then bluebell fade, the bugle quickly grows. It can tolerate shade and survives in summer woodland, but it grows to 10–30 cm in other places as well. From mid-May until the end of July, spreads of the plant appear almost everywhere. On short erect solitary stems, the small turrets of blue flowers and glossy green leaves, and its leaves of other hues, colour meadow and hedgebank, river bank, scrub, and shady woodland. Apart from being able to grow in the shade, bugle likes fairly damp, mildly acidic or alkaline soil; and it quickly spreads by long, creeping overground runners. The leafy runners root and new plants grow from the rooting points to form mats, even carpets of the plant.

Deep blue and just over 1 cm long, the flowers are very beautiful. Arranged in ascending clusters halfway up the stem, the delicate blooms whorl all the way to the top. With the upper leaves growing progressively smaller and the flowers rising in a dense spike, bugle appears to taper and is described as 'pagoda-like'. The flower has a long collar of sepals and, full of pollen, four stamens protrude. The petals present like tiny lips: the cleft upper lip is very small; the larger lower lip is three-lobed, with the central lobe notched. Colourwise, the plant can be confusing: while the stem and leaves are mostly green, and the flowers are blue, a spread of bugle looks almost purple.

RICHARD T. MILLS

The origin of the names 'bugle' or 'bugleweed' is unknown. Perhaps like the musical instrument, the plant takes its name from the shape of its flower. According to its other titles 'herb carpenter' and 'sicklewort', the plant was used as an ointment for the cuts and bruises caused by hammers, saws, axes, sickles, and other tools.

HERB ROBERT
Geranium robertianum

A true plant of May, herb Robert is commonly found in the shade of wall, hedgebank, in woodland, and about coastline and estuary. Growing to a height of 10–50 cm, its hairy stems branch from the base and the deeply divided, fern-like leaves have three to five lobes. Usually pink, always tiny, and notched, the pretty five-petalled flowers bloom from early May until September. The herb Robert is a wild geranium, a cranesbill. The cranesbills take the name from the shape of their fruit, which end in a long point like the beak of a crane. Classifed *Geranium robertianum*, the fact that, in autumn, the plant's leaves and stems turn a fiery red might account for the second part of its Latin name, *ruber*, meaning 'red'. Some say the plant gets its name from Saint Robert, an eleventh-century French ecclesiastic; and, when crushed, the leaves give off a pungent, unpleasant smell, which likely led to the name 'stinking Bob'. But the possible reasons for the name 'poor Robin' are the reasons I like best of all.

Herb Robert

In Scottish and English folklore herb Robert features prominently as the plant of the brownie or puck – namely, Robin Goodfellow. In Scottish folklore the brownie was a merry, kind-hearted little creature; shaggy and fairy-like, only a foot high, they like to live around farmhouses, and they often did the housework while the servants were asleep. If anybody offered to pay them, they went away. In many ways, they were like their English counterpart. However, Robin Goodfellow – Puck – a mischievous spirit, tormented people, usually in fun. He was also called hobgoblin. In 1595 Edmund Spenser included the 'pouke' among evil spirits, and Puck figures prominently in Kipling's *Puck of Pook's Hill* and *Rewards and Fairies*. In *A Midsummer Night's Dream* he is presented as a good-hearted elf; enjoying his pranks on human beings, Puck exclaims, 'Lord, what fools these mortals be!' And looking up at us, so says this little plant called herb Robert. In folklore the herb Robert is the symbol of steadfast piety.

HAWTHORN
Crataegus monogyna

With its scented white mayflowers and fresh green 'bread-and-cheese' leaves, the hawthorn brightens mile after mile of our countryside. For centuries the fast-growing, sturdy hawthorn – to fourteen metres – has bounded fields across the landscape. It will grow almost anywhere, and a well-made hedge of this bush or small tree, with spiny branches, can be impenetrable. It is very attractive too. Somewhat triangular, with five to seven lobes, the tiny green leaves look refreshing. Appearing in May, the white, pinkish flowers give the plant the name 'may tree'; and the greyish-brown bark allows it the name 'whitethorn'. But its most common English name is due to the fruit, the haws, which ripen to dark red in September for birds and hedgehogs.

In times past the haws were used for medical complaints: beaten to a powder, or by infusion in wine, the seeds of the haws were considered effective against internal stones, for unexplained internal pains, and for dropsy – the abnormal presence of fluid in the body tissues due to heart failure.

In Irish folklore, fairies loved to sit under the scented hawthorn tree. On May Day, people held hands and danced round a tall hawthorn. They chose a youthful person and garlanded him with fresh leaves and blossoms and called him Jack-in-the-Green, or the Green Man. Dressed in hawthorn foliage, this character sought food from the people. The gifts of food were tokens of sacrifice, given in hope of another fertile year; the hawthorn is the symbol of hope. And all over the country young May queens were chosen, bedecked with hawthorn, and paraded from house to house. There must be a folk connection in the familiar name 'bread-and-cheese', given to the leaves. I grew up with the notion. The leaves give a nutty taste to a salad, but they don't taste anything like bread and cheese.

The flowers and the leaves were important in superstition. To bring mayflowers indoors invited death to the house: a belief possibly derived from the vigorous nature of hawthorn seen quickly growing on farmlands abandoned after death through famine or plague. It was also thought that hawthorn leaves deterred witches, and it often forms part of the design carved into the bosses of old churches. Other stories tell of royal fairies and hawthorn trees, the property of the 'good folk' from time immemorial. An old lone hawthorn may be a fairy tree, never to be cut down. Under the hawthorn the king and queen, their family and subjects play music, dance and rest, and any mortal who disturbs or abuses this tree will suffer great misfortune.

Of course, probably the most famous story of all, is the legend of the Glastonbury Thorn, the hawthorn that grew from the staff that Joseph of Arimathea stuck into the ground on his arrival in England.

ASH
Fraxinus excelsior
Called the sylvan Venus because of its beauty of form, the ash is also a tree of great value and superstition. It is a graceful tree growing to forty metres, with airy leaves, black buds, and a smooth grey bark that furrows with ageing. Shaped like the hoofs of miniature sheep, the squat, velvety black buds are set in opposite pairs on greyish twigs with noticeable leaf scars. The leaves have nine to thirteen long-tipped, finely toothed leaflets. The purple-tipped male flowers and female flowers, as well as hermaphrodite flowers – sometimes all of them showing on the same tree – appear about three weeks before the leaves. Give or take a week, in any year, the flowers show towards the close of April and the leaves appear in mid-May. The ash comes relatively late into leaf and is always about three weeks after the oak – despite the old saying:

> Ash before Oak, there will be a soak,
> Oak before Ash, there will be a splash.

With long membranous wings called keys, that softly jingle in the wind and spin as they fall, the seeds are a favourite food of the bullfinch. The ash provides valuable timber, used for purposes where toughness and elasticity and lightness are desirable. In the past, it was the wood of the wheelwright and farm-implement worker. For DIY workers, its versatility still renders it the best (wood) material for oar, and handles for spade and axe; and cabinet-makers can use the veined roots. In medicine, superstition, and folklore, the ash has been the object of some peculiar notions. In *Culpeper's Complete Herbal*, first published in 1653, the ashes of the bark, made into lye (a soap), were said to cure scabs of the skin; the kernels would relieve 'stitches' and pains in the side; in white wine, a decoction of the young leaves would help cure jaundice.

According to Lady Wilde, in *Ancient Cures, Charms and Usages of Ireland*, the ash prevented and cured jaundice when the fairy doctors used the following procedure: out of sight of the patient, nine young shoots from the root were placed in a bottle; the bottle was buried in a secluded spot, and as long as it remained in the ground the patient was safe from the disease. But if the bottle was broken, the patient would die in a matter of days.

In Limavady, County Derry, I was given the following cure for earache:

Ash

Break several twigs which have large buds off an ash tree. Hollow the stems for about an inch at the broken-off end to form a little channel. Push the buds upwards into a hob fire. When the sap in the buds boils, it will run down the little channel and is easily caught in a large spoon. Sensibly pour this liquid into the sore ear.

It is said the ash was also used in curing ruptured infants. I take this to mean umbilical rupture when, perhaps, the newborn's cord had been cut too short, though I'm not sure. This particular superstitious practice involved a symbolic surgical approach. The trunk of a young ash was cleaved down its middle, and kept wide open with wedges. Holding her unclothed child, the mother stood on one side of the opening and the father stood on the other side. Then the infant was passed through the opening: mother to father and then back to mother. This done, both the bare infant and the cleaved tree – wedges removed – were tightly swathed at the same time. If the split tree healed, and this usually happened, the afflicted infant was similarly healed. In 1993 in South Normanton, Derbyshire, a deep scar in the trunk of a beautiful ash reminded me of the abuse these trees suffered in their youth – for the benefit of ruptured infants. Here in Ireland, fifty years ago, I clearly remember that a penny – firmly held *in situ* on a protruding bellybutton – cured the problem.

In England, another old cure involved what was called the 'shrew-ash'. Just as the split ash symbolised surgery, this 'old cure' approach was somewhat similar to the homeopathic notion that 'like cures like'. The practice centred on the pygmy shrew which was considered treacherously harmful to farmstock. It was thought that if the tiny shrew happened to creep over the limb of a healthy cow, horse, sheep, goat, pig, the limb of that visited animal would suffer loss of power. To protect their animals against the outcome of such an event, concerned farmers devised a ready-made remedy, or treatment for immediate use. They bored a hole – not too deep – in the limb of an ash, and while chanting or using some incantation, they pushed a live shrew into the limb and plugged the hole; and the shrew died. The tree became known as the shrew-ash and it was given much respect and relied upon, for when any animal presented signs of weakness of the limbs or poor co-ordination, all the farmer had to do was touch the afflicted limb of the animal with a handy twig from the tree and – if not straightaway – in time, the harmed limb of the animal would improve and get better.

Nowadays, similar features of illness can in fact be related to certain foliage ingested by animals. Ironically, studies show that poisoning may occur when animals graze near ash trees; that eating fallen leaves and fruit can cause incoordination – one of the signs of the condition formerly known in the English Midlands as 'wood evil'. It may be that innocent wild animals are still wrongly blamed for harming domestic stock.

In folklore the ash tree is the symbol of grandeur, and the twig of the ash is the symbol of festivity.

COMMON BEECH
Fagus sylvatica

With its strong smooth grey trunk and impressive many-branched dome, its slender, dark purplish-brown twigs with long and pointed buds, its colour-

Autumn beech

ful leaves and rich brown nutlets in bristly husks, and growing to a height of thirty-six metres, the beech is a magnificent tree.

The warm brown scaled buds grow long and swell and then release their crinkly leaves and yellowish-green male catkins in later April and the start of May. Short-stalked and shiny green with a wavy margin, the new leaves are fringed with silky hairs which soon disappear. The brilliant green of the beech as it comes into full leaf is a splendid sight. Its delicate canopy is delightful; and noisy with rooks. In early May the greenish-white female catkins become noticeable; and hanging like tiny tassels with purple tips, the male catkins soon fall away.

By mid-July the young rooks are beginning to look like their parents, and the beech leaves are showing their age as well. Much tougher now, with wavy margins and marked veins, the leaves are dark glossy green above and a paler green beneath. And with curly bristles, the female catkins are becoming hard. Into autumn the husk of the fruit, called mast, splits and reveals two rich-brown triangular nutlets. During late October into November another impressive spectacle occurs: the leaves turn yellow and copper-brown, and then, just before they fall, they become a deep orange-brown or reddish colour.

Throughout the seasons, the trunk of the beech, especially an old trunk, is a thing of art, with hollows and knobs or bumps and limbs that look round and soft; and where it's coloured with splashes of lichens, or hosting a velvety coating of dark green

RICHARD T. MILLS

Beech

moss, the olive-grey bark is picturesque. And, for practical purposes, covered with the pile of soft thick moss, a high-growing root often becomes a convenient seat.

The wood of the beech is very hard, heavy, closely grained and rather brittle, but it is used for a wide range of purposes. It makes strong chairs: most of the bentwood variety are of beech and so are the Windsor and other non-upholstered chairs; also table legs and various turned articles. It can be used for tool handles, mallets, planes, dowel rods, and woodwork benches; it was also used for rollers in wringing machines and mangles. And it may be stained to resemble mahogany or walnut.

Beech mast

RICHARD T. MILLS

The beech mast has a pleasant taste and is eaten by pheasants, badgers, squirrels, mice, and children. However, the mast can be poisonous. It is inadvisable to feed beech nuts to horses and cattle; and people are susceptible – the ingestion of fifty or more nuts can cause headache, abdominal pain, vomiting, diarrhoea, vertigo, and elevated body temperature.

In folklore the beech is the symbol of prosperity.

SILVER BIRCH
Betula pendula

Called by Samuel Taylor Coleridge the lady of the woods, the silver birch is my favourite tree. It is simply beautiful. Growing to a height of fifteen metres and shining through all surrounding scrub, its warm brown or silvery-white bark, long red-brown twigs, pointed buds and fresh green leaves always attract my attention. The ends of the branches droop slightly, hence the name *pendula*. On old trees the bark shows black diamond-shaped patches. Sadly the tree has a relatively short life.

The silver birch is one of the first trees to grow on newly cleared or abandoned ground; and, with the rowan, it grows higher up hillsides than any of our other deciduous trees. The leaves are very pretty. Small and somewhat triangular with regular toothed margins ending in a long point, the leaves turn bright yellow in autumn. The catkins appear in the autumn and the seeds are a favourite food of the siskin.

Birch tar oil may be used in making medicinal soaps. And cosmetically, a decoction of the leaves makes an astringent skin lotion.

Well known as whipping sticks, the young sprays were also used as the heads of brooms; and for making crosses against witchcraft. The wood was used for furniture, farm implements, packing crates, hoops for herring barrels, and firewood; and well-prepared sticks of birch charcoal made excellent crayons for drawing.

In folklore the silver birch is the symbol of meekness.

Crab apple blossom

CRAB APPLE
Malus sylvestris

Though the origin of the word 'crab' is uncertain and it describes the sourness of the wild apple, the tree itself should be exempted from the title. Even though, in hedgerow and thicket, the wild apple tree appears stumpy and graceless, to a height of nine metres, with ordinary short-stalked leaves, its masses of May blossoms are fragrant and very beautiful. The fragrance is similar to the scent of the honeysuckle and compared with most varieties of cultivated apples, each petite blossom displays curled and crumply petals, white and delicately tinged with varying depths of pink.

Also compared with cultivated apples, and wild escapees from orchards and gardens, the fruit of the 'crab' is small and squat, with deep sunken core ends and a long stalk. At first green and finely speckled white, sometimes acquiring a warm reddish tinge, the apple finally turns golden yellow and is speckled brown. I remember suffering cramps – the 'belly grabs' – as a result of eating too many hard sour crab apples. Nowadays, properly made with the thinly pared rind of a lemon and white sugar – and with their skins intact, their juice (verjuice) preserved, and a few pips thrown in – I prefer the fruit waiting in a jar labelled 'crab apple jelly'. Incidentally, cosmeticians write that the verjuice with malt vinegar makes a very good hair rinse.

In 1993 in County Armagh, visiting marvellous orchards and learning as much as I could, I soon discovered that commercial apple-growers hold the little crab apple tree in much respect. One grower showed me the direct descendant of a 'crab': the oldest tree in his oldest orchard full of splendid apples of different sizes, colours, shapes and tastes. Already the ancestor of Cox's Orange Pippin, the Bramley's Seedling and many other esteemed orchard and garden apples, the hardy rootstock of the crab apple tree continues to rear cultivated apples.

In folklore the crab apple tree is the symbol of temptation and its blossom is the symbol of choice.

JUNE

June is the month of strongest light, the end of spring and the beginning of summer – the month of the midsummer fire of Midsummer's Eve, when as a boy I helped gather wood for the bonfire and watched the celebrating. Everybody sang, and while the older boys and girls and parents danced the lancers, a quadrille, and reels to fiddles and accordion, the older folk sat and watched the goings-on, and laughed and talked to their satisfaction. In ancient times this same celebration was to honour Baal, the sun god, on the day of his greatest glory; when, at his decline, our ancestors climbed the hillsides for a last glimpse of the all-vivifying power. In some parts of the country rural folk still light bonfires and sing and dance, and enjoy themselves on Midsummer's Eve. Nowadays, the occasion also celebrates the eve of the birth of John the Baptist.

June brings many more ground plants to flower, and the fruit blossoms of bushes like the blackberry and the honeysuckle attract many insects – bees, wasps, hoverflies, butterflies, night-flying moths and many others, fly and creep and crawl about old walls, pastures, and woodland floors. And while birds continue laying, hatching, and feeding young, first broods are fending for themselves, and sparrowhawks and merlins are catching them. Starlings and jackdaws start imitating the whistles and voices of others. Mullet are swimming with sea trout and salmon in tidal water, and young otters and mink are watching them. June is also the month of our tiniest and commonest bat, the pipistrelle.

THE PIPISTRELLE
Pipistrellus pipistrellus

In the late summers of 1989 and 1991, by invitation, I visited private houses in County Fermanagh to see pipistrelles and long-eared bats. The breeding season was over, so I couldn't see myself doing the bats any harm. No matter; on both occasions, bat experts met me. Because I don't have any licence, I am not allowed to handle bats. Gone are the days when nobody seemed to mind children throwing stones at the 'blind bats' which flitted about during twilight. Due to serious reductions in populations, these small animals are now protected by law – a welcome and necessary development.

Yet bats and I have shared a few experiences. Looking through an old fishing

Dun Bunafahy, Achill Island,
County Mayo
KENNETH McNALLY

Pipistrelles

diary I find a pipistrelle reaching for one of my night-flies, and running rings around me.

12 JULY 1975

12.40 a.m. Casting very carefully because of a high bank behind me. Standing in about two and a half feet of water, surrounded by heavy bushes and low-hanging trees. As I was casting and bringing the flies from behind, I heard a 'brrr-rr-r!' above me – at the time the flies were passing over my shoulder. I thought it might be a leaf off a bush, snatched by one of the flies, but I was more convinced that it was frantic wing movements.

It was very dark but I could dimly see spidery ripples coming from the spot where my tail fly should be. I thought I could see something moving in the water, but could feel nothing along the line. I reeled in a short length and lifted the rod as high as I could above me. This hoisted a bat out of the water and it started flying 'around' me. It was attached to the line. It must have circled six or seven times, very quickly, as I warily waded towards the bank. I hoped to free the bat and was curious to see if it had reached for the fly or was caught on the head or body . . .

I didn't find out because the bat winged my leader into branches and the dropper fly was caught somewhere in the tree. This must have allowed the bat a fixture to pull against, because by the time I climbed the bank the bat had gone. I still had to get my flies out of the tree. In 1962, one evening between the lights another bat had deliberately seized one of my flies in the air and flew away upstream pulling line with it.

The bat is a unique animal: the only mammal capable of true or flapping flight comparable to that of insects and birds. Bat flight is slow and fluttering, yet it can hover, and fly and evade with great agility. One bright evening, just after tea time, I watched a Daubenton's bat being chased by a chaffinch and several greenfinches. The birds were no match for the bat: it out-flew and outmanoeuvred them by swooping to the level of the pool and then lifting itself to above the treeline with amazing speed. The display ended with the bat flitting away through high bushes. The finches seemed very confused.

The pipistrelle or common bat, sometimes called the blind bat, lives in trees, rock crevices, behind drainpipes and gutters, in old buildings. From early twilight its jerky flight can be seen over rivers, quarries, lanes, disused pastures. The Daubenton's bat, seen from late afternoon usually near water, also lives in trees, buildings and rock crevices. Other bats found locally are Natterer's bat, the whiskered bat, the long-eared bat and Leisler's bat. Despite being our smallest species, the pipistrelle's appearance, behaviour, and life style provide a useful general description of any of our bats.

When closely studied, the pipistrelle is a remarkable creature. It has a broad, flat head, with a blunt muzzle and a very wide mouth holding tiny sharp teeth. Sited just behind the angle of the mouth, the ears feel rubbery and are short, triangular-shaped structures, slightly notched on their outer edges. The body is round and muscular; the limbs are stumpy and membranous. The short tail enables crawling up or down a vertical surface. The pipistrelle weighs about 14 g and its head and body are about 35 mm long; the wingspan is 22 cm. Except on the ears and wing membranes, where it is blackish, the silky fur on the shoulders and middle and lower back varies from dark to light reddish-brown. The chest and upper belly have a paler fur and the underparts are scantily clad or bare.

The pipistrelle hibernates from November until late March, beginning April. It mates shortly before going into hibernation but fertilisation is delayed until the spring. After a gestation of thirty-five to forty-four days, the single young is born between late June and mid-July. After a month's weaning, the young bat is capable of independent flight.

Uttering high-pitched squeaks and capturing its food in the air, the pipistrelle usually flies at between two and thirteen metres from the ground. It is not totally blind. It uses its tiny black eyes to some extent but relies mainly on echo-location to find its way around and to capture insects – particularly midges and beetles. Its shrill squeaks bounce back from any solids, and by judging the

Pipistrelles

time taken for the echo to return, the bat is able to 'see' its surroundings. While standing in the dark, presenting a very fine fishing line to the water, I have watched the pipistrelle learning to avoid the line: between tip of rod and surface of water. The bat might touch the line once – but only once. It probably carries a sound picture of territory, comparable to the sight-memory of humans and other animals.

Although the pipistrelle eats mainly insects whose bodies contain high quantities of water, it does need to drink. To do this, it either lands on the ground, where it scuttles like a mouse, or it skims a pool – in the manner of swallows – dipping its lower jaw in the water while in flight. Some observers state that the pipistrelle can swim; they claim to have seen it rowing itself ashore, using its wings like oars – in 1975, when my tail fly and a hooked pipistrelle landed in the pool together, I nearly saw the same thing myself.

Bats have never been popular. Down through the ages they have been regarded as portents of evil. With their unearthly faces appearing in the fading light, this is hardly surprising. Many people still dislike them, saying, they're ugly; look like mice; spread infection; get tangled in your hair; bite you; and so on. Their looks apart, none of our bats is known to cause or spread disease harmful to humans, and they do their best to avoid us. Humans are their main enemies and have reduced bat populations to the extent that several species are in danger of extinction. The problem has been largely unintentional, however: the removal of old trees and demolition of buildings which housed bat roosts; the design of new buildings with no places to accommodate bats; the reduction of food as a result of improvement or greater use of once neglected meadows; and the extensive use of insecticides. Hopefully these kinds of activities and developments will slow down and change, for the protection programme – originally given only to certain bats – has now been extended to protect all species.

THE MULLET
Chelon labrosus

Mullet are beautiful fish, with silvery elongated bodies covered with small scales. Their average length is 60 cm, the females being slightly longer and more rounded than the males. Both male and female have broad mouths with thick, soft lips and a forked tail. They have two short, well-separated dorsal fins, and the paired fins are small. Their movements are slow and graceful, and apart from the arrangement of fins and shape of the mouth, mullet can fool non-anglers into thinking they are looking at salmon. On many occasions, arriving on a bridge, I have found excited angler-watchers pointing at what they called salmon. Often hoping to see a run of salmon below the spectators, I would find a shoal of mullet.

Mullet

RICHARD T. MILLS

These are mysterious fish. Year after year, mature mullet swim about the tidal reaches of rivers; but nobody seems to really know why they visit us. Many times I have watched holiday-makers and learner bait anglers deliberately trying to entice mullet, without success. Many thousands of times, experienced bait anglers have almost placed worms in the mouths of mullet, without a take. Because of its soft lips being torn in the struggle, anglers may have hooked and lost the fish without knowing it was a mullet; this is possible. But in my experience mullet in rivers do not seem interested in anglers' lures. During many years of bait fishing and flyfishing in tidal reaches of rivers, I've caught many trout, salmon, fluke, eels, roach, rudd, perch, and pike – but only two mullet. One fish was accidentally hooked in the back while I was night flyfishing; the other was caught in the gloaming on a fly called Blue Charm that had become coated with algae.

Mullet like algae. They scrape the fine, filamentous green plant from the surfaces of submerged stones and eat it. They also eat grubs, insects, molluscs, and decomposed matter. With their thick-lipped mouths, they suck up sand and mud from the river bed and extract rotting animal and vegetable food by straining the material through their gills. Anglers will often see individual mullet dipping up and down to the river bed, and coming up to the surface. The fish dip to suck up a mouthful of sand or mud, and expel the inedible particles as they continue swimming. They come to the surface with their mouths wide open to suck in grubs, insects and other small items of food. Despite the fact that anglers fail to entice them, the mullet do feed in our rivers. However, there is much more food available in the estuaries. Do they come into the rivers to spawn? To prepare to spawn? To recuperate after spawning?

When they enter rivers, mullet are fully grown and their visit seems purposeful; they usually come into the tidal reaches in June and leave again in the autumn. Although during the day they appear to stay in shoals, individuals sometimes temporarily leave the others and are seen swimming alone. At night the shoal disperses and each fish moves to its own location: the total membership spread over the river bed, all facing the same way. Finding young mullet, some 3 cm long, in tidal pools, observers are convinced that spawning takes place in shallow waters in the spring. However, little is known about the breeding habits of this fish.

THE BIRDS

GOLDFINCH
Carduelis carduelis

A widespread though thinly distributed resident, this very colourful finch (12–13 cm) is found about woodland edges, orchards, hedges, gardens and parks; it is also seen in fields of tall weeds, especially thistles. In winter groups are seen in open fields. The adult sexes are similarly marked with dark red face, black and white head, and a bright yellow wing bar which is conspicuous in flight. The upper body is brown with a white rump; the underparts are buffish-white, with white near the tips of the black tail. The flight is undulating, dancing, and erratic. The usual call is a liquid 'tswitt-witt-witt!' with a characteristic tinkling tone; it also offers a harsh 'geez!' call. The extended song comprises the tinkling call notes interspersed with very pleasant twittering. Because of its song, the goldfinch is illegally trapped, caged and crossbred with canaries.

RICHARD T. MILLS

Goldfinch

Taking seeds from thistles, the bird is often observed hanging like a tit from the plant head. Hidden by foliage and built on the outer end of a branch, five to six metres above the ground, the small and neat nest is difficult to see. Usually in orchards, but sometimes in high bushes and hedgerows, the nest is made out of fine twigs, rootlets, bark fibres, grass, moss and lichen, interwoven with spiders' webs and lined with thistledown. Pale blue with a few red-brown spots and grey streaks, the four to six eggs are incubated for twelve to thirteen days. With dark grey down at first, and creamy-white gape-flanges, the young remain in the nest for thirteen to fifteen days. The goldfinch has two broods: May–July.

STARLING
Sturnus vulgaris

With iridescent black and brown plumage, short and thin yellow bill and red legs, the starling (22 cm) is easily recognised. It is a highly successful species, forming huge flocks at favoured roosts outside the breeding season. The flight is strong and powerful, with glides; the diet comprises insects, leatherjackets, wireworms, and other pests, also seeds and fruit. The voice offers a variety of wheezing calls, and mimicry. Often described as a brash, aggressive bully of a bird, I find it comical, busy, and cheeky. It seems a proper busybody; and both its squat little body and the habit of swaggering and rushing about fit the bird for the part.

Starling

Starlings are excellent mimics. As well as their own whistles, gabbles, gurgles, wheezes, screams, and chuckles – as if life is one big joke – starlings can imitate the sounds of other things. Last June, when I whistled to my spaniels to come in from the back field, a cock starling on the roof of the house kept whistling the same way, and the dogs stood and looked up at him. There are other good examples of starlings mimicking. Once, when a fountain in a garden had been turned off, and the tinkle of falling water could still be heard, the sound was traced to a starling. The most remarkable example followed tree-felling – a power-driven saw was being used, and after this had been going on for several days, a starling was heard mimicking. A quarter of a mile from the tree-felling, the bird was making the sounds of a distant power-driven saw.

Nesting sites are in holes in trees, thatch on roofs, crevices in walls and buildings, under eaves, and similar places. Carelessly built with grass and straw-like material, the cup-shaped nest is lined with finer grass and feathers. Glossy pale blue and unmarked, the five to seven eggs are incubated for fourteen to fifteen days. Scantily clad with grey down, and showing pale yellow gape-flanges, the young remain in the nest for about twenty-one days. The starling may have two broods: May–June.

Starling at nest

Outside of the breeding season, their flocking and roosting behaviour make starlings noticeable. They live in flocks and roost in orderly formations. During the morning and early afternoon, all the starlings in the neighbourhood spread across different fields for feeding. In the late afternoon they begin to come together to prepare for roosting, and gather in small groups on tall reeds, bushes, fences, wires, and in trees. Then nearby groups join together. Soon large groups are formed and these join other large groups until a flock of a thousand strong takes to the air – like a cloud of smoke in the distance. Sometimes smaller flocks of hundreds will fly in formation, they turn and dive and wheel together with uncanny precision. At other times small groups of a dozen or so birds fly directly to the roost.

There are times when hundreds of starlings will gather in one tree in a noisy chorus. Then, suddenly, as if conducted, the chorus stops and seconds later all the birds fly away, except for the last five or six birds, which turn back, return to the tree and start singing again. Then others join them; and after flying in all directions for a while, more birds return and the chorus builds up again – only to stop suddenly once more, and the whole episode is repeated. This continues until all the starlings in the neighbourhood have assembled and roosted quietly.

JACKDAW
Corvus monedula

Our smallest crow – 33 cm – with black back and crown, grey nape and eyes, short stubby bill, and dark grey underparts, the jackdaw is gregarious,

RICHARD T. MILLS

Young jackdaws

forming flocks on derelict buildings, in towns, woods, hedgerows and sea cliffs. The flight can be very aerobatic, with soars, glides and dives. The diet comprises worms, grain, eggs, other birds' nestlings, and small mammals. The calls are a loud, harsh 'tchack!', or 'jack!', or a high-pitched 'keeya!' Nesting in holes in trees and buildings, quarries, cliffs, old nests of other birds, and in chimneypots, the nest is made out of sticks and straw, and lined with finer twigs and wool. Pale blue-green and spotted brown, the four to six eggs are incubated for seventeen to eighteen days. With sparse down and yellow gape-flanges, the young remain in the nest for five weeks. The jackdaw has a single brood: April–beginning June; and sometimes a replacement clutch.

The thieving habits of jackdaws are well known. It is even thought that the bird's cherry-picking – day after day, until the crop is gone – may be linked with the jackdaw's habit of stealing bright objects and hiding them. They are also renowned for their foolish and talkative nature. The bird's Old English name was *daw*, meaning 'silly person'. Then in the sixteenth century the bird became known as jack, after its call in flight. Since then the two words became joined to make 'jackdaw' – a name which became used to describe vain, foolish, thievish, and over-talkative people.

Jackdaws use a wide variety of call notes, many of them melodious and warbling. They can mimic various sounds: other bird calls, whistles and human speech. It was once thought that slitting a jackdaw's tongue would improve the bird's ability to speak, and many tame jackdaws suffered this senseless mutilation, for birds do not use their tongues to form sounds as humans do. However, while some jackdaws readily learn to 'talk', others never utter a word.

Jackdaw

RICHARD T. MILLS

According to Konrad Lorenz, a pioneer of the study of animal behaviour, jackdaws and other animals do not possess a language in the true sense of the word. However, every individual has a certain number of inborn movements and sounds for expressing feelings; it also has innate ways of reacting to these signals when it hears them or sees them in a fellow member of the species. Highly social species of birds like jackdaws have a complicated code of such signals, innately uttered and understood by every bird; this innate signal code differs fundamentally from human language, however, every word of which has to be learned.

Humans can still sense various feelings in others through body language; but signals and reactions are far from consistent. The 'tchack!' and 'keeya!' calls of the jackdaw are not comparable to human spoken language, but are similar to involuntary expressions such as yawning, frowning, smiling.

Concerning mimicry – this imitating is nothing more than the so-called 'mocking' found in many song birds. Learned by imitation, mocking consists of sounds that are not innate and are uttered only while the bird is singing, they have no meaning and bear no relation whatsoever to the inborn 'vocabulary' of the jackdaw species. Whistle at the jackdaw and it might return a similar whistle, that is all.

It seems that jackdaws are often very bold in their quest for bright objects and have found their way into many stories. There is the tale of the ex-sailor whose tame jackdaw would snatch lit cigarettes from his lips and then fly away followed by a torrent of nautical oaths. But the best story of all is told in the poem 'The Jackdaw of Rheims', by Reverend R.H. Barham, author of *The Ingoldsby Legends*, who died in 1845. This fragment tells of the theft of the cardinal archbishop's costly turquoise ring:

> The poor little Jackdaw, when the monks he saw,
> Feebly gave vent to the ghost of a caw;
> And turned his bald head as much as to say,
> 'Pray be so good as to walk this way!'
>
> Slower and slower he limped on before,
> Till they came to the back of the belfry door,
> When the first thing they saw,
> Midst the sticks and the straw,
> Was the ring in the nest of the little Jackdaw!

SPARROWHAWK
Accipiter nisus

Having survived the dreadful pesticides of the 1960s, this bird is relatively widespread and common again. Seen about woodland, field, hedgerow, and heath, the handsome sparrowhawk (30–38 cm) is a marvellous predator. Flapping its short, rounded wings for a few beats, then gliding low and very fast through bushes and along hedgerows – causing small birds to panic and scatter – the sparrowhawk takes its prey by terror and surprise.

The sexes look very different. Larger than the male, the female is brown above. She has a pale eyebrow and shows light grey barring beneath. The male is blue-grey above. He has a prominent eyebrow and is barred reddish-brown beneath. Both male and female have a long, square tail, banded grey and white; the legs are yellow, and the bill is black and hooked. Their direct flight is strong and always looks threatening; the call is a loud 'kek-kek-kek!'

The nest is easily seen. In mainly broad-leaved woodland it is usually observed in a conifer near the edge of a walk, glade, or ride, with a stream nearby. About seven to eight metres above the ground, and built close to the trunk, the untidy

Sparrowhawk at nest

RICHARD T. MILLS

nest is a flattened platform of local twigs, with a lining of needle-leaves and feathers. Ovate, bluish-white and heavily speckled purplish-grey and dark brown, the four to six eggs are incubated for about thirty-two days. With white, dense down at first, the young remain in the nest for a month. The sparrowhawk has a single brood: May–June.

MERLIN
Falco columbarius

Four summers ago in Dunfanaghy, after trying to contact the proper authorities, a farmer brought me an injured merlin. The cock bird was lying trembling in a cardboard box in a stupor; he seemed to be concussed. He needed some corner where he would be undisturbed, and warm and comfortable, and perhaps feel some sense of security. I went into the back field and gathered pieces of stiff grass, lichen and moss, and made an imitation merlin nest on the floor in a far corner of the garage. I put a soup plate of water near the nest, and I went to the butcher and got stringy meat. I chopped the meat and placed some of it between the water and the nest; then I put the merlin in the nest. Just before darkness I peered through the garage window, and seeing the merlin still in the nest, I left him alone. Early the following morning, the merlin was still there; he was alive and no longer trembling, but the food was untouched. I lifted him, opened his bill, and put a small piece of the raw meat into the corner of his mouth. He shook his head, corrected the position of the meat in his mouth and swallowed it, and easily swallowed several more pieces. Using the clear, hollow stem of a biro pen, I gave him a small drink of water. I fed him again in the late afternoon.

Female merlin feeding her young

After two days the merlin was moving his head and shuffling purposely; but he stayed in the nest. During the morning of the fourth day, while quite savagely attacking my fingers, he started taking food from my hand. He was much more bright and alert. That same evening, while holding his body, I let him weakly flap his marvellous wings. Now that he was recovering and could determinedly turn his head sideways to look up at me, and move his wings and legs, I called him Morag. On the fifth day, when I found him perching on a ladder in the garage, I brought him into the back yard, and again holding his body, I let him flap his wings. He flapped more strongly.

By the middle of the second week, when he was feeding himself, flapping heartily, flying about the garage and perching on the top rung of the ladder, and I feared he might be getting tame, I took him into the back field and let him go. I watched him crossing reed beds and waited for him to fall; but when he soared and glided, and then beat his wings, and flew away in the direction of the high ground known as Breaghy Head – his home territory – I knew he was well again, and that his wild nature was unharmed.

Merlin

Nowhere common, sparsely distributed throughout the country, with less than eight hundred pairs in Ireland and Britain, and with numbers declining

RICHARD T. MILLS

steadily, it is good to save a merlin; and Morag owed his life to the concerned farmer who found him and brought him in a cardboard box to the village of Dunfanaghy.

A beautiful small falcon of the hills, moors, estuaries, and freshwater marshy ground, the merlin (27–33 cm) quarters these areas in search of small birds. On sighting prey, the falcon rises and then quickly dives to kill with its talons; but it will also take prey in level flight. Smaller than the female, the male has blue-grey upperparts, the long wings are pointed, the face shows a hint of a moustache, the hooked bill is yellow, the underparts are reddish-brown and streaked, the short tail is blue, with a dark terminal band, and the legs are yellow and short. The female is dull brown above and the paler underparts are heavily barred and streaked. The flight is powerful and direct, with soars, glides, and aerial dives. The voice offers a chattering 'kek-kek-kek!'

Usually sited in a hollow among heather or rough grass on hilly ground and moors, the nest is a simple flattened structure of bits of grass and the stems of nearby plants, lined with fine, wiry grass, moss and lichen. Ovate, buffy and heavily marked with reddish-brown spots, the four to six eggs are incubated for about twenty-six days. Wearing white down at first, the young remain in the nest for a month. The merlin has a single brood: May–June.

BUTTERFLIES
Lepidoptera

Sometimes it is difficult to differentiate butterflies and moths. For June, I consider butterflies; for July, moths, even though they are also about in June. The division between butterflies and moths has no real scientific basis, but depends on a few straightforward observations. In general, butterflies are seen during the day, they have club-shaped antennae, and fold their wings vertically when at rest. In general, moths usually fly at night, and they close their wings horizontally. Both butterflies and moths possess two pairs of large, often coloured wings. The colour we see on their wings is not of pigment or any substance of that kind: it is light, broken and refracted, made visible by the creatures' arrangement of scales – too complex in design for any human eye to see. The larvae are called caterpillars, and the pupae or chrysalises, are the stage between larvae and adults – the immobile, non-feeding stage when changes occur to complete the meta-morphosis.

RICHARD T. MILLS

Butterflies and bees on thistles

Through June, our range of butterflies include the dingy skipper, green-veined white, peacock, marsh fritillary, pearl-bodied fritillary, common blue, small copper, meadow brown, gate keeper, small heath, ringlet, gray-ling, speckled wood; but, possibly, June's most common butterflies are the large white, small white, wall brown, orange-tip, red admiral, and the small tortoiseshell.

LARGE WHITE
Pieris brassicae

Well known to gardeners as a cabbage butterfly: upperside white, with a black apical border; the underside yellowish – especially the hind wings. It shows two black spots and a black bar on the upperside of the fore wings. Usually has two to three broods: April–October. The slightly hairy caterpillar is a conspicuous blue-grey, with yellow lines and dotted all over with black. As the name suggests, it feeds on cabbage-like leaves. Wingspan: 64 mm.

SMALL WHITE
Artogeia rapae

Distinguished from the large white by size and less pronounced markings, otherwise similar. The pale green caterpillar prefers the heart of the cabbage, but is often found on the outer leaves. Wingspan: 48 mm.

WALL BROWN
Lasiommata megera

Orange-brown on upperside, with dark brown veins, margins and transverse lines; white central eye-spot near the tips of the fore wings. It often rests on the ground in the sunshine. It usually has two broods: May–June; July–August. The caterpillar is whitish-green, dotted with white, and feeds on meadow grasses and cocksfoot. Wingspan: 50 mm.

Orange-tips

ORANGE-TIP
Anthocharis cardamines

White with outer third of fore wings a bright orange, excepting female. The female has black wing tips. The hind wings of both sexes are white and dappled green. The orange-tip has a single brood: May–June. The inconspicuous, bluish-green caterpillar feeds on green seed pods of various *Cruciferae*, plants of mustard or cress with four leaves suggestive of a cross, including cultivated rock cress and dame's violet. Wingspan: 45 mm.

RED ADMIRAL
Vanessa atalanta

A beautiful creature – fore wings black, with sub-apical white spots and a scarlet band. Widespread in meadows, hedgerows, downlands, breeding in late summer. Flies in summer and early autumn in a single brood derived from hibernated individuals or immigrants. And greenish to black, the spiny caterpillar eats nettles. Wingspan: 64 mm.

SMALL TORTOISESHELL
Aglais urticae

Upperside red-orange, with yellow and black patches; also dark borders with noticeable blue spots. The small tortoiseshell has two broods: June and August; and spiny, yellowish with black speckles and lines, the caterpillar feeds on clusters of nettles. Wingspan: 50 mm.

BUMBLEBEES
Hymenoptera

Following the close description of April's buff-tailed bumblebee, I want to mention some of our other bumblebees, busy through June: wearing two pairs of wings, waisted, with mouthparts for biting or sucking, and breeding legless larvae, or maggots.

COMMON GARDEN BUMBLEBEE
Bombus pascuorum
Widespread in hedgerows, pastures and agricultural lands. In early spring the mossy nest is built above ground in old bird nests and in walls. The queens and females show pollen baskets on hind legs. As with the buff-tailed, the females emerge before the males, and are red-brown; the males are light brown. Body: 14–18 mm.

SMALL EARTH BUMBLEBEE
Bombus lucorum
Black, with white tail, broad yellow bands on front of thorax and abdomen, this bumble is known to nest in bird nest boxes. Body: 14–23 mm.

Common garden bumblebees

EARLY BUMBLEBEE
Bombus pratorum
Resembles the small earth bumble but the tail is bright brown. Will nest in old bird nests. Male fluffy, with yellow-green hairs on body. This male appears earlier than other male species. Body: 13–18 mm.

RED-TAILED BUMBLEBEE
Bombus lapidarius
Orange-red on last three abdominal segments. Widespread in grasslands and hedgerows. The females emerge early and feed on dead nettles. The nest colony is underground; sometimes in holes in walls and banks. Body: 15–24 mm.

BEETLES
Coleoptera

Large to small, and generally compact, with a tough shell-like covering, vicious, biting mouth, horny protective front wings and a versatile body, our beetles are interesting creatures. Most of the larvae have developed legs on the thorax; those which burrow into vegetation are legless. June brings ground beetles, rove beetles, carrion beetles, ladybirds, chafers, and many more. Here I give a brief description of different types.

Devil's coach-horse

RICHARD T. MILLS

DEVIL'S COACH-HORSE
Staphylinus olens
This beetle is also called the do-ell, possibly derived from the Irish *diabhal*, meaning 'devil'. An old story tells that when the chief priests sent messengers in every direction to spy on Jesus, they asked the do-ell if he had seen Jesus and the creature replied, 'He was here today. He has not long gone away.' So the friends of Jesus killed the beetle, because he betrayed their master.

Found in woodland, meadow, and agricultural areas, this is a rove beetle: a predator – long and thin – it can run very fast to catch other insects. It has a flexible body and is also called the cock-tail. If disturbed it will erect its hind end and, while emitting a bad smell, it opens its jaws in a threatening manner. It can give a sharp bite. Its short, stumpy elytra, or front wings, expose much of the abdomen. Dull black, or black and orange, and often downy, the all-black beetle is usually the largest of the species. Nocturnal, it hides under stones during daylight. The larvae survive in decaying vegetation. Body: 20–28 mm.

GROUND BEETLE
Harpalus rufipes
Another predator and fast runner, this beetle is found in hedgerows and woodland. Black, with a striking bronze or green sheen, the antennae and legs are reddish. It is mainly nocturnal, and hides under stones during daytime. It feeds on insects and other invertebrates, but will also eat vegetable matter. The long larvae survive under leaf litter. Body: 14–16 mm.

VIOLET GROUND BEETLE
Carabus violaceus
Shiny black, with violet borders and noticeable black legs and antennae, and larger than most ground beetles, the violet is an active predator of insects and earthworms. Commonly found in disused ground, it lurks under stones during the day. The larvae survive under debris. Body: 25 mm.

COCKCHAFER
Melolontha melolontha
An attractive beetle with orange wing cases, black thorax and
abdomen, and red, fan-like antennae. It is seen flying at dusk and
often crashes into windows. The larvae feed on roots.
Body: 20–25 mm.

CARRION BEETLE
Oiceoptoma thoracicum
Found in hedgerows, meadows, and downs, this is a noticeable
beetle. It looks very flat but has strong lines, furrows and contours.
The shoulders are brown; rest of the body is black. It feeds on
carrion, fungi, and rotting wood. Squat, like a wood louse but with
fewer legs, the larva also eats decaying animal and plant material.
Body: 13–16 mm.

BLACK BURYING BEETLE
Necrophorus humator
This gruesome creature excavates ground under a cadaver – a
dead mouse, for example. The beetle keeps excavating until the
corpse sinks into the earth and is buried. The adult then lays eggs
in a chamber close to the buried animal. It feeds new larvae with
regurgitated carrion; the older larvae can eat the rotting animal.
The adult is black and angular, with red-tipped and clubbed
antennae. Body: 18–28 mm.

SEXTON BEETLE
Necrophorus vespillo
As the name suggests, this beetle digs graves. It behaves like the
bigger black burying beetle, and its antennae are red-tipped and
clubbed, but it looks more colourful. The wing cases have
attractive orange bands. Body: 15–20 mm.

I conclude June's insects with the common earwig.

COMMON EARWIG
Forficula auricularia
The dark brown body is 11–15 mm long, with short, hardened,
yellowish fore wings, ear-shaped hind wings, and prominent
pincers at the rear for attack and defence. The female's pincers are
straight; the male's pincers are curved. Feeds on flower heads and
ripe fruit. Nocturnal, it hides in flowers and under loose bark and
logs. It does not enter or damage human ears.

THE PLANTS

June brings many flowers to ground plant and bush: these include, white
clover, fairy flax, dog rose, yarrow, hogweed, water lily, rock rose, St John's
wort, oxeye daisy, stonecrop, mullein, meadowsweet, foxglove, thistle,
hawkweed, cat's-ear, ragwort, devil's bit scabious, bindweed, meadow cranesbill, purple loosestrife, pyramidal orchid, valerian – so many beautiful plants.
For special reasons I add a few others.

Agrimony

AGRIMONY
Agrimonia eupatoria

When I look at a church steeple, I think of Maybeth and her bunch of wild flowers. One June afternoon, nine years ago, I met an old lady with a bunch of limp flowers in her left hand, her good hand. Once a recognised artist, Maybeth loved the countryside and its wildlife. She especially loved flowers. Making a determined recovery from a stroke that paralysed the right side of her body and took away her power of speech, she was enjoying a stroll in the fresh air. I told her her flowers were beautiful, and she offered me her cheek to kiss. Then, before leaving me to stand and admire her efforts to steadily walk away, she graciously gave me a torn stem crowded with tiny yellow flowers, and tried to say 'church steeples'.

Maybeth had handed me a stem of agrimony, from the Greek *argemone*, poppy, a 'shining' magical plant whose wet fresh leaves, applied to the eyes, protected the Ancients against failing sight. Maybe it did. Today, experts in cosmetics and herbalism make known that an infusion of its fresh leaves, to bathe the eyes, makes the eyes sparkle; that, if sweetened with honey, and taken daily, a wineglassful of the same infusion will purify the blood and clear the skin of acute blemishes such as spots and pimples; that the leaflets can be used to make a stimulating tea and the small roots have astringent properties.

Curiously agrimony is not well known. Yet its attractive clusters of tiny, and starry, yellow flowers make it easily seen. In relatively neutral soil it is frequently found growing to 30–60 cm in hedgerows, field margins, woodland clearings, rough meadows, near scrub, and along roadsides. From early June through July and August, look for a slender unbranched hairy stem with alternate leaves, comprising coarsely toothed, feathery leaflets of varying sizes, and with a crowded 'steeple' of tiny sparkling yellow flowers smelling of apricots.

Bird's-foot trefoil

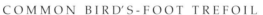

COMMON BIRD'S-FOOT TREFOIL
Lotus corniculatus

For my very first attempt to describe a plant on television I chose the bird's-foot trefoil. This little plant is well named: 'trefoil' means that the compound leaf has three leaflets; and the seed pods are shaped like the toes of a bird's foot. The red streaks or tips on its yellow flowers give the plant its other name – 'bacon-and-eggs'.

Bird's-foot trefoil grows to 10–40 cm in both acid and calcium-rich earth, and is commonly found in meadows, pastures and roadside verges. I have found spreads of it growing on the rocky island of Inishtrahull. The plant tends to spread on the ground, the green stems creeping and straggling before lifting their last few inches upright. The leaves and their paired, leafy stipules – where the stalk branches from the stem – are oval in shape. And in stalked heads, the pea-type, yellow flowers bloom from June until the close of September. Once widely used as a forage crop, the bird's-foot trefoil is now known to contain hydrocyanic acid, which will poison sheep and goats; and the milk from affected cows can taste bitter and look yellow. In folklore the common bird's-foot trefoil is the symbol of revenge.

WOODY NIGHTSHADE
Solanum dulcamara

I choose woody nightshade, or bittersweet, because it is beautiful and dangerous. It can poison both animal and human. All parts of the plant contain solanine, an alkaloid substance containing nitrogen. Most alkaloids have a bitter taste and can be very poisonous.

Woody nightshade is easily recognised. Showing through summer and autumn in hedges, ditches, copses – and trailing along the ground on disused land and seashore – the plant is colourful and attractive. Usually a climbing plant, to a height of 30–200 cm, its stems and leaves, flowers and berries are telltale. Woody at their base, the long and slender stems twist and twine round brambles, bushes and trees. Bearing dark green, smooth-edged, heart-shaped, pointed leaves, the stems' upper and lower leaves can vary in appearance. About 8 cm long, the lower leaves often show two noticeable lobes at their base; the upper leaves, often without lobes, may have leaflets. In delicate loose clusters the flowers have five purple petals and very bright yellow centres. These centres are the stamens that contain the pollen. Because the pointed petals curve back against their stems, the centres project as tiny cones. After continuing their display through summer into autumn, the flowers yield clusters of oval berries – green at first, then yellow, and bright red when ripe. Woody nightshade can be deadly, but it is not as dangerous as its close relative deadly nightshade, whose clusters of globe-shaped berries usually ripen to black, although some forms remain green or turn red. A search of literature finds the paper 'A fatal cause of solanine poisoning' in the *British Medical Journal*, 1948, which gives a detailed account of a woody nightshade fatal poisoning of a nine-year-old girl.

Woody nightshade

The plant's local names are apt: bitter when first formed, the red fruits turn sweet, perhaps to encourage animals to propagate the seeds. The old name 'mortal' probably warned that – before modern antidotes – the plant killed man and beast. It was called felonwort because the berry juice of woody nightshade was believed to cure felon, or whitlow – a painful inflammation of a finger or toe, usually near the nail. And to protect against spiteful witchcraft, and to ward off evil spirits, the plant was hung round the necks of humans and animals.

BOGBEAN
Menyanthes trifoliata

I fail to know why this plant is called bogbean, buckbean, bogbine. Why did our forebears, so accurately descriptive in naming other things and places, leave this plant without a suitable name? It's certainly a bogland plant, but it's not a bean. The name 'buckbean' is a translation from a Flemish term – *bocksboonen* – which means 'goat's beans'. There is possibly a reasonable connection in its alternative name 'bogbine', since the word 'bine' especially describes the creeping, climbing hop, and because bogbean was once used instead of the hop to flavour beer. The name 'marsh trefoil' describes the form of the leaves of bogbean. Still, not one of these local names is good enough for the admirable plant that brightens the margins of otherwise dull peaty ponds, squelchy ditches, and dark brown sheskins. Not many plants can survive in such anaerobic or airless muds, let alone flower beautifully.

The bogbean roots under water in peaty muds, or in wet bogland locations, where, from a densely rooted mat, its stems issue stalks that rise out of the dampness to grow leaves and lovely flowers to a height of 10–30 cm. The creeping stems allow the plant to become widespread in boggy ground. Sheathed at their base, the long leaf stalks present three-lobed leaves, oval and about 2 cm long. And through May and June, from a

cluster of pink buds, the flower heads open widely to show five fleshy petals covered with a bushy spread of white hairs.

In Ireland the stewed roots of bogbean were used to relieve ailments of the digestive system. And with treacle added to sweeten the infusion, the juice from boiled roots was a good tonic and cleansed the blood of impurities. Like the lesser celandine, it was used as a cure for king's evil, or scrofula, a form of tuberculosis that caused inflammation of the joints and glands, especially the glands of the neck. In the 1800s, scrofula was treated with the roots of rose-noble (hound's-tongue), burdock, common dock and

Bogbean

bogbean. The mixture of roots was boiled in water and the strained juice was bottled; the infusion was given to the patient three times a day.

BRACKEN
Pteridium aquilinum

Even though it does not like shade or waterlogged ground, and is rather sensitive to late frost, bracken, or brake, is probably the commonest fern in Ireland and Britain, and its numbers are increasing. With an underground stem, a rhizome, creeping through well-drained and usually acid soil, the fern flourishes in open woodland, spreads across hillsides and colonises neglected meadows. It has become very noticeable in upland pastures, and is beginning to crowd places where heather used to grow. Smothering both upland and lowland, and expensive to attempt to control, it is a serious pest to farmers; and it is very poisonous.

The plant withers brown and appears to die through autumn but the rhizome, or rootstock, survives and issues new fronds in the spring. The young shoots arrive like tiny croziers – curled tightly inwards from the tip. Uncurled, each shoot divides into frond-like branches and these branches are further divided into narrow segments. Brown spore-bearing structures, sori, form a continuous thin line round the underside margins of some of the segments. The margins curve back to protect the spores, which ripen through July and August.

Overall, bracken is an impressive plant – on a strong tall stem the fronds are almost triangular-shaped and sometimes reach two metres high. It was once called the poor man's thatch, and is used for animal bedding, for fuel, and it provides useful shelter for animals. But even after cutting and drying, bracken remains unsafe. In general, it can be a highly dangerous plant, causing acute and chronic forms of poisoning in animals and, possibly, causing cancer in humans. Studies concerning animal poisoning centre on conditions such as vitamin B_1 deficiency in horses and pigs; haemorrhagic diseases in cattle and sheep; tumours of the digestive and urinary tracts of cattle and sheep; blindness in sheep. Studies also attempt to identify other toxic constituents and their effects. Concerning the presence of carcinogens in bracken, the possible risks to humans are being investigated.

RICHARD T. MILLS

BRAMBLE
Rubus fruticosus

Bramble is an aggregate name for several hundred forms of *Rubus* known as blackberry bushes, each of which has its own pattern of thorns, leaf shape, and blossom colour – varying from deep pink to white. In Ireland there are more than eighty species of blackberry: all referred to collectively as *Rubus fruticosus*. Here I deal with the plant we all know as the blackberry, with thorny, pliant, woody stems that sprawl and trail and root to form new plants with green leaves of three to five leaflets, and show rosy flowers and bear 'clots' of fruit with many seeds. On prickly stalks some 90 cm in length, the flowers bud and bloom through summer; and green at first, turning red, then – from late August – ripening to a purplish-black and ready to eat, the sweet, juicy fruit are picked to make delicious pies and jam; and the wild birds scatter the raw seeds.

Bramble blossom

The long strong flexible shoots have been used for binding down thatches and in making beehives. The leaves are astringent. The ripe berries are a rich source of vitamin C and, in amounts, the berries have a purgative action. In folk medicine and superstition the blackberry earned much attention: here are a few treatments or 'cures'. While they are green, the buds, leaves and branches are said to be good for ulcers and sores of the mouth and throat, like quinsy, and for thrush and piles; unripe, the flowers and fruits ease diarrhoea; the powder of the root is good for kidney stones; the juice of the berries helps all sores, and as shampoo, boiled in lye (a strong alkaline solution), the leaves will heal itch and sore, and dye the hair black.

In 1890 Lady Wilde explained that in cases of sprain and dislocation, 'great virtue was attributed to the briar': a metre-long runner was taken and split evenly from end to end. The strips were held by two men who stood facing each other about a metre apart. A third man, a charmer, who knew the nature of plants, excited and caused the 'woods' to move, and as he continued his incantations the woods became so encouraged that they rose up and touched each other. Then, at the point of contact, a piece of wood was cut off and very firmly bound over the sprain or dislocation. The ligature was left in position for three days, after which the ailment was found to be cured.

Blackberries

In spring the buds of bramble were used to make a refreshing drink for sick people. As good as the buds, the roots in winter were boiled and simmered for twelve hours in an earthen pot. It was claimed that if a cupful of the infusion was frequently taken, a deep sleep would result, from which the patient would awaken perfectly cured.

Satan curses and sours the bramble. On Michaelmas Day, 29 September, the day he was expelled from heaven, the devil spits on all blackberries and leaves them sour, and turns them grey. After this day you must leave the berries for the birds. From the close of September, the fruit will cause very sore heads; thus it came about that to prevent children from eating them, the mouldy fruit were called scaldberries – for the devil himself clouts the berries with his club.

Also in folklore, the bramble is the symbol of lowliness, and a berry wreath of bramble is the symbol of reward.

BULRUSH
Typha latifolia

The name 'bulrush' was given to *Scirpus (Schoenoplectus) lacustris*, the clubrush. But ever since the Victorian painter Sir Lawrence Alma-Tameda depicted *Moses in the Bulrushes*, *Typha latifolia*, the plant formerly known as great reed mace, or cattail, became the bulrush in popular usage. And now, a century later the great reed mace has been officially renamed bulrush – from the Middle English *bule* and *rysche*, meaning 'stem' and 'rush'.

In flower, through June and July, the bulrush is a marvellous-looking plant: very tall, with pale, bluish-green leaves, and female flowers in a brown velvety cylindrical spike; and, above the female flowers, males showing like a golden plume. The bulrush grows in shallow water on the margins of lakes, ponds, canals, slow-moving streams and rivers, marshes and even ditches. It likes a clayey bed and it can tolerate low levels of organic pollution; stands of bulrush may even indicate polluted water.

At times two metres tall, erect and strong, the bulrush stem is sheathed, with long straight-lined leaves, both leathery and flat. As tall as the stem, the leaves measure nearly 2 cm across. The flowers – especially the female flowers – are the plant's most attractive feature. The female flower head is a composite of tiny hairy florets; the male flower head comprises clusters of stamens full of pollen. Without any gap on the stem, the flowers form a continuous spike of females and males; and the tiny hairs surrounding the florets are called down. After July, when the male flowers fade, the females are dark brown and ripe – and their seeds are scattered by the wind.

The bulrush rhizome spreads through the mud and rotting vegetation. In East Anglia this rootstock is the favourite food of the coypu, the 'swamp beaver', an orange-toothed rodent the size of a small dog. Native to South America and brought into Britain in 1929 to be cultured for their velvety underfur, escaped and released coypu settled in the Norfolk Broads; however, most have now been exterminated. The stems and leaves of the bulrush can be used with other reed-like plants in thatching. The flower down was used to dress wounds, and for upholstery, and during the First World War the down was used in the manufacture of artificial silk and cotton. Today the female spikes are used in flower arrangements and for Christmas decorations. In folklore the bulrush is the symbol of docility.

CHAMOMILE
Chamaemelum nobile

There are two species of chamomile with medicinal properties: German chamomile, *Matricaria recutita*, and Roman chamomile, *Chamaemelum nobile*, which is found in Ireland. Here I describe the latter, which is used for herbal teas, shampoos, and so on. Restricted to southwest Ireland, southern England, East Anglia, and south Wales, the plant is disappearing through land reclamation, and despite its many medicinal properties, the plant should be left alone – chamomile products are readily available in natural health shops.

A local plant of heaths, pastures and roadsides, on acid and sandy soils, chamomile takes its name from the Greek *khamaimelon*, literally 'earth apple'. It is a ground plant that forms dense mats and, carelessly crushed, it emits an apple-like fragrance. Yet, the flowers and the leaves have a bitter taste.

Chamomile is unmistakable. Flowering from June to August with white ray petals and a characteristic yellow centre, and 30 cm tall, it looks like a big daisy, although it clearly differs from the corn chamomile, oxeye and mayweed. With a much-branched stem divided into fine or thread-like segments, the leaves of Roman chamomile look feathery.

The medicinal properties of chamomile are concentrated in its flower – the yellow centre and the petals – and according to many sources, it can cure or relieve illnesses affecting every system of the human body. Its specific uses focus on stress relief and indigestion caused by tension. In general – as a tea, an oil, a poultice, or a shampoo, appropriately administered – chamomile has many uses: it is a sedative and it encourages sleep; it relieves tired limbs and counteracts fatigue; it relieves toothache and neuralgia, and is good for sprains and swellings; it relieves abdominal cramps and menstrual spasms; it aids digestion, settles upset stomachs and prevents flatulence; it helps kidney and bladder complaints; it is an antispasmodic, antiseptic, diuretic, and it reduces fever; it also stimulates the growth of hair and gives the hair a healthy sheen. In folklore it is the symbol of energy in adversity.

RICHARD T. MILLS

Honeysuckle

HONEYSUCKLE
Lonicera periclymenum
The honeysuckle is one of our most pleasing plants. Its enthusiastic twining and its tube-like flowers can be admired during the day; and at dusk the flowers' heady fragrance entrances night-flying moths. Through woodland, scrub, and along hedgerow the honeysuckle is unmistakable. Deciduous, it has hollow woody stems, oval leaves that are green above and bluish below, and clusters of flowers: creamy-white inside, purplish-red outside. As many as twelve long funnel-shaped flowers cluster in each terminal flower head, each with a four-lobed upper lip, and a tongue-like lower lip. Pollinated by moths at night and by bumblebees during the day, the flowers continue

from June to September, when the seeds are contained in red berries.

Honeysuckles are often seen low and trailing, and they may straggle the ground in woods, but they flower only when they reach good light. They do this by climbing, twining clockwise to follow the sun and they twine so tightly that they deform the stems or branches supporting them. They climb six metres high and make good 'barley sugar' walking sticks. The name 'woodbine' is from the Anglo-Saxon *wude bend* – 'bending round wood'. The derivation of 'honeysuckle' is clear enough.

Medicinally, in the 1600s, as a jam or confection, honeysuckle was taken to cure asthma, to promote the flow of urine, to help women in difficult labour, to relieve abdominal cramps, to allay fits and convulsions; and as an ointment, it cleared the skin of spots and freckles. In the 1800s, pounded and boiled in fresh milk, with oatmeal, and taken three times a day, honeysuckle was said to cure dysentry. Today, a lotion from flowers picked in the later evening cleanses the skin of impurities and leaves it soft and clear. Yet, be careful, for it is also known to cause dermatitis.

And in 1993 in Kerrykeel, County Donegal, I was reminded by a close friend that honeysuckle 'is best kept out-of-doors'; that to bring this plant into the house is 'to invite bad luck'.

RICHARD T. MILLS

Stinging nettle

STINGING NETTLE
Urtica dioica

The stinging nettle is covered with stiff hairs. Formic acid in the minute vesicles at the base of the hairs causes the sting and rash, which are satisfactorily treated by rubbing the affected place with a juicy leaf of curled dock. It is a marvellous plant, growing to a height of 152 cm, and too well known to need any detailed description. Yet the more pleasant, less well-known properties of the plant are worth mentioning.

The young tops make a tasty soup. Medicinally, the plant is valuable: its most important property lies in its ability to reduce blood pressure and to enhance appearance by removing that bloated look. Sweetened with honey, and taken internally, an infusion of the tops will purify the blood and clear the complexion. When applied to the face, it will serve the same purpose. An infusion also relieves arthritis, eczema, and mild diarrhoea. I am reliably informed that it also makes an excellent hair tonic, preventing the hair from falling out, and leaving it soft and glossy. To stimulate growth of hair, use a stiff brush and apply the juice of the nettle to the roots. It's worth trying!

JULY

———

The hottest month of the year, July is the time to enjoy our many birds, especially the mute swan. After July most of the woodland and riverside birds become less noticeable: they grow quiet, and some of them set off for other climes. Before old summer nests are with us for another year, it is the time to be watching and listening. It is also the month for lady's bedstraw, brooklime, wood avens, carragheen moss, centaury, and lesser burdock. The houseflies, moths, and other invertebrates grow numerous in the heat. And while children catch the minnow, stickleback, and stone loach in pools and streams of rivers, many other children play with sand and search rock pools at the seaside.

THE SHORELINE

The shoreline of Ireland is rugged and beautiful, and the waters that touch it are rich in micro-organism, plant, and fish. The variety of coastal habitat and wildlife opportunity is awesome, and conditions are ever-changing, and can be harsh for plant, bird, wild mammal, and human. The shoreline takes the full force and rhythm of the ocean; yet on a calm July evening, when the sea covers the shores, the pale green light is curiously restful; and when the tide retreats, beaches and estuaries are full of colour and activity.

Following the water's retreat from head of inlet as far as the low tide mark, much wild landscape is revealed – plant, animal and evidence of animal. The estuary hosts curlew, sandpiper and oystercatcher, probing for worms and shellfish. At the top of the shore, sand dunes allow marram grass to grow and hide snails, moths, rabbits and pipits; and moss and lichen cover tall rocks. Down the shore, different coloured wracks clamp to low rocks, where limpets and barnacles cling, and cormorants and shags rest, and in rock pools the blenny, goby, shrimp, and crab shelter. At the low tide mark the casts of lugworm appear in spaces between empty shells scattered about. On high, rocky ledges guillemot, fulmar, chough, and kittiwake look down at bather, wind-surfer, water-skier. Then the tide returns and the wild animals of shore and rocky ledge go out to sea and fishermen in boats follow them. This is the

The Gearagh, County Cork
RICHARD T. MILLS

nature of Ireland's shoreline, where the richness of the sea, meeting the opportunities of the land, creates a special wilderness.

RICHARD T. MILLS

Barley Cove, County Cork

THE BEACH

Formed where the power of incoming waves is checked in some way so that the carried sand and shingle find a resting place, often in bays between headlands, and slightly changing shape every day as the sand and shingle are moved in time to the steady rhythm of the tides, the general characteristics of our beaches have been the same for thousands of years. Often pure quartz stained yellow by iron, the sand under our feet may have been washed to the sea after the ice ages, when glaciers crushed underlying rock into fine particles. The pebbles may have arrived in the sea the same way to smash against the base of ancient cliffs to cause further erosion and sedimentation. And some of our beaches are formed almost entirely of fragments of billions of sea shells, worn a long time ago.

Walking towards the sea, the first notable feature is the dune: the mound of loose fine sand heaped up by the wind. After the dune comes the storm ridge: a line of shingle and shells thrown up parallel to the sea by storm tides. When incoming waves reach depths too shallow to maintain them, they break and run foaming up the beach. In stormy weather this rush of water, or swash, will pile pebbles, shells and sand at the head of the beach. Then, its strength exhausted, the water weakly retreats, carrying some sand but leaving the heavier materials where it placed them. Without a regular sousing in sea water, very little wild life uses the storm ridge, but it is a very good place to find a variety of pebbles and shells.

After the storm ridge it's interesting to heed the nature of the sand. The coarse sand quickly drains and dries under pressure – it becomes firm and white underfoot. A few steps further, where the grains are smaller, the sand becomes damp under pressure. Here, because little of the swash can soak through already waterlogged sand, the sea can retrieve much of the sand and other materials carried landward; and a clean, flat or very gently sloping beach is formed. However, on a predominantly shingle beach which usually slopes, material gathers. Because the water soaks through the pebbles, and the back-wash is too weak, and very little material is drawn back, the shingle beach keeps a strand line: an unpleasant mix of rotting seaweed, thrown-forward rubbish, debris, dead fish and birds, and a million flies.

SAND HOPPER
Talitrus saltator

Near the strand line, in dry sand, the burrows of sand hoppers are found. In the later evening, when they come out of these very tiny holes to search for food brought in by the recent tide, the sand hoppers will nip any obstacle – back, leg, buttock, elbow – anything blocking the way out of the burrow. Also called the sand flea, with three pairs of legs that enable it to hop or leap if disturbed, this little creature (20 mm) feeds and lives among the rotting seaweed on the strand line. It has upper and lower antennae and a narrow brown-grey or greenish body which curls under at the rear.

LUGWORM
Arenicola marina

Beyond the strand line, towards the low tide mark where the sand stays damp, the lugworm lives. The lugworm (20 cm) can spend its whole life in the same burrow: U-shaped and comprising a sand-filled head shaft, a gallery where the worm lives, and a tail shaft. It feeds by swallowing the sand at the base of the head shaft, causing replacement sand to slide down into the shaft. A slight hollow in the surface of the beach marks the location of the head shaft. Every hour or so, to leave room for more sand, the worm backs up the tail shaft to expel its waste: a coiled cast of moving sand for bird and angler to see; then, sometimes, the lugworm loses its tail.

About the low tide mark several types of shellfish live. These animals, for example, the cockle and the razor, are suspension feeders. Buried in the sand, they extend a pair of siphon-like structures. They suck in the water and its suspended particles of food through one of the siphons, and expel the filtered water from the other. Lesser sand eels are about the low tide mark as well. Buried in the sand, the eels wait for the tide to come in; then they swim the shallows in glistening shoals and keep diving terns busy. From atop low rocks at the water's edge, shrimps and tiny flatfish can be seen moving; and in amongst the rocks there are pools, like tiny aquariums.

THE ROCK POOL

A long time ago I used a tin bucket to rescue sea creatures trapped in rock pools. I enjoyed catching the shrimps, fish, and crabs. But the activity was also indebted to the notion that the next tide might not be strong enough to carry the creatures away. So I returned them to the sea myself, spending many days catching and carrying the rescued animals. They were not always easy to catch – a shadow cast across a pool would cause many of them to hide. Shrimps would retreat under the seaweeds, anemones drew in their tentacles, crabs sought the shelter of the weed or a ledge, gobies moved under pebbles. Still, learning their hiding places, and inspecting the many different crawling and swimming creatures in my bucket, allowed me precious insights into their strange world.

In each pool new discoveries could be made beneath every rock ledge and pebble and behind every curtain of seaweed. One pool was never really like another: the warm, green-fringed pools upshore of the strand line could never compete with those usually refreshed by ordinary tides. The middle and lower shore pools were very special. Crusting the hard rocks' contours, limpets and barnacles seemed immobile, while rubbery brown and red seaweeds clung waving. In the lower sides of the rocks, winkles and starfish tried to flatten themselves in tiny crevices; and down among the waving weeds – and some-times through the iridescent purple and brown moss of carragheen – tiny fish, snails, and worms lived. Amidst and behind the plants, the range of life was bewildering.

Many of the pools' creatures preferred to remain in the shelter of the plants or under rocks on a sandy bed. Others, out and about the sandy bed, blended with the background. Seen only when they moved, shrimps were often over-looked. But anemones were easily seen; and the commonest, the beadlet anemones – like red blobs of jelly – sometimes half opened their tentacles to show off a ring of bright blue spots.

With pink sides and floors, dashed with a fine coating of algae, some of the pools let most of their guests be seen, but the hermit crabs were always an exciting find. Squatting in the shells of others to cover their own soft defenceless backs and nether parts, the hermits – nimble despite their burden – often drew back their red and yellow fronts, and using the right claw to close the shells, they hid indoors. The middle and lower shore pools kept many other crea-tures as well: blennies mottled to match the brown fronds of seaweed; eel-like rocklings squeezed into tight crevices; slippery butterfish flattened under rocks.

KENNETH McNALLY

Rock pool

Too sensible to rescue marine creatures from rock pools any more, I just sit and look at them instead. The pools are not simply colourful places where sea animals stay, they are ever-changing aquariums, where a person can relax and observe a new set of acquaintanceships with the retreat of every tide. Because of the greenhouse effect the shoreline could change dramatically, and could change soon. According to the Institute of Terrestrial Economy, and assump-tions of other study groups, the sea levels around our coasts could rise 'five feet' over the next century; the rate of erosion of sea cliffs will greatly increase; familiar beaches will disappear and build up elsewhere along the coast; size-able rocks and wetlands will be drowned, and low-lying land will be flooded to create new water meadows and salt marshes.

FISHES IN A JAR

With school over for another while, July is the time to show our youngest freshwater anglers the stickleback, minnow, and stone loach. Instead of rods, use long-handled nets and, instead of bags, use jam jars to hold the catch, and fill them almost to the top with the stream's water. After admiring the fish, return them to their own territories. The lovely red-breasted sticklebacks are always difficult to let go.

Stickleback

RICHARD T. MILLS

STICKLEBACK
Gasterosteus aculeatus

Known locally as the sprick, possibly because of its sharp spiny fins, a stickleback will brighten up any jam jar. The male is a proud and fascinating creature. Between April and August – the breeding season – the male is colourful, aggressive, and demanding. When ready for courtship, he dons his spawning dress: his eyes are large and noticeably blue, and his throat and belly turn scarlet and make his whole body glow. Now a redbreast, he has taken over a territory and is watchful, vigilant, and kept busy chasing intruders – especially other male spricks.

In the centre of his territory the male will build a nest of tiny pieces of water plant, held together with a sticky substance secreted from his kidneys. He builds and secures the nest at the bottom of fine upright stems of water plants. When the nest is built to his satisfaction, he performs a courting dance to a passing female. Waltzing, with blue eyes shining and red breast and belly glowing, he entices the female into his nest and encourages her to lay eggs; then he chases her, darts into the nest, and fertilises the eggs.

The male looks after the eggs and the young spricks. He aerates the eggs by fanning the water over them, and after the eggs hatch – in less than a fortnight – he guards the young till they leave the nest. The young grow to be 4–5 cm long in their first year; and, in quiet water, they can survive three or four seasons.

The stickleback has a long body, sometimes up to 10 cm long, more usually less than 6 cm. The head is large, with big eyes and strong jaws.

Outside the breeding season the colour of both sexes is dark-olive on the back and silver on the belly. It has two dorsal fins, the first comprising three well-spaced, sharp pointed spines – for this reason the fish is called the three-spined stickleback. The second dorsal fin is similar to the anal fin, and the pectoral fins are well developed and strong; none of these fins is spine-like. But the stickleback has two other fins on its underside: these pelvic fins are long, sharp pointed spines. All of these spines are for protection and are felt when putting the stickleback into the jam jar. Despite this armature, many spricks are eaten, and among their greatest enemies are the pike and the kingfisher.

The stickleback mainly lives about the slower middle reaches of a river; it also lives in lakes and ponds. It eats almost any of our tiny freshwater creatures, including water fleas, shrimps, molluscs and their larvae, and sometimes fish eggs. It will take a worm as readily as any freshwater fish, and it prefers a tiny pink worm.

MINNOW
Phoxinus phoxinus

The minnow is the best-known fish to find itself in a jam jar: easily caught when it joins other minnows and they crowd sandy and gravel beds less than a metre from the river bank. In later July, after the females have each laid up to one thousand sticky yellow eggs among river-bed stones, the minnows gather in shoals.

Although seldom longer than 8 cm, the minnow is easily recognised in a river or stream. It has a blunt snout and a slender, cigar-shaped body, show-ing dark bars on its sides. Through the walls of a jam jar, the minnow looks almost transparent. It has large eyes and a down-turned mouth; the fins are short-based and rounded. Covered with very tiny scales, the upperparts are brownish-green to silvery grey, interrupted by fine dark side marks. The belly is cream-coloured.

Shoal of minnows

ÉAMON DE BUITLÉAR

Minnows hunt for water fleas, freshwater shrimps and insect larvae in the deeper parts of shallow streams. Their enemies include the heron, king-fisher, and trout. Indeed, trout anglers often successfully use an artificial minnow as a spinning lure.

STONE LOACH
Noemacheilus barbatulus

Face to face with it, there is no possibility of confusing a stone loach with any of our other tiny freshwater fish. In a stream its features are not easily seen; in a jar all is revealed. The most surprising thing about the appearance of the loach is its strange and ugly face. It has barbels, elongated, fleshy, dangling filaments, around a toothless mouth. It usually has three pairs of barbels, and the mouth is retracted beneath a heavy snout. Although seldom longer than 12 cm, the stone loach is obviously bigger than the stickleback and minnow. The shape of its body is different too. It has a slender, rounded body, cylindrical from snout to breast fins, then somewhat flattened from back down to belly. With tiny scales, the colouring of the body is olive-green

ÉAMON DE BUITLÉAR

Stone loach

above yellowish sides showing a dusky irregular marbling pattern. The belly is yellow.

The stone loach uses its barbels to hunt for food. The usual method of feeding is to comb the surface of the river bed, swallowing food matter and passing inedible particles out through the gills. The chief food is a mixture of insect larvae, algae, and worms.

Despite what I say about its lack of good looks, this little fish is likeable, shy, and interesting. In the jam jar it just lies and looks very bored. In the river or stream it burrows into the sand, mud, or gravel to escape notice. There is a story that it has the ability to foretell bad weather: the name loach is possibly derived from the Old French *locher* – 'to fidget', and the stone loach becomes fidgety twenty-four hours before a thunderstorm.

THE BIRDS

July is the prime month for watching birds and listening to their songs. Young peregrines are hunting, and twenty tufted duck use a lake where perhaps two pairs nested a year ago. From high in the sky, buzzards search the ground for fresh cadavers and rabbits to bring to the nest. Kestrels hover. The watcher also sees and hears coots, fulmars, greenfinches, wheatears, linnets, and others.

WHERE THERE IS COVER

The cock blackbird, with orange bill and orange eye-ring, his flight direct, song rich and fluty, and his alarm call a screaming chatter. The dunnock, a shy little bird, plump and thin-billed, with a grey head and streaked brown back and underparts; and a song which is a high, brief, and repeated 'seep!' The song thrush, with breast spots bold, flight fast and direct; the best of our songsters offering a series of repeated phrases with short, sharp interrupting notes. The robin, our best-known bird, with deep orange-red face and breast, flight low, and song rich, loud and warbly. The stonechat, with bright orange breast, black head and white neck patch, flight low, and song harsh and jangling.

ABOUT THE STREAMS AND POOLS

The dipper, with conspicuous white bib and chestnut belly; it can feed under water and walk on the river bed; flight fast and low, and the song 'clinking'. The grey wagtail, with upperparts blue-grey, underparts bright yellow, and long black white-rimmed tail; flight undulating, and song short and high. The grey heron standing motionless in shallow water, waiting for prey; looking mostly grey but with black markings on head and neck, and bill and legs long and yellow; in flight the neck is retracted and the long legs trail; the flight is slow and powerful; the voice is a harsh croak. The kingfisher, a beautiful bird, is unmistakable; the upperparts bright blue, with white chin and cheek patches; the underparts are orange and the legs are red; the rapid flight is direct and usually low; the call is a piping 'chee!' The moorhen, dark brown, with bright red and yellow bill and white undertail, prefers to run rather than fly, and the calls are loud and squawky.

Peregrine falcon

RICHARD T. MILLS

IN NEARBY FIELDS

Now rare, the corncrake, round-shaped and brownish with heavily streaked upperparts and barred belly, hardly ever seen but easily heard; however, the repeated 'crek-crek!' has become a privilege to hear. The lapwing, easily recognised by its flocking behaviour, aerial acrobatics, and wheezy 'pee-wee!' call, has a crest and greenish upperparts, and a white belly with a noticeable orange patch under the tail. The meadow pipit, flying up from the ground repeating thin 'seep!' notes, is brownish and streaked and has white-rimmed tail feathers; has a jerky, rising and falling 'parachute' flight as it glides to the ground, where it spends most of its time. The cock reed bunting, brown and heavily streaked, with a conspicuous black head and showing a white-rimmed tail during his jerky flight, offers a loud whistling call and a short, squeaky note. Rarely seen until flushed from underfoot, causing it to make a repeated harsh sound, the snipe is a brownish, long-billed bird, showing dark and pale stripes on the back and head; the flight is a zigzag and very fast; as it dives about, it can also make a drumming or vibrating sound caused by air rushing through the outer tail feathers.

ABOUT THE TREES

The collared dove, overall greyish brown with a narrow black half collar, has a direct and fast flight and a repeated 'coo!' call. The cock house sparrow, brown and heavily streaked with distinctive grey and red-brown markings and a black bib, has a rapid flight and voices a mixture of chirps and twitters. The rook, large, black, untidy looking with feathered thighs, and holding a heavy beak with a patch of bare skin around its base, has a direct flight with steady wing beats; and an extended harsh 'caw!' The starling, well-known for its mimicry and gregariousness, has a glossy, blackish plumage with a green and purple sheen, speckled, with a yellow bill; its flight is fast and direct, with glides; its song is a mixture of rattles, warbles, and whistles. The treecreeper, dark brown and streaked above, usually seen winding its way up the trunk of a tree – using its thin curved bill to eat many insects and spiders – has a flitting flight and a high-pitched squeaky call. The woodpigeon, softly calling 'coo-coo-coo!' and noisily flapping out of a tree in search of some barley field, shows noticeable wing bars and a white neck patch fringed with glossy green.

FLITTING ABOUT THE BUSHES

The bluetit, with bright blue cap – which differentiates it from other tits – and yellow underparts, has a kind of fluttering flight from bush to bush and a fine repeated 'see!' call. The tiny coal tit with a black cap, white nape, and double white wing bars, has a variety of piping calls. The goldcrest, our tiniest bird, with the flight of a tit and a thin 'see-see!' call, has green upperparts with black margins enclosing an orange cap; in 1988 I found five occupied goldcrest nests in a conifer planting of nineteen spruce trees

– about fifteen years old – outside the village of Donemana in County Tyrone. The great tit singing 'teacher-teacher!', showing a black head with white cheeks – the black continuing as a bold band down the centre of the yellow underparts – flits from bush to bush, but the flight undulates over longer distances. The willow warbler, the colour, shape, and size of a 'sally' leaf, has a jerky flight and a mild descending warbling, ending with a flourish. The wren, one of our most familiar tiny birds, showing a brown barred plumage and an erect tail, has a whirring and direct flight; a repeated 'tic!' call and a loud hurried song.

IN THE AIR

The house martin, with blue-black upperparts, white rump and underparts, flies high and calls 'chirrup!' Three nests adorn my house in County Donegal; sadly, I keep finding dead young, or scaldies, lying on the ground. Fluttering and erratic, flying high, and voicing sounds like the house martin, the sand martin has a brown breast and back and white underparts; this martin is a disappearing species. Also becoming fewer with every year, the skylark – streaky brown and crested, and showing white outer feathers on the tail; strongly fluttering skywards, offers a long-winded and very pleasant song from high above sand dune and old pasture. Distinguished from the martins by its forked tail, chestnut throat and forehead, the swallow is creamy underneath, blue-black above, and it shows a row of white tail spots during its graceful, swooping and acrobatic flight. The swift with long scythe-like wings, and dark colouring, to differentiate it from the swallow, utters high-pitched screams and seems to race every other bird over the streams; the flight is remarkably fast.

ABOUT THE EDGES OF WOODLAND

Handsome, shy, and rarely heard offering a mixture-maxture of notes, the cock bullfinch has blue-grey upperparts with a warm red below; his cap, wings, and tail are black, but white patches are visible on the wings and rump. The cock chaffinch, our most common finch with reddish-pink face and breast, grey cap and nape, brown back and white wing bars, loudly calls 'pink!' The goldfinch, our most attractive finch – both sexes similarly coloured – red-faced with cheeks white and black, upperparts brown and underparts pale, a bright yellow patch on wing seen during flight, has a pleasant liquid twittering call. The redpoll, a small, plump brownish finch seen flitting about the top-most branches of trees, uses a mixture of trills; the male has a red forehead and pink breast; the flight is dancing and high.

RICHARD T. MILLS

Goldfinch

HIGH UP AND LOW DOWN

The cuckoo is grey and slender, with a long tail and barring on the underparts. The normal call of the male is 'cu-coo!'; however, in 1977, while fishing for brown trout, the Reverend Stephen Kearney and I heard a repeated 'cuc-coo-coo!' from a male bird perched on a post in the southwest corner of Lough Ash in County Tyrone. 'There's a cuckoo with a stutter!' said Father Kearney. The hooded crow, with ash-grey on the back and belly; flies strongly with regular wing beats and has a harsh kraugh-like call. The magpie, unmistakable pied colouring and long greenish tail, offers 'chak-chak-chak!' calls. The magnificent sparrowhawk, especially the male, blue-grey above and pale red below, is usually seen gliding low and fast through bushes and along hedgerows, causing sparrows and finches to panic, scatter, and die.

Come August's Glorious Twelfth, when red grouse crow and try to escape from sight, most of our other birds become less noticeable. Meanwhile, I must mention the mute swan and its cygnets.

RICHARD T. MILLS

Mute swans and cygnets

THE MUTE SWAN
Cygnus olor

Through July many cygnets are born. Hatched from greyish-green eggs in a huge mound of sticks, reeds and other vegetation, the greyish-brown young leave the nest after a day or so. It is always a pleasure to see cygnets again, sometimes nestling among the feathers on their parents' backs while they swim. From now till autumn the family will stay close together – cob and pen parading their cygnets – with the pen leading and rooting up plants for her young to eat, and, following them, always vigilant, the cob ready to hiss and defend his family against other swans, animals, and even humans. Our resident mute swans are fascinating creatures. They mate for life and nest in the same territory each year. Sometimes violent fights take place when a new pair tries to usurp the territory. The 'pretenders' are usually defeated and they have to go elsewhere.

For eight hundred years from the eleventh century, all mute swans belonged to the Crown or to organisations or individuals who owned swans under royal licence. The value of the swan was as food and as status symbol. The sovereign's swan-master enforced the practice of swan keeping, and cygnets were marked on the bill or foot with various notches or more elaborate marks to indicate ownership. The practice was called swan-upping.

Nowadays they are found about the edges of lakes and along rivers, and about the shallow upper reaches of estuaries and in sheltered coastal bays. Truly designed for these relatively mild waters, the mute swan's body is shaped like a miniature longboat, tapering towards each end, and with little depth to it, broad in the middle; and underneath, the swan's strong short legs with paddle-like feet are set well back for speed and propulsion; and tall above the surface stretches the long, elegant, very muscular neck to reach down to fetch food from the shallows.

Weighing up to 18 kg and 152 cm in size, the mute swan is one of the world's heaviest flying birds. It finds difficulty taking off; but once in the air its flight is powerful, direct, and the wing beats produce a truly unmistakable sound. In flight a group of swans presents a spectacular sight and their great beating wings make a very unusual, throbbing, yet haunting, musical sound.

The name 'mute' is taken to mean that this is a silent bird, and compared to other birds, the mute swan is very quiet; yet it does have its own range of conversational yaps and angry warning notes, like snorts and hisses. And it can grow very angry. Despite its slow, graceful and serene appearance, the swan can be very aggressive – especially when nesting or protecting the cygnets. Then, if a stranger comes near, the swan will adopt its threat posture, full of promise to attack. Moving towards you, the swan's neck becomes noticeably arched, and the upper joints of the wings are raised to lift the flight feathers outwards and upwards over the back. When this happens, leave the scene to observe the swan and its family from a safe distance.

Swans have a special place in literature and legend. *The Ugly Duckling* is well known, and Andersen's tales *The Wild Swans* and *The Swan's Nest* are also classic. But the swan has occupied other marvellous minds as well: in Wagner's opera, *Lohengrin*, the mysterious knight comes to the king's court, borne on the river in a skiff drawn by a white swan; Cygnus, a northern constellation in the Milky Way, seen by ancient astronomers as having the outline of a swan in flight; and in Greek mythology Zeus disguised himself as a swan to seduce Leda. Yet my favourite is the sad tale of Fionnuala and her brothers Aed, Fiachra and Conn – the children of Lir – changed into white swans for nine hundred years by their jealous stepmother Aoife. And three hundred years they spent on Lake Derryvaragh, three hundred on the Straits of Moyle, between Antrim and Scotland, and three hundred on the Atlantic by Erris and Inishglory. Then the swans were gone and in their place stood an old woman and three old men, all dying. That same night the brave priest Mochaomhog, who baptised them before they died, dreamed he saw young Fionnuala and her brothers going to heaven. For her cruelty, Aoife's foster father Bodh Dearg turned her into a bird with a human head, destined to sweep the winds till Doomsday.

THE HOUSEFLIES

From spring till autumn many different kinds of flying insects come into the house: bluebottles, bees, wasps, moths, midges, flying ants, hoverflies, and others. Many of these are not true flies, which have only a single pair of wings. There are thousands of different true flies and a number of these come into the home. Most are accidental intruders which search the windowpanes trying to reach the open air again. Even the bluebottle, which comes into the kitchen to lay her eggs on meat, wants to quickly leave when her task is completed. However, there are two kinds of true fly which make themselves at home: the housefly and the lesser housefly.

Musca domestica, the housefly, is stoutly built and shows a greyish back, and in both sexes the abdomen appears yellowish. The lesser housefly – *Fannia canicularis* – looks like the housefly but is smaller and more slender. Lesser houseflies are a dull greyish colour and the males display a pair of semi-transparent yellow patches at the base of the abdomen. Both species pass their adult lives in houses, buzzing about and crawling over food. The buzzing is the sound of their wings beating – about two hundred times a second. Excepting minor differences, the breeding habits of the two species are similar. Both breed in the sort of refuse that accumulates around houses. The

Bluebottle

lesser housefly and larvae prefer food which is rich in nitrogenous compounds: they like urine, and loose or solid bird droppings – always abundant where pigeons and chickens live. The larvae of the housefly are less particular: they eat manure, compost, material in the soil from old-fashioned privies, and house refuse of most kinds.

White and about 1 mm long, the eggs are laid on suitable feeding places: a housefly may lay 1,000 eggs in batches of about 150 in different locations. In very hot weather the eggs hatch inside ten hours, but hatching normally takes two days. White legless maggots, the larvae feed rapidly and can become pupae in just under a week. The pupae then become adults. In very warm weather the cycle from egg to adult can take less than a fortnight; in cold weather the pupal stage might last two months. At a temperature of 15°C houseflies will breed continuously, the cycle from egg to adult taking about three weeks.

Lesser houseflies, becoming noticeable from late spring, appear earlier in the year than houseflies, which slowly build up their numbers and become abundant during July. Adults of both species live for about a month in summer; they live longer in cool weather when they are less active. Most adults die when the winter gets very cold, but many pupae stay alive to become adults in spring.

Flies and greenbottles

An annoying housefly is difficult to catch. To the sensory receptors of a fly, our swiping, clutching, and our fastest hand movements are very slow. A housefly has two large eyes that cover most of its head. The eyes are compound, made up of six-sided lenses, and there are about four thousand lenses in each eye. No two lenses exactly point in the same direction and each lens works independently. Everything a fly sees appears to be broken into small pieces. The insect does not have sharp vision but it can quickly see the tiniest of movements. In addition, a housefly has two antennae that detect any change in the

movement of air around it, warn it of danger, alert it to threat. Growing between the insect's eyes, the antennae – short, thick and highly sensitive – also help the fly to find food: to detect the appetising odour of chemicals in rotting meat and garbage.

Unlike midges and other biting flies, a housefly does not have piercing mouth-parts. It does not bite or chew; it cannot open its jaws; it cannot take solid food; but by dropping saliva onto its intended meal, the housefly can convert solid food such as bread or dung into nutritious liquids, which are sucked up the proboscis and delivered to the stomach. And a housefly with an overfilled stomach will leave little dirty spots of vomit on any surface.

The housefly is dirty and dangerous. It thrives under conditions of carelessness and squalor, in the kind of medium in which very harmful bacteria breed. Even from so-called clean locations, the housefly has been shown to carry a million bacteria on its body. These bacteria are not all disease germs but many of them are likely to be, and the fly can spread gastro-intestinal conditions such as dysentery and other diarrhoeal problems. Worldwide studies show infants and young children to be the most susceptible victims and the greatest sufferers. By spraying or exposing houseflies to specific chemicals, vast numbers are killed. Yet, like the bacteria they carry, they can develop a resistance to specific poisons. No individual housefly is likely to develop a resistance during its own lifetime but, if not exposed to a sufficient dose of the poison, it will survive to breed more resistant offspring. The immunity is inherited down through generations, until flies emerge with total resistance. For this reason many authorities are against the use of insecticides. For them, control of flies is best achieved by depriving the insects of breeding places. Water-borne sanitation, closed wheelie bins, and other facilities for good hygiene have gone some way towards controlling these pests.

MOTHS AND BUTTERFLIES

Having briefly described a number of butterflies in June, and delayed describing moths until July – when it is possible to see the cinnabar and six-spot burnet during daylight hours – I now describe the life cycles of the moth and the butterfly and offer further guidelines to help distinguish one from the other.

Lepidoptera, meaning 'scale-winged', is the scientific term used to describe the whole order of butterflies and moths. The term is relevant only to the fourth and final stage of their existence, and does not describe the larval stage and the process which allows a grub to become such a lovely flying creature. During each stage – egg, larva or caterpillar, pupa, adult – the insect undergoes a metamorphosis and leads a completely different way of life.

The parent lays the eggs on a plant that the larva can eat. Moths also lay eggs on feathers, cloth and other material that will serve as food for the hatched young. A sticky substance usually fastens the eggs to the leaf tissue or other material. The eggs of the different butterflies and moths are different colours – green, red, orange, yellow. A few days after an egg is laid, the larva begins to form, and when it grows big enough, it breaks out of the shell: some hatch after a few days; some take months to hatch.

After hatching, the caterpillar eats the broken eggshell, then begins to eat the material on which it was hatched; and as it grows, its skin splits and it slowly slips free. A butterfly caterpillar may shed its skin, or moult, four or five times; moth caterpillars moult from four to a dozen times or more.

It is during the larval stage that the insect causes damage. The caterpillar's strong jaws and other mouthparts are used for smelling as well as tasting and eating. The large head also holds tiny eyes and two short antennae, which the caterpillar uses to feel its way along a surface. On each side of the head, just above the mouth and arranged in a curved line, the eyes tell light from dark. A tiny structure, the spinneret, projects below the mouth, and delivers an almost continuous fine flow of silken fluid which soon hardens to become thread-like; this silken thread gives the moving caterpillar a 'foothold'.

RICHARD T. MILLS

Female emperor moth

The body of the caterpillar has twelve segments or parts. Continuous with the head, the first three segments form the thorax, each of which has two short legs, jointed and claw-tipped. These are 'true' legs – they later lengthen and become the legs of the adult. The remainder of the body – the other nine segments – forms the abdomen, from which pairs of 'false' legs, or prolegs, project downwards. These fleshy limb-like structures, tipped with tiny, hooked claws, are used when the insect moves to position itself on a suitable leaf or twig in readiness for the pupal stage, and are cast with the final shedding of the caterpillar skin.

Before changing into pupae many moths spin silken cases around themselves. However, already formed inside the caterpillar skin, a butterfly pupa swells, and its body curves and moves wave-like, and splits the skin. A hard shell quickly forms over the bare pupa. Some pupal shells have strange shapes, and many have bright colours arranged in patterns, often silvery or gold coloured – the chrysalis. The pupa looks inactive, but inside the chrysalis the structures of the caterpillar are changing to those of the adult moth or butterfly. In some cases the change may take a week, sometimes months or even a year. Then the adult emerges. At first trembling, with dull wings bent and scales too cramped for light, the moth or butterfly waits uncomfortably. But not for long: the tiny heart pumps and fills the veins of the wings to unfold like wrinkly petals, and new colour and radiance suddenly descend upon the new creature.

There are crude guidelines to help us tell butterflies from moths, and exceptions are always there to keep life interesting. In general a moth flies by night, a butterfly by day. This guideline holds good to the extent that butterflies never fly during the night, but there are moths such as the six-spot burnet and cinnabar which fly during the day. And in countries where night-flying predators of insects abound, most moths sensibly fly during the day. Both moths and butterflies possess two pairs of large, often colourful wings; but while at rest, the moth keeps its wings down flat or in a sloping-roof fashion; the butterfly reposes with its wings raised like snails. Yet some kinds of skipper butterflies, when resting, flatten out their wings like moths. Another guideline is that moths have fringed or feathered antennae, while butterflies have antennae that are clubbed at the extremities. Yet, again, exceptions exist: for example, a burnet's antennae have club-like ends; but in every other way a burnet has the physical features of a moth. In summary, it may be simple enough to see the difference between a clothes moth and a cabbage-visiting butterfly, but moths and butterflies may have common features and attempting to identify unfamiliar specimens can prove interesting.

Through July our range of moths includes the silver Y moth, death's-head hawk-moth, eyed hawk-moth, crimson and gold, magpie moth, ghost swift, common swift, brimstone, swallow-tailed moth, white ermine, puss moth, peppered moth, large yellow underwing, and many others. Yet, for me, among July's most attractive and interesting specimens are the cinnabar, the six-spot burnet, and the large emerald.

CINNABAR
Tyria jacobaeae
Found about hedgerows, neglected meadows and dunes, in places where spreads of ragwort or benweed, and groundsel grow, the cinnabar is a very attractive and highly poisonous moth. A member of the tiger moth family, renowned for their beautiful colouring, the elegant cinnabar gets its name from the vermilion lines and patches on its fore wings, and the crimson hind wings with their narrow black fringe. The coloration warns birds and other predators that the moth is inedible, so although nocturnal the cinnabar can also safely fly during the day. The moth's poisonous nature probably begins during its larval stage. In July and August the caterpillars feed on ragwort and groundsel, which contain poisons that do not harm the larvae but make them taste unpleasant. Brightly banded in orange and black, the colonies of caterpillars feed quite openly. Wingspan: 45 mm.

SIX-SPOT BURNET
Zygaena filipendulae
Like the cinnabar, the six-spot burnet is brightly coloured, poisonous, and flies during the day. With a whirring, bird-like

Six-spot burnets mating

flight, it is very active in bright sunlight. Commonly found in coastal meadows and grassy sand dunes, the moth is unmistakable. The six strong red spots on each of the moth's greenish-black fore wings are arranged in three pairs. The hind wings are a lovely deep crimson, with a narrow, blue-black fringe. The short, squat, yellow and black caterpillars feed on trefoil and vetch, which contain cyanide derivatives; and passed through the pupal stage to the mature moth, these poisons deter birds and other predators. The caterpillar makes a yellow, tissue-like cocoon on a stem of grass. Wingspan: 35 mm.

LARGE EMERALD
Geometra papilionaria
This beautiful moth is found in hedgerows and deciduous woodland. The wings are emerald green and show fine, white, wavy lines. The flight is noticeably fluttery. Although nocturnal, I have seen the large emerald in the daylight, but usually see it coming to the lighted window at night. The caterpillar hatches brown and then camouflages itself by turning green in spring, and feeds on the leaves of beech, birch, hazel, and other trees. It moves by looping: arching its thorax and abdomen, and then pushing the front end forward. Wingspan: 50 mm.

THE PLANTS

July's flowers include knotgrass, bindweed, hedge parsley, saxifrage, thistle, wild angelica, feverfew, bog asphodel, wild parsnip, tansy, monkey flower, cudweed, sea holly, harebell, sea aster, great willowherb. My favourites are: lady's bedstraw, brooklime, wood avens, lesser burdock, common centaury and carragheen.

LADY'S BEDSTRAW
Galium verum
Lady's bedstraw was once used to stuff mattresses and, when dry, its pleasant smell of new-mown hay discouraged fleas. In folklore the belief that the plant allowed uncomplicated childbirth and, in legend, that the Virgin Mary lay on a pallet of bedstraw, possibly led to the name 'lady's bedstraw'; because it was used to curdle milk in cheese-making the plant is sometimes called cheese rennet. The colour of its flowers gave it the name 'yellow bedstraw'.

Growing in dry, relatively neutral soil – slightly acidic, or slightly alkaline – lady's bedstraw is commonly found in disused meadow, hedgebank and sand dune. Although the plant sometimes reaches about a metre high, the structures and arrangements of its fine stems, leaves, and crowds of tiny flowers are very difficult to see. For me, a good magnifying glass is needed to know the beauty and design of the plant's different parts.

Eventually achieving an almost upright position, some of the slender, four-angled or squarish, slightly hairy stems are light brown. With single veins, the very narrow, linear, short-haired leaves grow in attractive whorls at each joint of the stem. Some of the whorls comprise eight leaves, others comprise as many as twelve. Bright yellow and tiny, the flowers are very

Lady's bedstraw

RICHARD T. MILLS

numerous in diversely branching clusters. Just 4 mm across the four joined and equal petals, the flowers bloom through July and August. Green at first, the very small and smooth, two-celled fruit turn black. And, with thread-like strands, the reddish roots creep here and there, but remain strong in the ground.

BROOKLIME
Veronica beccabunga

A mere scattering of marshy ground now remains in Ireland. Most of the wilderness areas of swamp and mud – especially the fertile, calcareous areas – have been drained for farming. Nevertheless, where heavy clay makes drainage difficult, and old ponds still abide, and springs keep oozing across meadows, and poorly dredged streams reach over their banks and soak ditches – these circumstances and conditions allow the brooklime to survive. The plant grows in the shallow margins of ponds, sluggish streams, damp ditches, and marshy patches in lowland meadows; and it takes the name brooklime from its habitat: 'brook' meaning 'a stream of water', and 'lime' from the Latin *limus* meaning 'mud', or from the Anglo-Saxon *lime*, meaning 'mud' or 'slime'.

This is an attractive plant, with stout, smooth stems, pleasant green leaves, and clusters of beautiful speedwell-like flowers. Creeping through mud, before bending upwards to a height of 20–60 cm, the hollow, succulent and fleshy stems produce roots and leaves and slim stalks for delicate flowers. The roots trail down from the stem's lower nodes, where opposite leaves begin and grow outwards. Some 4 cm long, the almost stalkless oval leaves have a glossy look and feel leathery. From where the upper leaves grow from the stem, the flower stalks, or spikes, also grow upwards, to display clusters of dark blue flowers, rarely pink. Less than 1 cm across, the lovely little four-petalled flowers help to brighten watersides and marshy places throughout summer.

Although bitter in taste, the plant can be eaten. Rich in vitamin C, it was once given to seafarers to protect them against scurvy; and like the water-cress which often grows alongside it, the brooklime can be used in salads. Internally, an infusion of the stems and leaves is said to cleanse the blood; and externally, it will remove unsightly blackheads and pimples.

WOOD AVENS
Geum urbanum

This interesting and attractive plant used to be called herb bennet. The name probably derives from the Latin *herba benedicta* – 'blessed herb'. In the later Middle Ages the little plant was in great demand and was kept very busy warding off evil spirits. Nowadays, as the wood avens, it lives in seclusion.

Preferring fertile, calcareous or limy soils, and damp shady places in woodland, hedgebank and streamside, the wood avens has pleasant features and qualities. It is a slim, upright plant, growing to a height of 30–60 cm, with downy stems and unmistakable foliage and flowers. Its palmate leaves have three dark green leaflets with toothed margins; and, in any leaf, the middle, uppermost or terminal leaflet is the largest of the three leaflets. At the bottom end of the leaf, where the stalk branches from the stem, a pair of tiny leaf-like growths are noticeable. Found on many plants,

RICHARD T. MILLS

Brooklime

these leafy growths are called stipules. At the very top of the wood avens, held erect on long stalks, the tiny flowers have five golden yellow petals, and dainty turn-down collars of sepals. The flowers are very pleasing and, during July, they grow brightly in the shade.

The roots are especially interesting: brown and about 5 cm long, they smell like cloves and can be used to flavour fruit pies and wines. The roots were also used to scent clothes and to repel moths; Wood avens

they are also astringent and have a high tannin content. Applied to the face, with the root of angelica, an infusion of the fresh or dried root of wood avens will leave the skin soft and smooth.

LESSER BURDOCK
Arctium minus

After a searching walk in the countryside, the clinging purple flower heads, or burs, of lesser burdock often have to be removed from clothing and from dogs' coats. The plant grows along woodland margins, hedgerows, roadsides, and on waste ground.

The name 'bur-dock' describes the plant's most noticeable features: the thistle-like flower heads and the large green dock-like leaves. But the burdock is neither a thistle nor a dock. For obvious reasons, it is also called the burr-burr and stick-button.

The lesser burdock is a coarse tall hairy plant, and can grow to a height of 120 cm. Rising from a stout taproot, the reddish, furrowed stem has numerous branches with leaves appearing to wind up them. Hollow-stalked and almost hairless on their surface, the scalloped, heart-shaped leaves are covered with white down underneath. From July till the end of September, the clusters of flower heads are packed with deep purple upright florets, which protrude

Lesser burdock

from cases of prickly bracts or burs. During autumn, the burs carry the plant's brownish seeds far and wide, and can be very harmful: apart from clinging to the coats of cattle and other animals – and sometimes causing skin irritations – they can fatally choke and obstruct the upper digestive tract of pheasants.

At one time an infusion of the leaves and stems of lesser burdock was applied to soothe burns and sores. And the plant's young stems were eaten in salads. Nowadays, a tea or infusion made from the fresh leaves, stems and flowers of the less common greater burdock *(Arctium lappa)* is recommended in the treatment of boils.

COMMON CENTAURY
Centaurium erythraea

Common centaury is an interesting little plant. Even though it prefers to grow near the sea, it does not like damp conditions. A frequent plant of sand

Common centaury

hills and cliffs, and grassland on mildly acidic to calcium-rich, well-drained soils, it grows locally inland, about woodland edges, open scrub and roadside verges. It flowers from June to October; and the pale red flowers dislike getting wet and open only in fine weather.

An Old World herb of the Gentian family, centaury has been tasted and tested for many uses, especially medicinal ones. The name 'chironia' is interesting and helps to explain the plant's Latin title *Centaurium erythraea*. The healing properties of the plant were said to have been divulged by Chiron, the centaur of Greek mythology. Unlike the other centaurs – lawless creatures of northern Greece – Chiron was a wise and trusted mentor who advised many Greek heroes, including Achilles. Hercules accidentally killed Chiron with a poisoned arrow, but Zeus placed him high among the stars. Some legends tell that Chiron became Sagittarius, the Archer; others say that he is Centaurus, the third brightest star in the night sky. Thus the name *Centaurium* derives from the Greek *kentauros*; and *erythraea* derives from the Greek *erythros*, meaning 'red', the colour of the plant's flowers. Despite the medicinal value of the plant, the name 'a-hundred-gold-pieces' is without foundation; 'gall-of-the-earth' is relatively modern and describes the very bitter taste of every part of the common centaury.

This is a pretty plant, but it is not outstanding. You have to find it. Usually it has a ground-level rosette of leaves and several stems with flowering branches that are 30 cm or more high. Sometimes it can be very dwarfed, with a single flowering stem only 5 cm tall. At the base of the stems, the rosette has pale green, pointed leaves with prominent veins. The square, erect stems have lance-shaped leaves in opposite pairs. The upperparts of the stems branch freely and, on short stalks, the dainty rose-pink flowers grow in dense clusters. The cylindrical petal tube extends beyond dark green, pointed sepals. And, as already mentioned, the petals close in wet and damp conditions.

An infusion of the fresh flowers in wine is said to reduce fever, is a tonic, and cleanses the blood. Applied to the face, an infusion of the whole plant, fresh or dried, will remove acne-like eruptions, ease soreness and leave the skin soft and smooth.

CARRAGHEEN
Chondrus crispus
Also called Irish moss and carragheen moss, this plant is not a moss at all. It is an edible seaweed, plentiful along the north Atlantic shorelines – on both sides of the ocean. With many-branched fronds, it varies in colour from violet to green, and grows on exposed middle shore of rock and shingle – not on mud. Even though it most commonly occurs along the rugged northwest coast of Ireland, the plant takes its name from the village of Carragheen, near Waterford, where it is also abundant.

Easily recognised, carragheen is a low bush-like seaweed, and can grow to a height of 15 cm. Its clusters of tough, flat fronds are regularly divided and forked six to eight times. The fronds form a broad fan shape that tapers down to a short slim main stem with a small tough disc-like base, by which it is firmly attached to rock. In deep water and rock pools at the tide's edge, carragheen shows a lovely violet or purplish iridescence. With exposure to light and air, the rich coloration fades, and the plant turns white if left high and dry.

RICHARD T. MILLS

Carragheen

Down through the centuries carragheen was gathered as food, and to cure lung diseases. Only fifty years ago, before the use of antibiotics and drugs such as Streptomycin for tuberculosis, it was used as a remedy for such chest complaints. The plant was thoroughly washed and soaked for several hours in spring water, and then it was simmered in milk for three hours – the recipe required a handful of 'moss' to a quart of spring water and fresh milk. The pasty mixture was strained and sweetened with sugar. Treated carragheen was also added to thicken soups and stews.

Carragheen is a valuable source of vegetable gelatine, a tasteless glue-like protein substance, easily dissolved in hot water and put to many uses. Exported from Ireland, it was used as a gelling ingredient for soups and desserts. It was used as a substitute for isinglass in blancmange and jellies, and for sizing walls and surfaces in decorating, and is still used in softening lotions and soothing handcreams.

AUGUST

Now into the height of summer, when insects are noisier and more numerous than in other months, and wasps are beginning to die, the days of August can be very warm; but the nightly fog or mist in low-lying pastures and river valleys signals the close of another season. Tall-growing summer flowers still brighten edges of meadows, damp ground, old laneways, and hedgerows, but the fruit on the oak, hazel, rowan and elder are signs of approaching autumn. Most of the bird nests are empty; and, no longer required to warble to claim territory or attract a partner, or chatter alarm calls to protect young, our best singing birds are quiet again. And the corncrake, the cuckoo, the swift, and many of our summer visitors, are on their way home to Africa. Out flying for the first time, young buzzards make loud mewling calls and seem to completely occupy the sky. People still holiday at seaside places, and some of them venture out to catch and tag the blue shark, and then set it free.

August is really the month of the moorland. Through July into beginning August, while bog cotton brightens marshy places and flowering and fruiting heathers give the whole landscape a lovely crimson-purple glow – and in special places hen harriers fly low to inspect the heathers – the hills and moorlands are pleasantly quiet; but come the Glorious Twelfth of August, shooting parties with double-barrelled shotguns, setters, pointers, and tail-wagging springer spaniels make this landscape dangerous and noisy. Then, while farmers and ramblers keep a safe distance, and snipe and hares flee for their lives, our precious Irish red grouse are shot dead.

THE HILLS AND UPLANDS

Our hills and uplands are very old and beautiful. The scenery is quite spectacular, with wilderness areas of peat bog and moorland reaching down from spur of rock and scrubby hillside to lush valley. Yet wildlife and domestic stock often find natural conditions difficult. Apart from gale, mist, freezing fog, snow and ice, summer rains can become heavy floodwater and wash the animals away; but the rich variety of life surviving there is a delight to see.

From the year's beginning, while farmers fear for their sheep and hooded crows watch them, foxes hunt rabbits across the moorland. In later January the foxes mate, and from the last day of February, frogs spawn in bog water and eyed ova of brown trout huddle together in the gravelly redds of upland streams. With spring, the grey-brown of the high slopes turns green and hares hurry about. A few hundred feet below the gorse is in bloom, the willows have let their catkins open and the blackthorn is blossoming.

The warmer weather brings the lark and pipit, and the kestrel appears. The grey wagtail and the dipper arrive back from lower streams and banks, where badger, otter, mink, and other mammals are nursing their young. And spent salmon and sea trout have started tailing down river on their way back to the sea, passing alder, birch, hazel, thorn and holly; with celandine, anemone, and primrose colouring the river banks. Through April into May, plover, snipe and curlew come up from the estuaries and, a short while later, the flowers of rowan begin to show. In later June, when the flowers of gorse are gone, the chicks of red grouse are eating bilberries and young heather shoots; and foxes and hooded crows eat the young grouse; and sparrowhawks, peregrines, buzzards, and, maybe, hen harriers are about.

Through July into August the scene grows quiet, but guns aimed at grouse soon put a stop to that. From the close of August into autumn, when the high ground grows quiet again, and silver eels leave deep holes in upland streams and lakes to return to the Sargasso Sea, farmers fence bog holes and make ready for another winter.

Ancient folds created by the earth's movement, and shaped by volcanic fire and glacial ice, the hills and moorlands have graced this country for a very long time. But Ireland's high wilderness places are now changing: countless artificial drains are beginning to mar the slopes; dark patches of coniferous plantation are too noticeable; areas of moorland are being reclaimed for grazing; peat bogs are being dried out and overharvested; and habitats for a variety of wild animal and plant life have gone or are quickly disappearing.

RED GROUSE
Lagopus lagopus

Once widespread in heathered uplands, the numbers of red grouse have seriously dwindled. Dumpy and round-shaped, both male and female birds are dark reddish-brown, heavily spotted and barred black. The male, 38 cm, is darker and larger than the female, and he has a bolder red wattle over the eye. The bill is grey, short and stubby; the dark tail is short and rounded. Red grouse feed on young heather shoots and take grit to aid digestion. Usually seen when flushed from heather, the startled escape flight is noisy, strong and powerful, before gliding silently with bowed wings to cover. The voice strongly offers the characteristic 'bec-bec!' call: 'Go-beck, go-beck, go-beck, beck, beck, beck!'

Red grouse nest on moorland which offers young heather, bilberry, crowberry, tussocks of grass and rushes. A hollow or scrape

Red grouse

RICHARD T. MILLS

on the ground, the nest is barely lined with dry grass, fibrous rootlets, and moss or lichen. Yellowish and blotched dark brown, the six to eleven eggs are incubated for about twenty-five days. Wearing a speckled pattern of light brown, chestnut, and dark brown down, the young leave the nest soon after hatching. The red grouse has a single brood: March–June.

Suddenly and loudly rising with wings whirring, then gliding with wing tips hanging from plump bodies trying to escape the hunters in August, but never straying too high or far from the safety of their heather, the red grouse are being shot out of existence – and we can never replace them. The Irish species is unique: different from the red grouse of Wales, northern England, and Scotland. (Some Irish birds have been introduced into parts of England, but they are still a separate species.) The Irish grouse probably belongs to the same species as the willow grouse of northern Europe, Asia, and Canada, but differing from the willow grouse by not having a distinct change of plumage: from rich red-brown in summer to white in winter.

Without grouse, our moors and hillsides have become poorer places. Once well-populated areas do not have grouse any more; elsewhere, the numbers of grouse fall with every year. Yet people continue to shoot the birds, justifying their actions by claiming that coveys need to be split to prevent runts through interbreeding. Even people who try to protect the Irish red grouse and ought to know better argue that the shooting man has kept the grouse going. But there is no getting away from the fact that packs have fewer birds these days. Stocks vary in different places and, of course, they grow less for other reasons as well – altitude and weather, soil fertility – yet much can be done to maintain and improve habitats. By husbandry it is possible to create conditions for grouse stocks to slowly increase; bad weather and the like may be impossible to regulate but providing more and better heather is manageable.

Heather provides the grouse with food and cover, and proper management of this plant is very important. Tender young heather shoots for food, and tall tough older heather for cover is the ideal get-together. Moorlands today mostly offer the older heathers, which provide plenty of cover but very little nutrition. The answer is regular rotational burning of heather. This requires the co-operation of hill farmers and other landowners, and then very careful planning and much hard work: for example, the marking and digging of 'muirbreaks' to control the spread of fire. This kind of management of heather is being carried out in different places, and in the Glens of Antrim, a few years ago, I was politely told not to walk across the uplands of Ounagh and Orra in case I would upset nesting birds.

BUZZARD
Buteo buteo

In Ireland the common buzzard is a bird of the north. Less than twenty years ago, it was confined to Rathlin Island and northeast Ulster. Since then, the numbers of nesting birds have increased noticeably. And while farmers, landowners, and gamekeepers leave the buzzards alone and are pleased to see them nesting, trespassing culprits shoot the birds. Nevertheless, the protection of the buzzard is a huge success story: birds are now breeding across the country from Antrim's Garron plateau as far as Donegal's Bloody Foreland.

This marvellous bird is our largest resident bird of prey, 50–55 cm. It

Buzzard

prefers hillsides overlooking wooded valleys and open fields, and is found in the Glens of Antrim, about the Sperrin mountains of Derry and Tyrone, and the hills of Donegal; it also frequents Fermanagh. It is a handsome bird, heavy and well built, with brown upperparts, rounded wings with dark patches, buffy underparts, and a short square tail with many narrow bars. The neck is short, the bill is black and hooked, and the strong, yellow legs have feathered thighs.

From mid-August into autumn, common buzzards are seen leisurely soaring high over moorland and woodland fringe, especially where tall trees grow on small hills. Parents and young, three, four, or five birds together, sail in high wide circles and make mewing 'pee-oo' calls. Looking up at them, the buzzards seem dark, their brown backs and pale breasts are difficult to see; but their relatively small heads, short, wedge-shaped or fanned tails and broad, 'finger-tipped' wings are enough to identify them as *Buteo buteo*.

Buzzards take small mammals such as mice and rabbits but, from the sky, they spend a great deal of time looking for fresh cadavers. Within a range of about four kilometres from the nest, every day, they watch the ground from early morning into the gloaming, and they miss nothing. Occasionally, from a carefully selected perch, they will drop to the ground to take more lowly things like grubs and worms.

The buzzard nests in tall trees – deciduous and evergreen, particularly larch – often in a broad fork of a tree growing on the fringe of woodland; but sometimes it will nest on rocky ledges. The nest is usually about eighteen metres above the ground, about 70 cm wide, and built with branches, bracken, heather, and lined with pieces of bark, leaves and moss. Because the birds keep adding fresh branchlets and green leaves to the outside of the bulky nest, and it blends into the foliage of the tree, it is not very noticeable. Dull white, showing some reddish-brown and purplish-grey markings, and slightly bigger than the eggs of farmyard hens, the buzzard's two to three eggs are incubated for five weeks. The eggs may be laid at intervals of two days; likewise, the young leave the nest in turn. With sparse greyish and white down at first, the young leave the nest after six or seven weeks. The buzzard has a single brood: April–June.

Buzzard

HEN HARRIER
Circus cyaneus
This magnificent bird of prey is a rare sight. The hen harrier (43–50 cm) breeds on high ground up to three hundred metres and is found about conifer plantings surrounded by moorland and heather. Throughout Ireland and Britain there are only five hundred to six hundred pairs. Recovering from near extinction at the start of the twentieth century, the hen harrier returned to its old haunts, but since the early 1970s the numbers have declined again and, in Ireland, most of the birds are probably breeding in the north. In recent years I have seen pairs in the Glens of Antrim and mid-Tyrone. Almost any wild bird or small mammal, including the hare, is fair game for this predator, and centuries ago, when it was more widespread, the bird preyed on poultry – hence the name hen harrier.

The male bird is pale grey above, with black wing tips, white rump, long and square grey tail, grey throat and breast, and white belly. The bill is black

RICHARD T. MILLS

Hen harrier at nest

and short; the legs are yellow. The female and juveniles are brown above, with noticeable white rump, and streaked light brown below. The hunting flight is low and undulating over heather and moorland; but the harrier also hovers, soars, and glides. Except for squealing and cackling sounds during courtship, the bird is silent.

On damp ground in moorland, hidden in heather or other low vegetation, the nest is a platform of twigs, heather, bracken, or nearby stems, and is lined with grass. Chalky white and unmarked, the four to six eggs are incubated for about thirty-two days. With white down, becoming grey, the young remain in the nest for five weeks. The hen harrier has a single brood; April–June; and sometimes a replacement clutch.

THE BLUE SHARK
Prionace glauca

In August 1991 I went fishing for blue shark. With some of Ireland's best shark anglers, I fished the Atlantic, about fourteen kilometres off the northwest coast of Donegal, for two full days, and we boated eleven shark. For research purposes, we recorded their weight, measured their length, tagged them, and let them go again. They were unharmed and quickly swam away.

The blue shark has a worldwide distribution, with fish weighing over 430 lb coming from New Zealand waters, and fish weighing almost 220 lb caught in British and Irish waters. However, due to overfishing in home waters the blue shark has shown a marked reduction in average weight, with numbers of fish of 30 lb to 50 lb taken. Blues should always be speedily returned alive to the sea.

Normally found in semi-tropical waters, the blue shark migrates during summer to European coasts. Nobody really knows why; but they possibly move north in the warm water of the North Atlantic Drift to feed on mackerel, herring, and other shoaling fish. In some years this seasonal migration extends further north than in others, but while the sharks rarely reach the north of Scotland in any numbers, packs of them are usually found off the northwest coast of Donegal – especially during August.

During my 1991 fishing trip we hooked the most aggressive fish with a single 6/0–10/0 Seamaster hook hidden in a dead fresh mackerel – kept near the surface by a balloon pegged to a stainless steel leader – and then nearly crippled arm and back playing the fish with stout rods and expensive, many-geared multiplier reels. We decked the sharks with tailers and quickly took their statistics before letting them go. Experienced shark fishers bait hooks in a way that prevents the fish swallowing or throating the bait; it is hooked in the lip, and this greatly reduces the risk of harming the animal.

We enticed the sharks with rubby dubby, a bloody, ghastly, smelly, sticky mixture of pulped, chopped or filleted fresh mackerel in bran and blood or fish oil. The mix is put in onion bags attached to the side of the boat, and held dangling in the waves to create a slick to fetch sharks from somewhere before the horizon. Within half an hour somebody's reel creaks a few times, and then starts screaming. On my two outings the biggest caught blue shark was two metres long and it weighed 109 lb; and after exactly thirty-four minutes of give and take, a big strong man, and the shark he caught, lay on the deck – exhausted and blue. The smallest fish caught was 40 lb.

The blue shark is slender and streamlined, with long pointed snout, wing-like pectoral fins, a true 'shark-like' upright dorsal fin and a very long, sloping caudal fin. It has a brilliant blue back and clean white belly, and its mouth bristles with extremely sharp, tearing teeth. The blue attacks and savages humans. Truly wild and ferocious animals, they are not as huge as the great white but they are big enough to seriously hurt a body. I watched a big blue shark crossing about fifty metres of turbulent ocean to attack a balloon, be-cause the thing vibrated a little. Sharks like blues are detector machines – you can't hide from them in water. It has been said that attacks on humans are caused by one of the animal's senses becoming confused. Experienced shark fishers laugh at such a notion, and insist the blue will reach for a human arm or leg and strip it, and eat it. When I suggested to my fishing companions that this was a bit of an exaggeration, I was told by the skipper, a retired university teacher of marine biology: 'Think what you like! All over the world the blue shark is a known man-eater. Why should it change its nature just because it's a few miles from your house.'

A hunting blue shark homes in on the body electricity given off by prey; injured prey transmit more electricity – signals of their vulnerability. Even if prey keep still or hide in sediment on the ocean floor, the shark will detect their presence. The sharks have many other sensory talents: they can detect any water movements caused by the muscular twitchings of prey; they can hear the slightest sounds made by a swimming fish; their eyes are ten times more sensitive to light than human eyes; they can find prey by smell alone, scenting blood from half a mile away. They are special animals.

INSECTS AND INVERTEBRATES

COMMON WASP
Vespula vulgaris
Everybody knows the common wasp (22 mm) with its black and yellow stripes, slim waist, petulant nature, and unbarbed burning sting that can be reused. They are blamed for stinging people – just for the sake of stinging. This is not true. Except in August, when they are dying, wasps will only sting people if the nest is threatened or in any way disturbed. I know all

Common wasp

about it – I once leapt headfirst into a deep pool to get a hundred wasps off my face and out of my hair. After seeing a salmon turn and climbing down to entice the fish, and unknowingly standing ready to cast a fly beside a wasp nest in a sandy bank, I soon heard and watched hundreds of wasps flying out past me and then suddenly returning to try to sting me to death. Despite my dip in the pool, I arrived home that evening with a very sore head, a puffy face, and closed eyes. If, so mercilessly punished, I can agree with wasps, anybody can.

Individuals will sting when they are frightened or unnaturally confined, inside human clothing, for example. Otherwise, they are very helpful insects, doing more good than harm. They sting to death innumerable harmful caterpillars and flies to bring home to the nest, and they feed on nectar and fruit juices and help fertilise plants.

Like the bumblebee, the queen wasp stays with her eggs and larvae. And in return the offspring supports the queen and looks after her future broods. Unlike bees, wasps do not make honey. Bumblebee and wasp nests are very different in design and fabric, but both are social insects and the organisation of the colonies is similar.

Round or pear-shaped, with several storeys or combs, the wasp's extraordinary nest is usually in the ground or inside walls, or sometimes attached to slim branches of bushes. They build their nest of papery cells from a mixture of old wood and tough plant fibres, chewing the material to a pulp and, using saliva, forming it into 'wasp paper'. The felt-like material is real paper, made of cellulose; the Chinese invented paper after watching wasps at work.

In their social arrangement many wasps live in the same nest. Most of the individuals are sexless female workers, which kill caterpillars, aphids, flies, especially bluebottles, and other insects to feed the larvae and the queen. The workers feed on nectar, fruit juices, and drops of a sweet liquid exuded from the larvae. The workers also enlarge and repair the nest.

The communal life of the wasp is similar to that of the bumblebee, but there are ten times more workers in a wasp colony. From spring until the end of summer the colony employs about two thousand female workers. Drones and fertile queens are hatched during August. Born to fertilise the young queens, the drones die soon after mating. The workers and the old queen die with the first frosts of later summer, beginning autumn. Only the young queens survive the winter. At the close of 1990, on Boxing Day morning, I saw a young queen wasp crawling about the garage floor. Somebody had unintentionally disturbed her winter sleep. Unfortunately, she probably died that same evening.

BLACK GARDEN ANT
Lasius niger

This ant is the species found in gardens, banks of hedgerows, pastures, river banks, heaths, woodland, old walls, and on plants hosting aphids such as greenfly. The black garden ant is a dull brown colour and has the physical structure of other insects: head, thorax and abdomen. The head has two long, joined antennae used for the senses of taste, smell and feel. The ant

RICHARD T. MILLS

RICHARD T. MILLS

becomes almost helpless if the antennae are damaged. The eyes play a secondary role. The jaws are used to cut, dig, push, squeeze, crush, and carry. The thorax supports the ant's wings and three pairs of legs. Young queens and males have wings, sterile female workers do not. The abdomen begins with a slim waist and holds the digestive organs. Ants do not have lungs: for oxygen intake they have spiracles, tiny openings along the sides of the thorax and the abdomen, from which air passes into tracheae tubes, that branch into all parts of the body.

Black garden ants

Like bumblebees and the common wasp, the black garden ant is a social insect. The colony has a mother queen, larvae, pupae, callows or infant ants, sterile female workers, drone-like males, and potential queens. Larger than the males and workers, the mother queen is 13 mm long (the male is 6 mm long; the worker is 5 mm long). The sterile workers feed the queen and take care of her; and they have other duties. Work is divided according to age: newly hatched workers remain inside the colony as cleaners and nurses, while the older ants go out and find food, or defend the nest. (Strangers are recognised by their odour.) The food gatherers forage in plants for the sweet honeydew exuded by aphids; and to protect their source of food, the ants sometimes protect the aphids from predators such as ladybirds. Workers will also visit houses in search of sugary food. Males hatch from unfertilised eggs, and live only a few weeks. They do not work: their only function is to mate with the young queens.

Black garden ants are usually inconspicuous. However, during the still warm days of August, winged males and young queens swarm in the air on mating flights. They mate in the air, for the first and last time. After mating the males die, and the queens spend the rest of their lives laying eggs. Before laying, each queen chews off her wings and looks for a place to start her own colony. She usually builds her nest under a flat stone, an old log, or in shallow moss or grass covering a rock; sometimes at the base of a crumbling wall. In time the nest becomes a complex arrangement of tiny rooms or chambers.

At first she digs a tiny hole and seals herself inside by closing the entrance with soil. Then she starts laying eggs and remains with them. Without any food, she may eat some of the eggs; but, now redundant, the strong muscles that moved her wings become fatty, and she uses this fat to keep up her energy and strength. The eggs hatch into tiny white larvae, which shed their skin after a few days' growth. After several moults the larvae become pupae, shaped like ants, with legs and antennae folding against the body. The pupae are almost immobile and do not eat, but they change physically. When these changes are complete, the infants break out of their pupal skin and are tended by their mother.

Because the queen has only her own saliva to feed them, the first workers are smaller than later ones. Soon, however, the young workers leave the nest and return with food for the queen and her new brood of larvae. As the colony grows tasks are divided among the workers. During summer, a number of the baby ants are young queens, and some are males; and during August, they crawl out of the nest and rise into the air and mate – and so the life cycle continues.

Froghopper in cuckoo spit

RICHARD T. MILLS

FROGHOPPER
Philaenus spumarius

Called cuckoo spit because it was once believed that cuckoos spat on plants, the foam of the froghopper is found all over the countryside. In April, shortly after the first cuckoo is heard, blobs of frothy white spittle appear on plants. Inside each blob, a nymph of the froghopper sits, sinking its proboscis into the skin of the plant and sucking sap at such a rate that the liquid quickly passes through its digestive tube and out the other end. There the excreted fluid mixes with a secretion from glands on the underside of the nymph's abdomen. The sides of the abdominal segments are extended to curve under the body, enclosing a cavity into which air is collected through spiracles. The cavity opens to the rear through a valve, and the froth or spume – the cuckoo spit – is caused by expelled air and the fluids mixing. The adult (5 mm) does not make froth but leaps from plant to plant; and its large head and movements earned it the name 'froghopper'. Related to the aphids, the froghopper can be a nuisance, causing plants to dry up and wilt.

Froghopper

RICHARD T. MILLS

TRUE FLIES

Having described house flies in July, I now briefly mention flies found out-of-doors. They are immensely varied in size, colour and shape. The adults are distinguished by a single pair of membranous wings, which may be patterned but are usually transparent; the hind wings are reduced to become short balancing structures. The mouthparts for sucking liquids are often modified for piercing purposes. The larvae, or maggots, are legless. From some five thousand species which live in Ireland and Britain, here are a few of the more common flies of August.

DADDY-LONGLEGS
Ctenophora atrata

Also called the crane fly, the long, slender body (12–21 mm) is conspicuously banded with black or yellow. It has very long legs, transparent wings, and flies slowly. Mostly nocturnal, it is easily disturbed during the day. The larva, or leatherjacket, is greyish, thick-skinned, feeds on the roots of plants, and is a pest.

CLEG
Haematopota pluvialis

The cleg (8–10 mm) is a slender nuisance, especially the female which lands so lightly and silently that its victim is unaware, until it pierces the skin to suck blood, and causes a painful red swelling. At rest, the wings slope roof-life over the body. Found on farmland, the general coloration of the cleg is dull. A tuft of long, black hairs covers its head and the eyes are an iridescent, purplish colour. The carnivorous larvae live in soil.

BLACK FLY
Simulium ornatum

Bothersome swarms of tiny black fly emerge in the heat of August. They are common in pastures and near water. It is a tiny humpbacked insect (2–4 mm) with noticeable antennae. A silvery abdominal segment interrupts the black body; it has yellow legs. The female bites. The larvae are aquatic.

RICHARD T. MILLS

Daddy-longlegs mating

HOVER FLY
Syrphus ribesii

This attractive and helpful fly (11–13 mm) is sometimes mistaken for a wasp. Its brilliant yellow and black markings make it conspicuous. Commonly seen in woods and along hedgerows, in bright sunshine it hovers over flowers. The maggot-like larvae feed on aphids.

BLUEBOTTLE
Calliphora vicina

This well-known fly is a dirty nuisance. Common in hedgerow, woodland, farmland, and about rubbish tips, the female often comes into the house to lay her eggs on meat. Outside, she searches for rotting, dead animals, dung, or putrid organic material; and she transmits disease to human food. The adult male feeds from flowers. Strongly built, hairy, and a gleaming metallic blue-grey colour, the bluebottle (10–12 mm) flies like a bullet and makes a loud buzzing or humming. The larvae, or maggots, feed on rotting animal tissue and excrement. Coarse anglers use the live maggot as bait.

RICHARD T. MILLS

Hover fly

GREENBOTTLE
Lucilia caesar

Except for its metallic green colour, the greenbottle (10–12 mm) is similar to the bluebottle in its habits. However, the female rarely enters houses. The eggs are laid on carrion and the larvae are important decomposers.

THE EARTHWORMS

Earthworms are very important. By ventilating earth, recycling minerals through different layers to the surface, bringing rotting vegetation underground and creating humus, worms keep the soil loose and fertile. And fed upon, they provide a nutritious diet for many mammals, birds, and fishes. Earthworms are very numerous. Many feed on soil and burrow deeply, digesting its organic matter, others live in compost and rotting vegetation on the surface of the ground. Hermaphroditic, having both male and female reproductive organs, worms mate to exchange sperm. When they separate, their eggs and sperm are then deposited in a mucous cocoon, which is secreted by the clitellum, the soft smooth saddle-like band located along the worm's segmented body. Fertilisation occurs within the cocoon, and small worms hatch.

Garden worm

RICHARD T. MILLS

GARDEN WORM
Lumbricus terrestris
Also called the common earthworm, lob, or dew worm, this animal is usually about 20 cm long but may grow to 30 cm. It is the largest and one of the most abundant of our species. It is found in gardens, pastures, woods, and even crawling along a pavement after a night of heavy rain. But it prefers clayey soil, and lives in a deep tunnel, dragging down dead leaves for food. A fallen leaf protruding from a tiny hole in the lawn probably has a resting lob at the leaf's underground end. This worm is dark brownish-red to violet above, and yellowish underneath. It has an orange-red clitellum; the garden worm's long, soft cylindrical body has a flattened rear end.

BRANDLING
Eisenia foetida
Found in compost heaps, manure and dead leaves, this worm is usually about 10 cm long. The soft body can be red, purple or brown, with noticeable red-brown and yellow bands. It has an orange clitellum. Sometimes called the dung worm, when hurt the brandling ejects a sour-smelling yellow fluid. It is a favourite bait of both trout and coarse anglers.

PINK WORM
Allolobophora rosea
Found under stones, leaves, logs, or near the surface in meadows, this lively worm is a favourite of trout anglers. Just 8.5 cm long, the slim body is firm and pink, with a reddish front. The clitellum is orange.

GREEN WORM
Allolobophora chlorotica
Commonly found in shallow tunnels in fertile soil and heavy
compost, this sluggish worm is soft and green or greenish-yellow.
Just under 7 cm long, it has a pink to orange clitellum.

THE PLANTS

August's many attractive flowering and fruiting plants include the true heather, or ling, bell heather, cross-leaved heath, cranberry, crowberry, common reed, crested dog's-tail, quaking grass, false oat grass, marram, Yorkshire fog, knotweed. But August is better known for its early fruit-bearing bushes and trees: the oak, hazel, rowan, and elder.

OAK

At the head of our native trees stands the oak: old, strong, durable and exceedingly useful; and hallowed by superstition, legend and folklore. There is much evidence of the importance of the oak tree in Irish placenames. Derry or *doire* means 'oak grove' or 'oak wood'; Derrybeg means 'little oak wood'; Derryduff is the 'black oak wood'; Derrybane, 'white oak wood'; Derrygarriff, the 'rough oak wood'; Derrynahinch, the 'oak wood of the island or river meadow', and so on.

In Ireland two forms of oak tree are commonly found. In one tree the acorns are supported on long stalks called peduncles; in the other the acorns are described as sessile: without any stalks, the acorns are directly attached to the branch. A few other differences between the two trees have led botanists to regard them as two distinct species, namely, *Quercus robur* and *Quercus petraea*.

Oak branch

RICHARD T. MILLS

In *Quercus robur*, the pedunculate or common oak, while the acorns are stalked like the tree's tiny female flowers, the leaves are sessile; also, the leaves have ear-like lobes at their base. This is our most common oak, standing up to thirty-five metres and famous for its broad trunk, massive crooked branches and spreading crown, and found mostly on fertile lowland.

In *Quercus petraea*, the sessile oak, while the acorns are sessile like the tiny female flowers, the leaves are stalked, or pedunculate; also, the leaves do not have lobes at their base. The sessile oak is more commonly found in upland, less fertile areas. Standing to a height of forty metres, it tends to be taller than its lowland relative and has a longer, straighter trunk. The male flowers are similar on both trees.

As these differences are practically unimportant, and as the history of the two trees is almost identical, I prefer to simplify the matter by generally speaking of them as simply the oak.

Apart from the yew tree, the growth of the oak is possibly slower than that of any other native tree, and may take several hundred years to attain its full

grandeur. The young trees may take fifteen to eighteen years to produce their first acorns; under more suitable conditions, they will fruit before fifteen years. The acorns were once very important. Just over a century ago our grandparents were grateful to use acorns as food. When conditions improved and cereals became available, the acorns were fed to horses, cattle and pigs. Nowadays, although it is normal for domestic stock to eat acorns as a highly nutritious pre-winter feed, it is known that – without a mix of hay and bran – poisoning may result from excessive ingestion of the fruit. Still, wild animals such as badgers, squirrels, jays and wood mice thrive on acorns.

Acorns

The name 'acorn' seems to derive from the fruit's use as a cereal: *ac* being the Saxon word for 'oak'; so that 'acorn' is possibly 'oak corn'. And just as the names of many Irish towns and villages have been derived from the Irish *doire*, a similar explanation of placenames is found in England: Acton is 'Oak-town'; Acrington is 'Oak-ring town', and many others are examples of places associated with the oak.

Oak timber has been used for at least five thousand years, and as an essential material in the building of early dwellings and boats, it has played a most important role in our evolving civilisation. Except for the pine masts, everything on a ship could be made of oak. The wood was also used for wheels, barrels, carts, farming implements, and furniture.

The oak is well known in superstition, folklore and legend. The Greeks fabled that Jupiter took the oak under his protection, giving the oaks of Dodona the power of speech and prediction. The Romans used wreaths of oak leaves as civic crowns. The Druids looked upon the oak as sacred and many of their rituals were performed in oak groves. In folklore it was claimed that a handful of acorns mixed with oats and given to black horses would alter their colour to a fine dapple grey after a few days; this change in colour was caused by the vitriol or acid in the tree. Regarding the medicinal, astringent, quinine-like, and other properties of the oak – prescribed in the 1600s – only a few are accepted and safely used today, and are generally associated with galls – tiny swellings or tumours of different shapes and colours, made by insects like gall wasps, and found on leaves, stalks and branches: decoction of galls applied to the face and neck removes wrinkles; an ointment of galls has a soothing effect on the skin; because galls contain gallotannic acid, they can be used in tanning, ink-making, and dyeing. In folklore the oak leaf is the symbol of valour.

An oak tree hosts a vast variety of wildlife: birds and squirrels, but especially butterflies, moths, beetles, gall wasps, and hundreds of other insects. No part of the tree is without guests. The greater number find food and shelter in the foliage, but some eat into the wood, and some mine under the bark. Others feed on the inner surface of the leaf, inserting themselves between the upper and lower membranes which they leave uninjured; this activity produces the bladdery-looking blotches often seen on the leaf. Gall wasps lay their eggs somewhere in the foliage: in the twig, the bud, the midrib or the stalk of a leaf. When the larvae hatch, their feeding and secreting cause the surrounding plant tissue to swell and grow into a variety of shapes, green at first, then turning red or yellow. More numerous on the oak than on any other tree, galls protect developing larvae. Many insects hatch out of their galls during summer; for others the gall turns brown and the larva spends the winter inside. However, within each gall there are usually other insects which parasitise the owner – the best-known gall, the oak apple, has been found to contain dozens of different insects, as well as the gall wasp larva. The pretty 'oak spangles' and 'silk buttons' that stud the underside of the oak leaf, and the little currant-like spheres attached to the flower stalks, are also the work of gall wasps.

COMMON HAZEL
Corylus avellana

This marvellous native shrub is found in mixed woodland and interesting hedgerow. Although in terms of tallness, it might be considered tree-like, the hazel bush is best seen as part of the underwood, in a grove, especially a coppice, for left alone, even in high summer, a hazel can look bare, straggly and unhealthy. I was sorely tempted to include the hazel in later February into March when it heartens us with the promise of spring, but I looked forward to its early fruiting in August, late summer and beginning autumn.

Hazelnuts

All year round the hazel is pleasant to see. Standing nine metres high, with a shiny brown bark and downy shoots, it is easily known. The leaves are shortly stalked, broadly oval or nearly round, somewhat heart-shaped, 7.5 cm across, toothed and sometimes slightly lobed, and downy on both sides when young. In spring, as tiny swellings contained within the leaf buds, the female flowers are tipped reddish-pink; and before the leaves appear, the long yellow male flowers, or 'lamb's tails', shed their pollen during later February into March. The leaves start appearing during the second week of April; and through summer, the bush swells with lovely bright green foliage. During the second week of August look for clusters of three or four green nuts enclosed by deeply toothed leafy bracts. During August the raw, green nuts are eaten by the grey squirrel. Into September, the nuts turn brown and are eaten by the red squirrel, wood mouse, and human.

Hazel scrub

About their medicinal properties: made into a powder and taken with honey in water, the parted kernels help a persistent cough; a pinch of pepper added to the powdered seeds relieves catarrh. Prescribed by Dianecht, chief physician of the Tuatha Dé Danaann, a porridge has been handed down the ages for ailments such as colds, phlegm, catarrh, and intestinal worms. The porridge consists of hazel buds, dandelion, chickweed, and the wood sorrel, all boiled together with raw oatmeal. Taken in the morning, this porridge is said to make your troubles go away.

The leaves of hazel have been used as fodder for

cattle; and hazel shoots were especially useful: long and pliant, they were used for making crates, hurdles, hoops for barrels, floors of currachs, garden seats, baskets, fishing rods. All fifty years plus, the best fishers I know claim they learned their skills with hazel rods and bent pins; and they all read Mark Twain. The hazel rod continues to divine water and metal. Obtained by coppicing, the slender shoots are still used for purposes in which flexibility, toughness or strength, and regularity of size are desirable qualities.

In Irish folklore and superstition the hazel is fascinating: one of the most sacred trees in Ireland, it is thought to be effective against demons and witches. To protect oneself against evil, take a hazel stick and mark a circle around yourself, for no evil thing dare enter that circle. Saint Patrick used a shoot of hazel to rid Ireland of snakes, except for the one that plunged into the great lake of Killarney and remains there to this day waiting to be released. In other folklore the hazel is the symbol of reconciliation.

Rowan

RICHARD T. MILLS

ROWAN
Sorbus aucuparia

On bare hillside or behind a drystone wall, or standing up to twenty metres over a mountain stream, or along some old track leading down to the stream, or upright on the side of a deep cut through rock, or beside a derelict cottage, or in a hedgerow – anywhere in the Irish countryside – this lovely, graceful and open tree, with smooth grey-brown trunk, branches and twigs, is noticeable through all seasons.

In winter, the twigs hold large pointed purplish buds, with long grey hairs. The spring foliage is airy and ash-like with long, fresh green leaflets, stalkless and delicately notched towards the point. Although the rowan is called the mountain ash, and has leaves like those of the ash family, it is in fact related to the whitebeam and the wild service tree. With the birch, the rowan grows higher up mountainsides than any of our other deciduous trees. In early summer every branch is dressed with tufts of fragrant cream-like flowers. But the time of the rowan's greatest and most characteristic beauty is late summer when the fluffy blossoms have changed into dense clusters of fruit. Attracting birds, especially thrushes, the berries progress from yellow through glowing orange to bright scarlet by mid-August. Through September the leaves turn red and often fall before the close of October.

Medicinally, a distillation of the fresh leaves was once used for bathing sore and tired eyes; but the rowan's real power was against witchcraft and evil. From early times the tree had a wide reputation for its magical powers, and the Druids used it for protection. A stump of the rowan has frequently been found in the burial places and stone circles of the Druids, probably a relic of a tree planted by them for its sacred shade. In Irish superstition it especially protected cattle and infants against evil fairies and witches – if a witch looked upon a baby, it was doomed to die, unless a branchlet of rowan was tied to the cradle. The first three days of May were considered very dangerous for cattle. During these days, certain fairies held great devilish power and protection was achieved by securing rowan leaves to the animals' horns or necks and tails. The rowan tree was very sacred and, on May Day morning, pieces of the foliage were hung over doors, cradles and churns to keep away evil spirits. Through autumn the berries were also used as charms to protect against evil.

Apart from superstitious practices, both the wood and the berries served a variety of useful purposes. The wood was excellent for making bows; however, it was chiefly used for making cogs for wheels, spoons, handles for cutlery and various other turned objects, and walking sticks. And the rowan berries can still be used for making ale and beer, and a pleasant jelly to flavour game.

ELDER
Sambucus nigra

Although found apparently wild in hedges and woodland edges, the elder must have been a thoroughly domesticated tree, for it is most commonly found outside broken walls, in waste ground, old orchards, and close to derelict houses. I seldom find an elder far away from where people used to live. Most elders are bush-like, three to four metres tall, but given sufficient room and light the elder can grow into a fine tree. Famous for its wines and jellies, I must warn against its berries. When nine years old I ate raw juicy elder berries and became extremely sick. Cooked, the berries are safe and pleasant.

Elderberries

Compared to my favourite trees, the silver birch, the wild cherry, the elegant ash, and so on, I still find a place in my heart for the elder. It looks old before its time and it is neither graceful nor handsome, but it is a tree full of character, an energetic, working-class tree, one of the first trees to come into leaf – in mild years often starting before the end of winter. Ragged-looking, with a deeply furrowed trunk, a greyish corky bark, and often bent as if from years of toil, its many branches contain a soft pith, stained yellowish-brown, like the filter of a cigarette. The scaleless leaf buds are purplish on a light brown twig, and with five to seven oval,

RICHARD T. MILLS

Elder flower

RICHARD T. MILLS

toothed and pointed leaflets, the compound leaves smell unpleasant when crushed. Animals seldom eat the elder, possibly because of its unpleasant odour – just as well, because the bark, leaves, and berries have poisoned mammals and fowl. In June the elder presents flat-topped flower heads of numerous sweet-scented and creamy-white flowers, which make a delicious cordial. These develop into dense clusters of purplish-black globular berries, which hang down in August and September.

Extremely hard, the old wood of elder may be used by the engraver. As a boy, I hollowed out the stems by removing the pith to make good whistles and haw-shooters, even though a teacher had once warned my class to apologise to the 'Judas tree' before harming it. Knowing that the elder was feared in superstition, and that old people used to make crosses of elder for good luck, I carried on regardless, and exchanged my shooters for war medals or sold them for threepence. Nowadays, when I look at the elder, I wonder at my youthful recklessness.

The elder was once used as a cure for epilepsy: cut a shoot of the elder tree into nine parts, string the pieces together, and tie round the patient's neck; but should the necklace fall and touch the ground, it must be burned and a new one made.

Like practitioners of long ago, today's herbalists claim that elder flowers are therapeutic: taken three or four times daily, an infusion of two teaspoonfuls of elder flowers in a small cup of hot water is good for troublesome catarrh, acute cold and influenza. In folklore elder is the symbol of mercy.

SEPTEMBER

September brings the close of summer, but images of the brightest season are worth reflecting. For me the summer of 1993 began on Sunday afternoon, 23 May, on a bank of Upper Rooskey in northwest Donegal. In bright sunlight I sat by the lakeside and looked around. On the ground about me I saw tiny tormentil, dog violets, ribwort plantain, primroses, dandelions – some in bloom, others holding 'clocks' – and on the stem of one there was a green lacewing. Delicate, with golden eyes and gauzy transparent green-veined wings held roof-like over its slender green body, the lacewing rested there for twenty-five minutes; and I wondered how a creature with such a short life could spend so much time doing nothing.

Young ferns were about, heather too, and frothy cuckoo spit smothered a leaf on a small bucky rose bush. A large white butterfly landed, then a wall brown, and on a tall rock glossy green ivy clung. Bees buzzed and one came close; greenbottles sped like bullets across bramble. Insects and spiders were everywhere. In my mug of coffee tiny flies floated.

Behind me, a spread of gorse bloomed, and to my left, beyond a wire-and-post fence, alder, ash, willow, birch, sycamore and oak wooded the steep bank. A few yards to my right, a cock chaffinch was calling from a blackthorn bush, which was white and fragrant with many blossoms. Beyond the blackthorn, a rowan tree bloomed creamy-white, and bog myrtle stood between me and the lake's edge. More than two hundred metres away, across the lake, a woodpigeon flapped out of a tall hawthorn, and blackbirds, thrushes, robins, and finches were singing. In a brae-field a cow and her calf grazed and, high above them, darkening the skyline, fifty conifers looked unpleasant. Then the cow moved down into the lake's shallows to drink, and water rippled away from her and crossed the lake and slapped rocks below me.

For three metres out the lake was clear, then, beyond sloping bedrock, it grew very dark. Some of the rocks hosted white worm-like crustaceans, others held green algae. On the surface of the water, dandelion seeds floated like tiny white caenis flies, while real flies – orange, green, white, black, yellow – swam hopelessly, and plopping trout ate them. A green frog appeared from long grass and then leapt out of sight beneath the bog myrtle. From the south side of the lake, to the left of me, as they came out of reeds, and through lily leaves, and moved along the lake's surface, dabchicks made long gargling sounds. Ravens, rooks, and hooded crows were noisy all the time, and across the lake a cock pheasant crowed every ten minutes. Behind my right shoulder, in the far distance, a cuckoo kept calling – a few times it gave a single abrupt 'cu!' as if startled. Chickens clucked in a farmyard nearby, and a dog barked. Then, overhead, a lone herring gull silently glided.

The sky was blue and the clouds were white and fluffy. I sat sideways to the sun and looked at Muckish Mountain, velvety grey. I looked at the colours about the lake: green, white, yellow, purple, pink, blue, brown, violet; I could not see anything red. Then the rod's tip plunged and half a minute later, I saw red freckling on the sides of a brown trout.

During June I heard corncrakes and watched kingfishers, badgers, mink, otters, foxes, buzzards, peregrines, stonechats, sea birds, seals, nesting swans, gorse losing its bloom. In July, holiday-makers arrived and enjoyed the sun; I caught three salmon on two outings; the heather started flowering; meadowsweet, purple loosestrife, harebells and fuchsia became noticeable; I watched a calf being born and called him Julius; but on Lake Sessiagh nearby, the pair of swans failed to have cygnets.

During August the rowans berried; bog cotton flowered in damp places; ragwort covered disused meadows; the corncrake, cuckoo, and swift went home to Africa; grey wagtails were everywhere; I caught another three salmon; and I watched rare choughs, and saw corn being harvested, and thistles spreading seeds, and I looked into old summer nests.

On Monday 30 August I returned to Upper Rooskey and found the lake quiet and lower than usual. Not a trout showed. The day was overcast, dull, grey, with a changing breeze, threatening showers. The lily leaves held a scattering of white flowers, and a few tufted duck – and a mallard – stayed among the reeds. Not a blackbird or thrush or robin made a sound, then a chaffinch cheeped twenty times and went quiet again. The ferns had grown tall and a few daddy-longlegs staggered about, and a lone bumble buzzed. Across the lake, sheep bleated, and a dog whinged in the farmyard nearby. The heather was losing its colour; some of the trees showed shades of brown, red, yellow, and leaves were lying about. Several sycamores suffered black spot. Rowans and hawthorns were bright with berries and I found green sloes on blackthorn, green berries on holly, green mast on beech, black pods on gorse and orange-coloured galls on the leaves of an oak. A hazel grove was full of young fruit. Then the breeze gathered and the lake rippled beneath an unpleasant glare; and a heavy shower flattened the lake's ripples, and more leaves fell.

RICHARD T. MILLS

Sloes, hawthorn and blackberries

Now in late September, sometime between the twenty-first day and the twenty-third, when the sun crosses the celestial equator to move south, autumn starts. Most of our wild plants have lost their flowers and the birds are quiet; but much is still happening. At sea, congers set off on their spawning migration. On grassy banks grasshoppers quiver and chirp. In gardens and woodlands spiders spin marvellous webs. Parents and children go looking for ripe 'chessies' or conkers under horse chestnut trees; and in other trees they may see the shy red squirrel or the cheeky grey.

THE SQUIRRELS

These attractive animals are rodents. Like the rat, the squirrel's chisel-like front teeth continually grow and can become blunt, cumbersome and useless. To keep them short and sharp, squirrels gnaw on the bark of trees. The word 'squirrel' comes from the Greek *skia*, 'shadow', and *oura*, 'tail'. Across the world many kinds of squirrels have short tails and never climb trees; collectively these are ground squirrels and include chipmunks and marmots. Of more than three hundred kinds of squirrels, Ireland has two: the native red and the alien grey – both tree squirrels.

Expert climbers and very acrobatic, tree squirrels quickly and easily move about trees and other tall structures such as pylons, roof tops, and overhead cables. With light bodies, strong limbs – especially hind limbs – curved claws, and bushy tails to give them balance when they jump, they spread and straighten their limbs to leap from one branch to another. They have two homes: a permanent home that is warm and dry, and a temporary place that is cool and airy for very hot days. The permanent home may be located high above the ground in a hollow tree trunk, or it may be a sturdy drey built on a high branch. Lined with dry leaves and strips of bark, the permanent home is made of layers of twigs and leaves tightly packed to keep out rain, snow and wind. The temporary home is usually a loose pile of twigs and leaves; it is easily torn apart by strong winds, and a squirrel may have to build several during a hot summer.

Squirrels eat a variety of fruit, including berries, seeds and nuts. From early September they spend much of their time eating and gathering food for winter. Both kinds of squirrel hide food in holes in the ground and in hollows in trees.

Red squirrels are famous for the many pine cones they cut and store in hollow stumps, or pile around a log or a stone, which they cover with leaves. Neither the red nor the grey hibernates, so storing food is a useful behaviour. However, to the surprise of many naturalists, the squirrels often ignore their hoards. One explanation is that, in dry winters, the stored food loses its aroma and the squirrels may fail to find it. In the case of red squirrels, the importance of their hoarding behaviour is overstated. In truth, while they will come into gardens to eat wheaten bread, I have often watched numbers of red squirrels happily eating newly cut pine cones during winter.

RICHARD T. MILLS

Red squirrel

RED SQUIRREL
Sciurus vulgaris

Heard chattering or scolding in lowland and aged coniferous plantings, especially Scots pine forests, but also in deciduous woodlands where tall beeches grow, the native red squirrel is a delight to see. With rich fiery-brown fur, white underparts, big bushy tail, noticeable ear tufts, orange-brown feet and lower legs, the animal is unmistakable. During autumn the tail becomes a pale cream colour; and during winter the long silky coat turns chocolate-brown and the ear tufts lengthen. Meanwhile, the month of September is a very good time to watch the red squirrel.

Some 38 cm long, including an 18 cm tail, the red squirrel has become a rare sight. Until the 1940s it was relatively common; since then it has completely disappeared from some usual haunts. The decline is thought to be due to some unknown disease, and the spread of the grey squirrel; but red squirrels have disappeared from woodland where there are no greys. It may be that humans are partly to blame: apart from removing trees, it is worth remembering how people slaughtered the reds.

From the beginning of the twentieth century until the start of the Second World War, foresters, gamekeepers and hunting clubs killed thousands of red squirrels because they damaged trees and bushes. Soon the grey squirrel, introduced in 1876, colonised woodland once used by the red, and then refused to let the native squirrel return.

The native red squirrel survives in old and private woodlands, and it is a privilege to see the little animal – with grand tail upright – sitting on a stump where it likes to feed, dexterously turning a pine cone in its tiny paws and, with good teeth, stripping the hard cone from the base in a few minutes, then scampering away to find a toadstool for dessert. It is also an unforgettable experience to see the squirrel's startled reaction when accidentally disturbed while it is searching for fungi or some other delicacy on the woodland floor. On the ground it is watchful and busy: with tail outstretched, it moves in short leaps and bouncy runs; then it pauses, sits back on haunches, and sniffs the air before moving on.

The red squirrel has a very acute sense of smell, and it finds most of its food with that sense; but it also has excellent sight, with a wide angle of vision, and it will run for the nearest tree trunk the moment a stranger appears. It will leap on to the trunk and, immediately moving round to the side out of sight, with sharp claws gripping, it will climb the tree in seconds. Moments later, propelled by its powerful hind legs and balanced by its big bushy tail, the squirrel will leap from branch to branch, and cling and swing with an astonishing ability and agility.

These skills apart, for the squirrel-watcher – including the fox – the red is a vulnerable little animal. Like any creature that lives in a confined environment, its territory and behaviour are soon known. On the ground, decapitated fungi, pine cones stripped from their base, and tree stumps used as 'dining tables' are evidence of squirrel. Its ability to quickly climb a tree saves it from the fox and the dog. Yet, just as its ground territory is easily found, the obvious dreys, even dens, and familiar routes through the tree-tops leave the red squirrel an easy target for humans.

During summer the red might eat a hundred pine cones a day; sometimes it robs birds' nests. During autumn it will eat beechnuts, hazelnuts, acorns, sweet chestnuts, fungi and seeds. It will dig up bulbs, and turn leaves to eat insect pupae. Through winter it strips the bark off saplings, and in suitable woodland, pine cones are readily available through winter.

Red squirrels are very active around Christmastime. Except during late summer, they can mate throughout the year; and although second litters are born during midsummer, the squirrels seem to be at their busiest, sexually, from midwinter till beginning spring. Twice a year the red will deliver three to four young; gestation is about six weeks. Weighing some thirteen grams – less than half an ounce – a newborn red squirrel is naked, blind, and deaf; its eyes open between twenty-six to twenty-eight days after birth; it is not fully weaned until nearly seven weeks old; even so, fully furred, after eight or nine weeks the squirrel is out of the nest exploring the world.

Grey squirrel

RICHARD T. MILLS

GREY SQUIRREL
Sciurus carolinensis

Found in mixed woodland, parks and large gardens, the grey squirrel is easily recognised. About 45 cm long, including the 20 cm tail, this squirrel is grey above and pale beneath; it does not have ear tufts and the tail is bushy and grizzled. During summer the coat has a yellowish-brown tinge; during winter it is silvery-grey. In the trees the grey has a rasping, chattering voice, but compared to the red it spends a great deal of time on open ground, where it can bound along at 29 k.p.h. Unlike the shy red squirrel, which prefers to stay high in the trees, the grey comes within easy reach of humans. Even with an abundance of natural food close by, the grey will visit litter bins and take food scraps from people. In 1993 on a bright sunny day in the outskirts of Castledawson, County Derry, I watched grey squirrels eating trash food like potato crisps; and in Gosford Forest Park in County Armagh I watched them stealing bread crumbs offered to penned birds. Left alone, the greys eat nuts, buds, fungi and woodsap. Unfortunately, they eat the raw fruit of beech, oak, hazel, and others, and hardly leave any food for the native red squirrels, which like their food ripe.

Introduced from northeast America by wildlife enthusiasts, and thought of as a lively and lovable little animal, the grey squirrel has been badly abused. Brought to Cheshire in 1876, and then from England to Ireland, it was allowed the pleasure of grand estates. Ironically, while the more beautiful, less harmful and shy native squirrel was suffering slaughter at the hands of humans, the bigger and fiercer, attention-seeking grey squirrel was enjoying our admiration. But in the end human privilege turned against the once welcome grey – blamed for the disappearance of the red and for destroying trees, in the 1950s, in Britain, it had a price on its tail: two shillings, or four shotgun cartridges, for every tail turned in. To blame the grey for the noticeably reduced number of the reds is unjustified, but without any doubt, by stripping off bark to get at sapwood, grey squirrels do kill many saplings and even mature trees. By the time these accusations were being fired at the new squirrel, however, the animal was well settled in many of our woodlands.

Powerful for its size, and most agile and acrobatic, the grey squirrel has to be admired for both its ferocity and its winning ways. Using sharp teeth, claws, and strong hind legs, it will kill rats and rabbits and fight a stoat; yet it will behave like a pet for a piece of dry bread. A true tree squirrel, it displays quite amazing skills on light, leafy branches: clinging and swinging, running and leaping, and all the while, scolding, especially when chasing other males in competition for a female.

Breeding takes place in spring and summer, when the female builds a dome-shaped drey, lined with soft moss, grass and leaves. After six weeks, three to eight young are born. Naked, blind, and deaf at birth, these young squirrels are survivors. Three weeks after birth they have heavy fur, and ten days later they can see and hear. At two months old they are weaned and are learning to forage. After four months the young are ready to leave the drey and seek their own territory.

Another lovely and interesting animal to add to our short list of wild mammals, it would be unforgivable to attempt to destroy the grey squirrel.

PAUL KAY

Conger

THE CONGER
Conger conger

Congers are commonly called conger eels. This is incorrect. The name is from the Latin *conger*, meaning 'sea eel'. Because of its utter lack of scales, the conger can be distinguished from the freshwater eel. However, like the freshwater eel, the conger spawns once and then dies. It spawns near the Sargasso Sea in depths approaching one thousand fathoms; and its spawning migration mainly occurs in early September.

In 1990 in the Northern Ireland Aquarium in Portaferry, County Down, I enjoyed a long and close look at a conger from Strangford Lough. This was a special experience because the creature usually lurks in rock crevices or wrecked ships on the sea bed, where it waits to reach for prey. Since then, using rod and line, I lost a good-sized conger. A strong stout-bodied animal normally about one and a half metres long, but sometimes over two and a half metres, the conger can weigh up to 65 kg. The skin is scaleless and smooth, and the usual coloration is brown to slaty-grey on the upperparts, with silvery underparts. The body colour can vary with the animal's local environment: living on a sandy bottom, it may be light brown; on a rocky bottom the body is dark.

The conger's body is elongated, slimy, and eel-like. The pectoral fins are small but quite noticeable; there are no pelvic fins; and starting near the head, the dorsal fin continues along the back and meets the anal fin. The head is fierce-looking, with large eyes and formidable jaws, which have a vice-like grip. The lower jaw protrudes and the deep, broad mouth gapes. Extending back to below the eye, the mouth houses rows of dangerous, sharp teeth; very close together, a row of teeth in the upper jaw is set to sever. The cutting nature of these teeth is famed in stories of fishermen having lost fingers while carelessly sorting a catch in which a conger lay hidden. The animal's face has two pairs of nostrils: on the snout, the front nostrils are tube-like; the second pair are near the front rim of the eyes. The large gill openings reach to the underside of the body.

The shape of the body enables the conger to swim easily and gracefully. From the head backwards, along the dorsal fin to tail, a wave-like action allows the animal to cruise gently. When chasing prey, stronger side-to-side movements give the conger greater speed. Carnivorous, it will eat carrion and almost any animal that moves on the sea bed: squid, octopus, lobster, crab, and other kinds of fish, including smaller congers. Crabs and lobsters are held and smashed against rocks before being swallowed.

The congers of Irish waters spawn near the Sargasso Sea. They stop feeding before spawning, become almost black, and their eyes grow very big. The female lays between 3–8 million eggs, which float in the middle layers of the ocean and sometimes reach the surface. A conger larva was first recorded in 1763 by William Morris of Holyhead, and named *Leptocephalus morrissii*. But it was not until 1886 that Yves Delage, the French zoologist, proved beyond doubt that *Leptocephalus morrissii* was a larval conger – he watched it change in an aquarium.

On reaching our coastal waters, after crossing the Atlantic, the larvae lose their teeth and change into young eels. The body becomes rounded and shortens slightly. Until they reach a length of 38 cm, the young congers, or straps, are pale pink. Then they slowly take on the dark colour of the adult. When about half a metre long they move into deep water and spend most of their time near the sea bed.

On Saturday 11 January 1992, near Marble Hill in Donegal, I saw five congers floating with the tide. The animals were alive. I went home and consulted the books. According to literature, congers will float when their swim bladders are too full. In *Curiosities of Natural History* Frank Buckland describes the observations of a surgeon made during January and February 1855. Living at St Leonards on the southeast coast of England, the surgeon was told about congers floating in the sea. During a period of cold, a few miles offshore, thousands of congers were seen moving about on the surface of the water, seemingly unable to descend. Consequently they were easy prey, boatmen catching them with hooks on long sticks. Eighty tons of congers were captured – eels of all sizes, some two metres long and surprisingly round. The surgeon opened one and found the swim bladder fully distended with air, 'so as to completely close the valvular opening. It was this, evidently, that buoyed them up.'

RICHARD T. MILLS

THE SPIDERS

Finding delicate sheet, or hammock, webs on dewy September mornings brings me to the spider. Everybody knows what common, harmless spiders look like, yet many people act as if they are afraid of the things. Their reactions to spiders are difficult to understand. Except for the tiny 'money spider', which is allowed to dangle on silken dragline from a person's ear because it might bring good fortune, the majority of people do not want spiders anywhere near them. Most admit that it is not really a fear of the spider itself, but the thought of the thing crawling over them. In *Manwatching* zoologist Desmond Morris believes that our reaction to spiders is possibly inherited: creeping into our ancestors' company, the poisonous spiders were the creatures most likely to produce the sudden shudder, or protective reaction which still lurks in the mind of the modern human. Morris also states that by the time of puberty, spiders are more hated by girls than boys. He relates this to body hairiness, something frightening to the adolescent girl; and the spider is the animal embodiment of this feeling. Anyway, just when it is time to switch off the light and go to sleep, the house spider which appears on the ceiling has to be flicked out the window; and the spider which falls from inside the cold water tap will often cause a scream and a hurried departure from the bathroom. However, spiders found in Ireland are harmless to humans, and because they kill insects, such as disease-spreading flies, they are helpful.

Seen everywhere they can find food – in fields, woods, hedges, heaths, dunes, walls, fences, buildings – spiders may be stumpy, round, flat, or long and thin; most of them are brown or grey but some are beautifully coloured and marked, their bodies covered with a tough skin clothed with hairs or bristles.

Spiders are not insects. They are classified as arachnids, which differ from insects in structure and behaviour: spiders have eight legs, insects have six; most insects have wings and antennae, spiders do not; insects usually have three body divisions – head, thorax, and abdomen – a spider has two – the cephalothorax, which is a fused head and chest, and a well-developed abdomen, which is separated from the cephalothorax by a very narrow waist.

Crab spider

RICHARD T. MILLS

The spider's eight legs grow from the cephalothorax; and it has silk glands within the abdomen. Attached to the rear end of the abdomen are finger-like organs called spinnerets, which the spider uses to spin silk. The tips of the spinnerets comprise many tiny tubes, through which liquid silk flows from the glands in the spider's abdomen. Some of the glands produce silk that dries and hardens outside the body; other glands produce a sticky silk. Spiders use their different silky secretions for particular purposes: spinning webs, making draglines, building nests, covering eggs, wrapping victims. The name 'spider' possibly stems from the Old English *spithra* – meaning 'to spin'.

Spiders are animals of extraordinary skill and interest, from web-making and mating behaviour to catching prey. Different species of web-spinning spiders make webs of different sizes, shapes and patterns, and some webs are sticky, some are dry; webs also vary in their angles. The garden spider spins an orb web; the money spider has a web like a hammock in grass or low in hedgerows; the house spider has a large triangular-shaped web; the daddy-longlegs spider builds a three-dimensional web, like a tiny scaffolding attached to a wall. Some spiders do not spin webs to trap prey. For example, when her eggs are ready to hatch, the wolf spider only spins a web as a nursery in which to place her egg sac.

At mating time the female is violent and very dominating, and the sexual activity puts the usually smaller male at risk – he appears to die of exhaustion. The same ferocity is exercised in hunting and killing. All spiders are predators and they have fangs; and most kinds of spiders have poison glands. A single spider bite can kill an insect. Some catch their prey by waiting in ambush, others stalk insects and then leap at them from a distance; others simply let their victims struggle to death on sticky webs, and then suck the insects dry.

RICHARD T. MILLS

Garden spider

GARDEN SPIDER
Araneus diadematus

Also called the cross spider, the garden spider (13 mm) is one of our commonest orb-web spinners. A hairy spider and easily recognised by the white cross on her back, the female is bigger than the male. She spins the web and the male survives by scavenging off it. Dry at first, then made sticky, the web has a loosely meshed outer spiral, and a tightly meshed inner spiral or centre. The female normally hides behind nearby foliage and rushes into the web to take insects. Sometimes, especially at night, she rests at the centre of the web waiting to hurry across the outer structure to seize trapped prey, usually midges. By coating her feet with an oily exudate, she avoids sticking. Any live insect is paralysed with venom, injected with juices to make it digestible, and bundled in silk. Every few days the web is eaten by the female and a new one is spun. In late September she lays a mass of eggs which hatch in the spring.

HOUSE SPIDER
Tegenaria domestica
Dark brown or grey, and hairy, this spider (10 mm) is found about dark outdoor places as well as in sheds and houses. The house spider visits the bathroom because it is attracted to water but if it slips down into the bath, it cannot climb back out. Also found in sinks, it has very long legs; and organs on the legs detect water. The familiar dense triangular non-sticky web may be 20 cm across, and the spider quickly seizes entangled flies and other insects that fail to walk across the web.

MONEY SPIDER
Erigone atra
One of many tiny money spiders, usually blackish and sometimes with odd-shaped heads, *Erigone atra* (2.5 mm) is often seen ascending into the air, pulled up by a silk thread. The non-sticky web is the familiar sheet web low in hedgerows or in grass – easily seen when dew has fallen. Upside down, the money spider patiently hangs below the web waiting for small insects to land on it, and while attempting to walk across the strands, the insects are grabbed from below.

MESH-WEB SPIDER
Amaurobius similis
Dark brown with light abdominal marking, the female (11 mm) builds her web to suit the location: a small hole in a fence, tree, wall, or in the ground. The bluish, non-sticky mesh web is made of exceptionally fine strands of silk, which produce a tangled and durable network of snares, and has a tiny tunnel, inside which the female sits, waiting for beetles and other crawling insects to trap themselves. The male spider strums on the web to make known his presence.

FOUR-SPOTTED ORB SPIDER
Araneus quadratus
This attractive spider (20 mm) is found on low bushes, heath and rough pasture. The orange, brown or red female has a large round abdomen with four noticeable creamy-white spots on her back. The orb web is spun between low plants such as grass or heather, and sometimes on gorse.

DADDY-LONGLEGS SPIDER
Pholcus phalangioides
Also called the long-bodied cellar spider, the name 'daddy-longlegs' is more appropriate: covered with long, fine hairs, the legs are five times the length of the body (10 mm), which is pale yellow with a grey abdomen. This spider likes warm conditions and it lives indoors. In the corner of a room, it hangs upside down, and the female may be seen carrying a cluster of eggs in her jaws. The flimsy web is like a tiny scaffolding against the wall.

WOLF SPIDER
Pisaura mirabilis
This spider does not spin a web to trap prey; it is a hunter and

uses its power of speed to chase, pounce and kill. Once caught, the victim is quickly paralysed by venom injected through the spider's fangs, then the insect is sucked dry. Seen running across the woodland floor, the wolf spider is easily recognised. It has a long body (15 mm), with a yellow or white line on the back, and the forelegs are close together. The female carries her silk-covered egg sac until the eggs are ready to hatch; then she spins a web as a nursery for the ripe egg sac. Before mating, the male offers the female a 'gift' – usually a dead fly wrapped in silk – which prevents the female from eating him instead.

THE GRASSHOPPERS

September is a good time to find grasshoppers – animals which are heard but seldom seen. In amongst the grass on knolls, and in marshy ground, and about woodland clearings, while camouflaged by their green, olive-brown, and sometimes mottled colours, the males sing their different chirrups or ticking songs to attract females. They sing loudly on sunny days, but are often heard after the close of September. The different courting and mating calls are made by the males rubbing the bases of their front wings together, which causes special areas of the wings to vibrate and make a loud sound; the calls are also produced when a row of tiny pegs on one of the strong hind legs is rubbed against the stout veins of the fore wing. Females hear the calls with 'ears' – special organs on the sides of the abdomen or below the knee joint on the front legs.

RICHARD T. MILLS

Field grasshopper

Grasshoppers are insects. They have antennae, six legs, and two pairs of wings. Apart from the meadow grasshopper, which has reduced wings, our other grasshoppers can fly and leap; some can leap 40 cm, which is twenty times the length of their body – in human terms, a long jump of nearly forty metres. Their main enemies are birds, wood mice, spiders and beetles.

Like other insects, the body of the grasshopper has three divisions – head, thorax and abdomen – and is covered with a shell-like skin. The head has two antennae which are used to find vegetation, and to examine the food before it is eaten. Powerful jaws with sharp teeth behind two lips are the main parts of the mouth; however, on the sides of the mouth and on the lower lip, fine finger-like appendages, palpi, contain the insect's taste buds. On each side of the head, a pair of compound eyes – consisting of thousands of independent lenses – allows the grasshopper to see to the front, to the side, and to the back. The two pairs of wings and six legs are attached to the thorax. When resting, the grasshopper lets its wings lie flat, closed fan-like, with the elbows of the tough front legs protecting the long thin hind wings. In flight, the grasshopper mostly glides; when walking, it uses all its legs. Apart from using its front legs to protect the wings, these legs hold the food when the insect eats. And the longer and much stronger hind legs used for singing also give the insect its power to leap and its lift to fly.

At the rear of the abdomen female grasshoppers have ovipositors, strong, sharp projections, which they use to dig holes in the ground – or in the low leaves or stems of plants – to hide their eggs. Grasshoppers start laying their eggs in late September and the eggs hatch in spring. Although tinier than adults, and without any wings, the newly hatched infants look like their parents. In different species, during the first six to seven weeks of growth, grasshoppers moult five or six times. With the last moult, the wings are complete and the insect is mature. Given the similar appearance of young and adult grasshoppers, and their process of development, any attempt to identify the different species by size alone is a useless exercise.

MEADOW GRASSHOPPER
Chorthippus parallelus
Even though it cannot fly, this is our most abundant grasshopper and is found in damp grass. It cannot fly because the wings are severely reduced: the fore wings are very short and the hind wings of the female just reach the abdomen, while the fore wings of the male reach mid-thorax. The colour is green to olive-brown. The female (20 mm) is larger than the male. In September, when the young are fully grown, the wings can be telltale, but the song or call is the best means of identification. The song is a very short chattering 'chirp!' which lasts one to three seconds. As a boy, I learned to identify our grasshoppers by their calls.

FIELD GRASSHOPPER
Chorthippus brunneus
Mostly found on dry grass or wasteland, this grasshopper flies with long wings in warm sunshine. The body colour is variable – green to olive-brown according to habitat. The female (20 mm) is larger than the male, but the rhythm of the call is unmistakable. When I was young, my father told me that field grasshoppers taught referees in boxing rings how to count the seconds for a knockout. The common field grasshopper produces a chirrup a second – almost exactly, ten chirps evenly spread over ten seconds. Yet, because this species is gregarious and there is usually a loud chorus of calls, the listener must be attentive. On a sunny day, a grassy knoll can be alive with calls – I often wondered how the females decided which was the most attractive. Sadly the field grasshopper dies with September, leaving eggs in the earth to survive the winter.

COMMON GREEN GRASSHOPPER
Omocestus viridulus
Appropriately named, this grasshopper (20 mm) is the specimen most likely to find itself in a jam jar or a matchbox. Distributed on grassy knolls, it leaps, makes its presence known and is easily watched, followed and captured. 'Put them back where you found them!' my mother scolded. Experts say that because of their coloration these grasshoppers are difficult to find. No matter; for identification purposes the call is telltale. Quivering, this grasshopper offers a continuous 'chirrup!' for twenty seconds or more; and the call ends abruptly.

Common green grasshopper

MOTTLED GRASSHOPPER
Myrmeleotettix masculatus
Found in dry moorlands and heaths, this tiny grasshopper varies
greatly in colour. The antennae are quite clubbed; the fore wings
are dark, never green; and the body (15 mm) varies from dark
mottled grey-green to purplish-brown, but it is always mottled,
and well-camouflaged. It flies in sunshine, and offers isolated
bursts of repeated 'chirps'.

LARGE MARSH GRASSHOPPER
Stethophyna grossum
This is the largest grasshopper in Ireland and Britain. In
Connemara in 1989, sitting beside a bog hole, near bog cotton, I
saw *Stethophyna grossum* and easily caught it – the most colourful
grasshopper I have ever seen. Its antennae are noticeably short; it
has a cream-white line along the front edge of its fore wing; the
body (35 mm) is greenish-yellow and, from foot to thigh, the leg is
yellow, black, and red underneath. It is active in sunshine, and
offers a short, slow ticking song.

THE CHESTNUT TREES

In Ireland there are two kinds of chestnut tree, the sweet chestnut and the
horse chestnut. The trees are not related, and neither is native. Also called
the Spanish chestnut, the sweet chestnut has been in Britain since Roman
times, when the soldiers were fed on porridge made from imported nuts. It
was introduced to Ireland from Britain. However, it is only an ornamental tree.
Our summers are too cool for the nuts to ripen; when half-grown, they fall
during early September and are eaten by grey squirrels and wood mice. Nuts
for human consumption are imported from southern Europe. Used for fence
paling, the timber is comparatively worthless.

The horse chestnut was brought from the
Mediterranean in the late seventeenth century. The tree was planted for ornamental
purposes – neither the wood nor the fruit are
of much value. It does, of course, provide
conkers for children and parents to play with;
and from the rich brown shiny fruit – after
removing the hard polished skin – juice is
extracted and used in bath oils for a bath
foam that will tone the skin and make it
supple. But the nuts are bitter and inedible
for humans and, except for burning as fuel,
the soft weak timber is used for only a few
other purposes where neither strength nor
durability are required.

I failed to discover which of the trees is the
true chestnut. Looking at the sweet chestnut through the seasons, and the
nature of its fruit, I can see how it might be compared with the beech; but, until
now, the name 'chestnut' is just a word, possibly derived from Old French

Sweet chestnut

RICHARD T. MILLS

chastaigne, or Latin *castanea* or Greek *kastanea* – origin unknown. No matter; despite popular protest, the sweet chestnut might be the true chestnut tree.

SWEET CHESTNUT
Castanea sativa

This is a beautiful tree. Of Fagaceae, the family of the oak and beech, the rich foliage of the sweet chestnut is unrivalled. The glossy green leaves are definitely superior, and in old trees the deep rugged clefts give the often spirally twisted trunk much character. Yet the age which gives such strength to the indigenous oak brings weakness and decay to the alien sweet chestnut. Planted, the chestnut is more commonly seen in private estates, but it is found in parklands and many wooded areas now left open to the public. Looking at the tree through the seasons, it has unique and lovely qualities.

Sweet chestnut

In winter, standing to a height of thirty metres, its bare outline is dark and bold; and, spirally set, its large pointed red-brown buds lie close to the body of the twig, which is stout with angled ridges. In beginning spring, the twigs look pinkish-brown and the appressed buds are greenish-brown. By the end of the first week of April, the buds are swelling, and before the close of April, the leaves have unfolded. In summer, especially in July, cream-coloured catkins with their female and male flowers appear. Some catkins bear only male flowers; some have both male and female, but it is uncommon to find both sexes on the same catkin. At the base of the catkin – close to the stem – the female flowers, larger than the male, have tufts of cream styles, the fruit-producing organs. Along most of the catkin's length, in tiny bunches, the male flowers show yellow anthers, the fertilising organs. Meanwhile, the leaves have become lance-like and shiny green, with prominent parallel veining and large saw-like teeth. Sometimes lobed at the base, the impressive leaves may be 25–30 cm long.

Into August the male flowers die, and the dried-up catkins remain; but the females have produced small rounded husks of fruit. In September these husks are densely covered with yellowish-green spines, but because of our unfavourable cool summer climate, the fruit abort and fall from the tree to present three empty nuts in the open husk. With a concave face, each nut still holds a tuft of styles at its apex. From the close of September, when the nuts are dead, the leaves become a rich yellow, which gradually turns brown. Then the leaves fall.

In folklore the sweet chestnut is the symbol of luxury.

Sweet chestnut

HORSE CHESTNUT
Aesculus hippocastanum

This large broad-headed tree, with scaling bark and standing to a height of thirty metres, is common in parkland, where grooming makes it look very stately and upstanding. Sometimes seen growing wild in woodland, the untouched horse chestnut looks its true self, with lower branches sweeping down to the ground before turning their ends upwards again. Splendid in September, the tree has something special to offer the whole year round.

During winter, its strong bare fawn-coloured branches arch and bow, and their twigs curl upwards to present large and shiny reddish-brown buds. Light or red-brown and speckled all over with tiny breathing pores, lenticels, the stout twigs support the horse chestnut's famous sticky buds. Coated

Horse chestnut

RICHARD T. MILLS

with resin, the glistening buds are arranged in opposite pairs, with the largest and most noticeable bud at the tip of the twig. Below each bud, on the surface of the twig, there is a definite leaf scar shaped like the print of a miniature horse's hoof. Approaching spring, when the days grow warmer, and the dry resin begins to dampen, the buds become truly sticky.

Horse chestnut candles

After mid-April the buds release their crinkly leaves, densely covered with light brown sticky threads, which disappear as the leaves unfold. By the close of April the new leaves are seen spreading and separating their leaflets. Fully open, the bright green, palmate leaves have five to seven leaflets. In May, the tall candles or spikes of flowers arrive, and all over the tree the flowers appear white, but when closely seen, they show many lovely colours. With five sepals, the individual flowers have five frilly petals and eight long stamens. Lemon-yellow at first, the centre of each flower becomes orange to pink and then crimson, and the white stamens have orange anthers. At different stages of development, but all present at the same time, the beautiful tall hyacinth-like flowers and the splendid leaves give the horse chestnut an appearance superior to any of our other large trees in late spring.

Through summer the leaves turn dark green, and, fully grown, they are some 40 cm across. During the start of autumn, while the tree holds clusters of fruit, the leaves begin to change colour: from dark green to bright yellow, coppery-brown, red, even crimson. The fruit appear as round pale green husks, sometimes smooth but usually covered with soft spines, which split at the close of September, revealing one or two seeds – the famous glossy brown conkers.

So called from having been used in the treatment of respiratory disease in horses, in folklore the horse chestnut is the symbol of amusement.

Horse chestnuts

OCTOBER

From mid-October, when game fishing ends and anglers put their rods away for another season, and most of the poachers put their nets, gaffs and other contrivances out of harm's reach, salmon, sea trout and brown trout move further upstream to the beds of their parents – to spawn in December.

I would rather the angling season closed with September. On Saturday 30 September 1989 I saw a soldier fish, a cock salmon in full spawning dress, being administered the last rites on a river bank. Not anything like his usual self – changed in almost every way in readiness for courtship and spawning – once hooked, the male salmon was easily played, landed and killed. He hadn't a chance. October salmon – hens and cocks – are not difficult to catch. Their hormones make their excitements grow, they become aggressive, careless, easily tempted; and their bodies change too. The hen salmon becomes blackish on the upperparts and dusky underneath. Apart from discoloration, and a distended belly with maybe five thousand eggs inside, she keeps her usual appearance and good looks. The cock fish is very different: the silvery-green lustre of his back and sides changes to a dull dirty copper and red colour; the black spots on his back and sides grow larger; his white belly turns greyish-yellow; coral-like, his skin grows hard and his scales become embedded in it; his lower jaw and snout lengthen and the upturned kype on the lower jaw grows taller to touch the roof of his mouth. The cock salmon, turned ugly, angry, and not at all tasty should be left to shed his precious milt and to guard his mate's redds until February's floodwater drowns and washes him away.

Ever since autumn leaves began floating down Irish rivers, wild Atlantic salmon dressed for the occasion have moved up river to shed ova and milt in their own place of birth. Mid-October's cold winds and falling leaves have always heralded the run-up to spawning. October is also the month of the Irish wild trout and their many species: different brown trout, black-finned sonaghen, powerful dollaghan, lazy gillaroo, strange ferox, and magnificent sea trout.

In the woodland, last year's fallen leaves, crisp until mid-spring, have turned into mould for fungi, worms, snails and others to use; and while the litter feeders eat and grow and burrow, litter hunters attack and feed on them. In the dampening earth the ferns are inclining to brown and some fungi are turning black, and others are showing their fruits of coloured mushrooms and toadstools. And while their fruits are enjoyed by maggots, beetles and snails, the real fungi – caught beneath the mulch and mast – are still feeding mites and

West Cork
RICHARD T. MILLS

nematodes. But trapped fungi apart; not even the wood lice and centipedes and millipedes, which can hurry and hide from the light of day, can escape the hunting spiders, and beetles of various kinds.

Everywhere and all the time, through day and night, October's woodland floor is a busy generous place. For while microbes, with heat and damp, continue to mat and turn leaf into mould for worms, and beetles hunt the worms, others search and listen to strike for food. From dawn till sunset, robins and other soft bills search through the litter for insects and their pupae, blackbirds cock their heads and take struggling worms, and thrushes use anvils to smash open handsome banded snails; and from sunset till dawn, when slugs and millipedes and low wood lice move through the night, hedgehogs and pygmy shrews and newts, all feasting or searching, are taken themselves by badger, fox, stoat, mink, and owl.

Now with a chill in the air, the swallows, swifts and all other summer visitors gone home, our own birds quiet, the pipistrelles and other bats out of sight, the silver eels away to spawn in the Sargasso, the badger and otter – pregnant already, and due about St Patrick's Day, the mink in rich winter coat, the vixen down from the hill, pike up to no good, long-tailed field mice busily storing, lamprey heading in towards brackish water to cut redds for the spring, the heron standing still and lonely, watching the salmon and trout running past, and the misty evenings drawing to an early close, the different leaves have changed colour. Now the bronze, yellow, copper, purple and rich scarlet leaves will help to keep the woodland bright and full; their fall – important and necessary – will leave the place dark and bare, and old bird nests will seem sorry sights. Still, the conifers, evergreens, holly, ivy, and tiny patches of orange, red, yellow or white lichen and fungi on soft bark and empty branch, and brown galls for hibernating larvae, will lighten the gloom. And the berries, drupes and fruits of many kinds, ripening and growing more colourful until October's end, will keep the woodland somewhat awake and bright – and resident and immigrant birds and the red and grey squirrels plump – until the evenings grow longer from winter's solstice day, when in the gravel beds of nearby streams tiny black eyes will begin to peer through the transparent walls of salmon and trout eggs. Meanwhile, red deer stags are gathering harems.

Red deer

RICHARD T. MILLS

THE RED DEER
Cervus elaphus

Found in forest and moorland parks where herds flourish, but sometimes allowed to roam in old woodland, the red deer is our largest land mammal. The size of the animal depends on where it lives. Naturally a browser – a nibbler rather than a grazer – feeding mainly in the morning and evening, the

Red deer

RICHARD T. MILLS

body mass and the size of antlers in red deer living in open parkland are far less than those of deer living in forests. They feed on grass, young shoots, and the bark of trees. The stag is up to 120 cm at the shoulder, and the hind, the female, is 114 cm tall. The mature stag may have antlers 80 cm long; the hind does not have antlers. The summer coat is fiery-brown with light underparts; the rump is buff-coloured and the tail is short. In winter the coat is brownish-grey.

Normally red deer are quiet, private animals. Apart from a mild bark-like call or bleat when alarmed, the hind is silent. In distress, the calf utters a high-pitched bleat; and, except during the rutting or mating season, the stag seldom voices any sound – sometimes he offers a gruff bark. During the rut he bells to the hinds and roars defiance at any other stag that comes near the harem. Outside the rutting season, stags and hinds live in separate groups, each keeping to a well-defined locale.

At the close of September, when antlers have reached their peak for that particular year, the sexually mature stags want to mate. Their whole attitude changes: they become aggressive and noisy; they roar and fight among themselves, butting foreheads and sparring with clashing antlers, but they seldom fight to the death. Once the group of stags separate, the strongest always makes known his superiority and invites rivals to fight again. With strong head thrown back, he roars: demanding his rights, announcing his desires for hinds and territory – bellowing his serious wants to the whole world. Now and again, he keeps quiet to listen to the roars of rivals; then once more he loudly calls for other stags to dare come forward and challenge him.

Soon afterwards, he chases brave adolescents and butts and clashes his antlers with mature animals. Victorious, the master stag secures his territory and rounds up his harem, including three-year-old hinds, which are sexually mature; and continually patrolling the boundaries of his territory – thirty metres or more across – he roars warnings to other stags. Quite often while he is with a hind or engaged in physical combat with an older rival, a four-year-old stag – now capable of sex – will mate with the hind on the furthest edge of the harem. In any case, after about a week of mating, although he is in prime breeding condition for another fortnight or so, the stag may leave his hinds to younger and more vigorous rivals; and the mating season continues through October.

On the last day of October 1991, between the lights in a clearing in Ards Forest Park in Donegal, a red deer stag appeared and stood for a moment beside a berried rowan tree. Robed in rich fiery-brown with head held high and crowned with burnished branching antlers, the stag was majestic. Then raising forelegs in turn and lowering them almost deliberately, he moved across the clearing, slowly, before picking up speed with a run of stiff-legged growing leaps to bound away between ash and beech. This was a satisfied stag, quiet and easy-going. After the rut, he wanted to be alone.

After a gestation of about eight months, the hinds separate and calve in May to mid-June. They drop their single calf, sometimes twins, in a secluded spot among bracken or in some other low sheltered place. On Inishtrahull I found calves hidden under low overhanging rocks. Newly-born, the calf is able to stand after a few minutes, and it can run a few hours later. Still, it is required to stay where the mother puts it; and it remains there. The red deer calf is truly lovely: brightly covered with fawn hair, its sides are dappled white. The spots fade before the calf is eight weeks old. Calves are weaned after eight months, and while young females remain in the mother's herd, the weaned males leave their mother the following autumn. In Ireland, apart from the fox, dog, and large predatory birds, or ravens and hooded crows which will attack a runt calf, the enemy of the red deer is human.

Soon after young stags are born, two hair-covered bumps called pedicles appear on each side of the forehead, above and behind the eyes. The roots of the antlers, these are permanent features of the male deer's skull. Depending on suitable nutrition, an adequate diet with proper mineral salts and vitamins, the development of antlers starts when the male deer is one or two years old. When the two pedicles appear, the young stag is called a knobber. The following year he grows a pair of simple horns or spikes and is called a pricket. After the spikes of the second year of antler growth, in the third year – on each spike – the stag grows a branching point, or tine, known as the brown tine. Then, after shedding, he grows new antlers with two branching points called bay, or bez, tines. The next year he has brown, bez, and trez tines; and in the succeeding years when he has three tops on the spike – six tines on each antler – he is a 'royal' and has 'all his rights'.

Obvious appendages of the skull, the antlers are shed every year between February and April. As soon as the antlers are cast, flesh starts to grow over the stump pedicles, and is richly supplied with blood vessels which bring all the mineral salts and vitamins required for the growth of bone. In May or June, bony tissue begins to form; this is the antler tissue. Like the branches of a tree, the enriched flesh-covered stumps grow upwards and outwards until the antlers are full grown. During this period, with the antlers clothed in a fleshy skin rippling with blood vessels, the stag is said to be 'in velvet'. When the antlers have reached their peak, the blood supply is cut off: thought to be due to a ridge of bone sealing off the circulation from the skull to the antlers. The velvet dies and untidily begins to separate from the antlers, which the stag rubs against the branches of bushes and young trees until they are clean and burnished. Formidable and strong through autumn and winter, the antlers fall like dead branches in early spring.

THE TROUT
Salmo trutta

For over fifty years I have angled for wild trout. I have also tickled wild trout. Indeed, some of my fondest childhood memories of summer find me watching and following brown trout, which move to hide under sizeable stones in shallow pools and streams. On hunkers, or sitting in the water, I would use small stones or pebbles to block all exits – to keep the trout in its hiding place. Then I would carefully inspect the stone's tilts and its safest angle from the river bed, and set about using this spot as my entrance route to tickle the fish. After gently removing a few of the pebbles, I would hurry my hands under the stone and find and stroke the fish, before working my fingers into the unfortunate animal's gills; this done, the trout was mine to keep or let go. After becoming expert, I always let the small trout go.

The beauty and sheer strength of all wild trout cause me great feelings of excitement. Nowadays I try to protect rather than harm them. Yet other anglers must learn to know what's best themselves. I've had my days and nights! Fishing for sea trout in the still of night is quite unlike any other experience. You stand in the darkness retrieving line when, all of a sudden, a trout takes and the rod tip bends and the reel screams. The take seems stronger than usual, and the scream of the reel seems louder, as you peer about the pool or try to see the bend of the rod to discover the location of this wild trout. Night or day, a silvery trout home from the sea, a tiny resident trout, dark bronze and speck-led red from moorland stream, or, from a tarn under the mountain, a trout gleaming like copper is a sight to see.

In Ireland there are wild river trout and wild lake trout. The common river trout are the brown trout, dollaghan and sea trout; the lake trout are the brown trout, sonaghen, gillaroo and ferox. All members of the Salmonidae family, in general, trout are classified as *Salmo trutta*.

Despite their different behaviours, all trout eat the same kinds of food, spawn in freshwater, and have a similar body structure. They feed upon the

Rainbow trout

KENNETH McNALLY

River Erne,
County Fermanagh

larvae and pupae of waterbred flies, as well as the mature insects. Other food comes in the form of insects blown onto the surface of the water: these include the alder fly, dung fly, beetles and grasshoppers. Trout also eat freshwater shrimps, snails, worms, minnows, loaches, sticklebacks and alevins. In the Atlantic sea trout feed on herring, eels and planktonic crustacea. Apart from differences in size and coloration, wild trout have the same physical structure.

All trout have a fleshy adipose fin on the back, in front of the tail, the function of which is not known. Between the adipose fin and the tail is the tail wrist, which terminates in the fan-like tail or caudal fin. A trout also has anal, ventral or pelvic, pectoral, and dorsal fins. Apart from the adipose fin, all of these structures function as balance and poise instruments controlled by the lateral line and the swim bladder. Initiated at the head, the undulatory movement of a trout comes about through the flexions of the whole body. Running the length of the centre of each flank, the lateral line is an arrangement of 110 to 120 specialised cells; it is a sense organ which is connected through the lateral nerve endings to the general nervous system, and is sensitive to variations in water pressure, and concerned with equilibrium and co-ordination of general fin movement.

A trout uses its swim bladder to hold its position in various depths – or weight and pressure – of water. With gaseous adjustment, the expansion or contraction of the bladder affects the specific gravity of the fish, and equalises the weight, or bulk, of the fish with the weight, or bulk, of the water pressing against it.

The trout has vision, smell, taste, and possibly hearing. Of these senses, sight is probably the most important. There is much speculation about trout vision, and because a trout's eye is structurally similar to the human eye, it may be that trout and humans see things similarly. However, given that trout and humans live in media so distinct as air and water, it is unlikely that a trout and a human appreciate colours in the same way, or to the same degree, and it may be that trout can see colours outside the human's spectrum. They see best in dull conditions, and are almost blind in very bright sunlight.

The many thousands of trout anglers should keep low when approaching a deep trout pool, or fish from the shallows. It might also prove useful to consider the colour of the water and its hatching insects; the use of non-spectral colours – black, brown and grey – in dull conditions and night flyfishing; the effect of tinsels on artificial and coloured fly-bodies; the use of violet, indigo and blue in dull conditions with occasional sunlight; the use of blue, green and yellow in bright sunlight; the use of yellow, orange and red if the conditions are very bright.

The importance or value of the other senses is not so readily explained. The reason that trout show preferences for certain kinds of flies and worms may be because some of these foods move better, or smell or taste better than others. Trout will take brandlings and ignore other worms – the reason for this remains unknown. It is doubtful whether the sense of smell is of much use: tests demonstrate the sense of taste as being more powerful than smell. Little is known about a trout's sense of hearing. The auditory mechanism seems to be connected to the lateral line sense, and a trout probably appreciates vibrations rather than sound – it is unlikely that it can hear sound made in the air. (Without a special microphone, a human cannot hear a sound made underwater.) It may be that sound made in water can be heard by an ear designed for that medium; if not, it is difficult to account for the underwater sounds of whales and dolphins. Of all its sensory structures the most important are the lateral line and swim bladder, then sight.

A trout obtains its oxygen from water passing over the surfaces of its gills, which will function only when a trout is facing the current. Such knowledge is an advantage to the angler fishing eddies in a spate. The successful angler will always heed the fact that the current running through a backwater flows in a reverse direction from that of the main stream, causing the trout to face downstream or in a downstream angle across a heavy pool. It makes sense to cast across and below an eddy, and to retrieve the fly or worm along the whole length of the backwater.

Through October, trout move to feed-in burns and sidestreams to spawn, where the gravel is small and light. The nest, or redd, is a scooped-out trough about 5 cm deep and 30 cm across, constructed by the female by shifting the gravel with her tail. The stream must be shallow, but not likely to run dry; and it must be brisk enough to aerate the developing eggs, and to keep them free from sand and silt. When the time for spawning has come, the female positions herself a few feet upstream of the redd. The male then lies beside her, and when he exhibits a quivering behaviour the female extrudes her eggs, which float down into the redd. The male then sheds his milt and this is carried down into the redd to fertilise the eggs. Trout sperm can only survive for about a minute in the stream, so fertilisation must be almost instantaneous. The alternate extrusion of eggs and fertilisation continues for about a week. Then spent, the exhausted parent brown trout, kelts, move into deeper water to recuperate before returning to their lake or main river in March. By the end of April, their silvery coats restored, the kelt sea trout are moving out of estuaries to Atlantic waters.

Given the proper conditions, which include a water temperature of about 5°C, it takes seventy to eighty days for the eggs of different species of trout to hatch. The small round eggs are rich pink or orange-pink at first. Less than two months after fertilisation the embryonic fish can be seen in the egg, or the eyed ova. Just before hatching, the tiny embryo secretes an enzyme which breaks down the inner lining of the egg 'shell'. The fish then bursts its way out of the egg and moves into the gravel bed, where it stays for three or four days. Now called an alevin, scaleless and colourless, it obtains its food from the yolk sac attached to its belly, which takes two to three weeks before it is absorbed. At this stage the trout are fry, feeding on protozoa and very tiny organisms.

About 2 cm long, pigment cells begin to develop in the skin, and then scales grow, which begin along the sides of fry as lateral lines. The pigmentation becomes noticeable and takes on the appearance of vertical marks on the flanks. Like thumb prints, these pigmented areas are called parr marks, and the tiny fish is known as a parr.

Trout and salmon parr are often confused, but in trout the upper jaw extends behind the eye, and the adipose fin has an orange tinge; the adipose fin is greyish in salmon and the upper jaw only reaches the eye. The tail wrist of a trout parr is relatively thick and the tail fin is only slightly forked. The tail wrist of a salmon parr is slim and the tail fin is deeply forked. There are nine or ten parr marks on a trout, and four or more spots on its gill cover. A salmon has ten to twelve parr marks, and less than four spots on its gill cover. However, there does not appear to be any difference between brown trout species and sea trout at this stage, except that brown trout parr are larger than sea trout parr.

Scales continue to grow until the body is completely covered and, when about 15 cm long and two or three years old, the fish looks like an adult. At this stage, while brown trout species stay in their parent rivers and lakes, young sea trout, or smolts, are ready to migrate to the sea to mature. The age at which a trout becomes a smolt is influenced by factors such as a suitable water temperature, an adequate oxygen and food supply, and the good fortune not to be eaten by kingfishers, herons, eels, bigger trout, and other predators.

Sea trout smolt

ÉAMON DE BUITLÉAR

THE RIVER TROUT

There are three different trout in our rivers: the migratory sea trout, the migratory dollaghan, and the resident brown trout. The sea trout is known as the 'white' trout, and the brown trout is called the brownie. Confined to the Lough Neagh system, the dollaghan keeps its own name.

SEA TROUT

Silvery, a sea trout is easily distinguished from a brown trout and a dollaghan. It looks very like a small salmon, and it is sometimes difficult to differentiate large sea trout and small salmon. The back is blue-grey, the flanks are silvery, and the belly is white. The body is covered with black spots and sometimes a few red spots. The average sea trout weighs 1–2 lb; very good specimens weigh 5 lb. Like the salmon, a sea trout is born in a freshwater stream and then migrates to the ocean to feed and mature physically and sexually, before returning to spawn in the river of its birth. The trout does not eat on the spawning return. It is less marine than the salmon and for most of its sea life it possibly remains near the coast. Until more is known about its behaviour and feeding habits, the life of the trout in the Atlantic can only be described in a general way.

By the end of April, in some rivers not until the second week of May, the trout smolts leave the freshwater river for the estuary,

Sea trout

ÉAMON DE BUITLÉAR

where a number remain during their first year out of the river, going to sea for their second post-smolt year. The trout kelts are well-mended in the spring following spawning: they fed in the river and feed at sea and may return in the same year to spawn again. Because the meat of the sea trout is similar to the pinkish meat of maiden salmon, the trout probably takes the same kind of sea food as salmon – herring, eels and planktonic crustacea. It is argued, however, that the feeding grounds of sea trout are not far from the coast and, compared with salmon, they have fewer problems finding the parent river. Yet not all sea trout return to their parent river: trout kelts tagged in one river have been recaptured in other rivers as fresh-run trout. On their return to freshwater they stop feeding and begin moving up river to spawn in sidestreams. The main runs into freshwater occur during the second and third weeks of June, and numbers tail off after July. Claimed to be due to pollution in headwater streams, and epidemics of sea lice caused by fin-fish farms located near the coast, the recent serious decline in sea trout numbers is being thoroughly investigated.

RIVER BROWN TROUT

Non-migratory, a brown trout spends its life in the river. Much smaller than the sea trout, its back is medium to darkish brown-green; the intensity of brownishness varies according to the local environment. The flanks are light brown and the belly is creamy-yellow. Including the gill covers, the body is beautifully freckled with red and black spots. The usual river brownie weighs under a $^{1}/_{2}$ lb, but 1 lb fish are taken.

Most river brown trout live in rough mountain streams or along the upper reaches of rivers. These little fish are truly native. Because of the nature of their environment, they do not grow big, but I greatly admire them. The habitat is usually a floodwater stream. After heavy rainfall, soon followed by drainage from mountain slope and moorland, the stream swells and rises rapidly and washes most things away. During a lengthy spell of dry weather the stream is little more than a trickle from springs; yet the trout manage to survive. When the stream is in freshet, running higher than usual, the trout lie in shelter, waiting for food carried to them. They lie behind boulders or in tiny bays of slower water close to the banks. Except during the breeding season, when they move upstream to spawn in light gravel, and during the evening when they move to the throat of the stream to take flies, river brownies lead a solitary existence in their lie, or lodge, resting and feeding on whatever food comes along. Because of the broken and diverted flow down a mountain stream, caused by its boulders, some parts of the stream offer more shelter and present more food than others. The trout compete for these better locations, and the bigger trout win.

Slightly acidic from peaty moorland, a stream like this offers

ÉAMON DE BUITLÉAR

River brown trout

little of the kinds of salts – for example, calcium – that give trout good skeletal growth; and the absence of these minerals also means that few plants grow in the mountain stream, and the few that grow suffer through spate and low water conditions. Not many insects hatch and grow for trout to eat, so the trout are small.

The dark coloration of the brown trout is probably for camouflage in the peaty, deep-amber water. Against the bed of gravel, the heavy speckling of the body and sandy, yellowish belly help camouflage the fish when the water is low and clear. The streamlined body and large tail fin help it to withstand the sudden and heavy rush of floodwater. It has a dark tail which is unspotted, and the adipose fin has a deep orange tinge. A mature trout might be 3 cm long and weigh ¼ lb. Still, it is a lovely and courageous little fish.

DOLLAGHAN

This magnificent wild trout is found in the tributary streams and rivers of the Lough Neagh system. It is a migratory fish; but instead of going out to sea as a smolt, it spends its adult life in the lough. Born in the gravel beds of headwater rivers and streams like the Ballinderry and Orritor, it spends about three years in a mountain stream and then moves down river to Lough Neagh where it feeds for nearly two years. Five years old and physically and sexually mature, it returns to the parent river to spawn. The run upstream, and spawning behaviour, are similar for the dollaghan, the sea trout, and the brown trout. The dollaghan and the brown trout have the same coloration and marking, but the Lough Neagh trout is much bigger than the brownie. The average weight is 1–2 lb, yet very large fish are caught; in May 1994 I saw a dollaghan which weighed 20 lb, was 95 cm from snout to end of tail, and had a girth measuring 50 cm. Because of past pollution and large algal blooms in Lough Neagh – which almost certainly lowered oxygen levels and diminished the range and amount of food life for trout – it's likely that the dollaghan suffered; as well, widely reported fish kills in the lough's headwater streams greatly reduced their numbers. However, in recent years the survival of this marvellous trout is in the very capable hands of the Ballinderry River Enhancement Association.

THE LAKE TROUT

All over the country there are lakes – in uplands and in lowlands, some tiny, others large. There are peaty lakes and limestone lakes – some are shallow, others are deep. A number of lakes are set on major river systems, but there are countless others where feed-in streams are little more than trickles. With few exceptions, in all of these lakes there are varieties of brown trout. The trout often appear to be quite different, and several subspecies can be found in a big lake such as Lough Melvin; but usually the coloration of the trout's body and its flesh are due to the nature of the diet, and where the trout spends most of its time in the lake. The darkest-coloured trout frequent deep holes near banks, where burns run in from peaty moorland; lighter-coloured fish mostly live about parts of the lake where the bed is sandy or holds fine gravel. Brown trout with typical coloration and bold markings usually frequent the reed beds about lake margins. The silvery bodied trout live in deep water, where they feed on animal plankton.

Like the river brownie, the lake trout's growth, size, and the colour of its flesh are influenced by the nature of the water and the supply and kinds of food eaten. Taken from deep water, trout displaying proud red speckles and pink flesh are probably feeding on tiny planktonic crustaceans. The shallow margins of lakes offer freshwater shrimps, and trout feeding on these have strong red markings and pink flesh. A diet without carotenoids – the orange-red pigment found in crustaceans – leaves trout with faint body markings and pale flesh. Still, unlike the $^1/_2$ lb brown trout that are confined to narrow streams, and sometimes very low water conditions with very little choice of food, some lake trout grow to a weight of 4 lb or more.

LAKE BROWN TROUT
The typical brown trout found in lakes has a dark brown back, a red-orange adipose fin, flanks that display bright red and black spots, and a golden belly. In prime condition, a 6 cm long fish will weigh about $1^1/_2$ lb; the body is firm and well built, bright with health, and the flesh is reddish-pink. A lake brownie is still in very good condition at 3 lb weight, and it is one of our most beautiful trout.

SONAGHEN
A very special fish, the sonaghen trout is found only in Ireland's Lough Melvin. It is a distinct species, and because of its black fins, it was once classified *Salmo nigripinnis*: *nigri*, 'black', *pinnis*, 'fins'. The sonaghen is different from other lake trout in both appearance and behaviour. It is a small streamlined fish, seldom longer than 4 cm and weighing under 1 lb. Less colourful than other lake trout, its overall coloration is silvery-blue; the back is darker and the body is mainly speckled with subdued black and red spots. The fins are very black, and the splendid tail is relatively large. The sonaghen's mouth is also proportionally large.

Except during the breeding season – when lake trout spawn in feed-in rivers, or streams and tiny burns – the sonaghen spend their lives in Melvin's deepest water, where they feed on shoals of tiny crustaceans called zooplankton. Because the diet comprises individuals too tiny to eat singly, sonaghen swim with open mouths, taking in thousands of tiny organisms. The large tail fin enables the small trout to follow the zooplankton on their own searches. However, as Lough Melvin anglers know, sonaghen also come to the surface after flies.

GILLAROO
Found in lakes such as Conn, Corrib, and Melvin, the gillaroo is our most colourful subspecies of lake brown trout. Feeding in the shallow margins of loughs, this trout's blend of colours – bold black, orange, reddish-brown, and red spots, merging together with the overall golden coloration – allows it to escape notice on the brightest day. It is a very lovely trout and its flesh is rich red.

The gillaroo searches about the surfaces of rocks and the stems of reeds and other aquatic plants. Its main diet comprises water snails and freshwater shrimps, but it will also take fly life. Once classified *Salmo stomachicus*, because the walls of its stomach were considered so strong and rough that they could grind gritty food, like a gizzard, this feature of the gillaroo is also found in other trout which feed for a long period on tough food items.

FEROX

This strange, long-living, fish-eating lake trout has the huge head and monstrous long powerful jaws that would identify other old trout as being 'cannibal'. With a silvery or plain dull brown colouring, showing fine dark speckles, the ferox trout is a big carnivore and it does eat fish. It attacks and eats salmon and sea trout kelts that have to pass through a lake where it feeds; it kills resident trout as well. In times past it was not uncommon to hear of a 10 lb wild brown trout being caught in lakes set on major river systems that run to the sea; but big ferox have become very rare. It might be argued that falling sea trout numbers could be a reason for the scarcity of ferox trout; yet, not enough is known about this trout. Little is known about its spawning behaviour; but, not surprisingly, during the breeding season in streams where the ferox dallies, no other trout are found.

CENTIPEDES, MILLIPEDES AND WOODLICE

Although not much heed is given to these creatures, they are important, and they certainly deserve mention. However, compared to animals such as trout, they have a limited interest, so I confine myself to very general comments and to common individuals.

COMMON CENTIPEDE
Lithobius forficatus

Although the name centipede means 'a hundred legs or feet', this is very misleading: any centipede has a pair of legs to each body segment, and some centipedes have 150 pairs of legs. Yet our common centipede (30 mm) has fifteen to sixteen pairs of legs. Like insects, centipedes have a hard skin, but they do not have the waxy, waterproof layer of covering that allows insects to preserve their body moisture. To prevent dehydration, centipedes do not expose themselves to the sun, or dry air: they live in dark and humid surroundings. During the day they lurk under stones, logs, in leaf mould, wet compost heaps, and similar places. At night, when the air is moist and cool, they emerge to kill and feed on spiders, worms, wood lice and other small prey. Without eyes, centipedes rely on vibration, touch, and speedy scuttling to catch food. They paralyse and kill with 'poison claws' that inject venom into the victim. An egg-layer, the centipede can live for six years.

Common centipede

RICHARD T. MILLS

COMMON MILLIPEDE
Polymicrodon polydesmoids

Although the name millipede means 'a thousand legs', common species have forty to sixty pairs of legs – two pairs of legs to each body segment. Most of our millipedes (21 mm) are black, grey, dark brown, or brown; and like the centipede, they are nocturnal. During the day they live under stones and in leaf litter and emerge at night to feed. Unlike the centipedes, however, which are venomous carnivores feeding on insects, worms and spiders, millipedes feed on decomposing vegetation.

COMMON WOODLOUSE
Oniscus asellus

Locally called the slater, the woodlouse is the only crustacean fully adapted to live on land. It is liable to dehydration and must live in dark humid places such as rotting tree trunks, logs, in old walls, under stones, and similar places. They come out at night to feed on decaying animal and plant matter – including wood bark, fungi and moss. Until the miniature woodlice hatch, the females carry the eggs in a brood pouch on the belly. Wearing a shell-like skin of body segments with defined ridges and different colours – grey with paler patches, sometimes orange or yellowish – the woodlouse (15 mm) is related to the shrimp, the crab and the lobster.

THE PLANTS

Before moving on to November and describing that month's many fungi, and then to December, the time of the holly and conifers, I leave October, briefly describing the sea buckthorn, larch, and ivy.

SEA BUCKTHORN
Hippophae rhamnoides

Growing naturally, but very locally, along our eastern shores on sand hills and exposed cliffs, the sea buckthorn is a sprawling deciduous shrub, usually two metres tall with tough roots, stout thorny branches, remarkable green and silvery leaves, minute inconspicuous flowers, and bright berries.

The mesh of their roots makes sea buckthorn thickets very strong and also helps to stabilise sand dunes, like those of County Down's Murlough Nature Reserve, where the buckthorn is plentiful though invasive and can become a nuisance. The branches hold lateral thorny twigs or sideshoots. In March and April the twigs show tiny green flowers on separate female and male bushes. The female flowers grow in tiny clusters at the base of the lateral thorns; though quite ordinary, the more elaborate male flowers are in small catkins. Pollinated by the wind, the flowers appear before the leaves.

Willow-like, hence the name 'sallow thorn', the leaves are adapted to

Sea buckthorn

RICHARD T. MILLS

retain moisture and reflect the sun's heat. About 8 cm long, the slender lance-shaped untoothed leaves are green above and silvery underneath. During October the female plants present bright orange-yellow berries which – if not devoured by birds – remain throughout winter. The juicy berries are rich in vitamin C; they have a pleasant acid taste and can be used in making marmalade.

LARCH
Larix decidua

From the higher mountain ranges and valleys of central Europe, the European, or common, larch has been planted in shelter belts, coniferous forests and, recently, in amenity areas throughout the country. An ornamental hardy deciduous tree, it likes plenty of light and open space; and it successfully grows on low lime, mineral soils. In the right place it is a good plantation tree, and because it likes space and light, plantings of European larch are normally thinned as they grow, providing valuable and versatile timber.

A lofty pyramidal tree, it can reach a height of thirty-eight metres. The light brown bark shows thin regular plates, more noticeable on elderly trees. On mature trees, the lower trunk is bare of branches – higher up, the branches are thick and strong and almost horizontal. It is an impressive tree. Interesting too. Unlike the spruces and other firs, and the pine – conifers that are evergreen – the larch drops its needle leaves in October and stands almost bare through remaining autumn and in winter when, viewed against the sky, its cones give the larch a curiously spotted appearance.

In mid-spring, April into May, before the needle leaves appear on the straw-coloured twigs, the flowers show. Erect and purplish-red in clusters, the remarkable female flowers are called larch roses; reddish-yellow and hanging, the proud male flowers are simply called catkins. Then the leaves grow: fresh green needles in rosettes, sometimes singly, shooting from stumpy straw-coloured buds. Into May the larch looks lovely with a beginning delicate clothing of bright green leaves contrasting with the various woody shades of trunk, branches, twigs, and true tree flowers. Through summer, when so many other beautiful plants claim attention, the larch still catches the eye. In late September, beginning October, when the leaves turn a golden colour – so brilliant against the usual heavy dark green background of evergreens – the larch is special and lovely to see. Then the needles fall, leaving the tree with bare branches and egg-shaped fruit: pale cones with tightly packed scales; and, in truth, when this happens the larch becomes a sorry sight.

The heartwood of the European larch varies from a yellowish-white to an attractive reddish-brown, and is usually straight grained. Its lightness and durability once brought it into use for railway sleepers, coal-mine props, scaffold props and good ladders; while in carpentry, it still has the merit of being comparatively free from large loose knots. Its straight branches are welcome to the amateur and commercial flower-grower for pergolas, arches, supports of different kinds and, for the landscape gardener, attractive rustic bridges. Creative farmers can use the wood in many ways: with their base charred, creosoted, or treated with preservatives, bits and pieces of the common larch can last many years.

Ivy

IVY
Hedera helix

The ivy is one of our few native climbers to arrive at any great height: thirty metres with support. The stems have innumerable fibrous and adhering roots, which allow the plant to clamber over walls, rocks, up trees; and ivy is planted to climb the gables of houses. Dark green and shiny – sometimes purplish in winter – three to five lobed leaves are borne on non-flowering stems. Flowering stems grow leaves without lobes; on these, in October, the green flowers have an abundance of nectar and are pollinated by flies and dying wasps. The fruit is a black berry.

Medicinally, ivy had many uses in the seventeenth century. The berries were said to cure jaundice, to stop the spitting of blood, to kill intestinal worms, to prevent the evil plague, and even cure sufferers. Boiled in vinegar, the fresh leaves – applied warm to the sides – gave relief to persons troubled with ailments of the spleen, or ache, and stitch in the side. The concoction, applied to the temples and the forehead, eased a persistent headache. Boiled in wine, the leaves would successfully clean obstinate ulcers of the skin, and heal infected wounds, and burns and scalds. Sniffed, the juice of the berries cleared the head; the same dropped into the ears cured infection and running. For a hangover from consumption of a certain wine, the best and speediest cure was to 'drink a draught of the same wine, wherein a handful of bruised ivy leaves were boiled'. And musically, in the right hands, the ivy leaf could be a lively, versatile instrument.

Ivy berries

In the 1990s *Hedera helix* is listed among plants that may be harmful to animals and children who eat the berries; and the sap of the plant can cause dermatitis, sometimes with severe blistering and inflammation.

In superstition, during winter, villagers gathered ivy to keep the house goblins or evil spirits away until Candlemas Eve, 1 February. In folklore the ivy plant is the symbol of friendship; the black berry is the symbol of warning; the spray is assiduous to please; and the wreath is the symbol of reward. And the person named 'Ivy' is likely to have a clinging nature.

NOVEMBER

Coming between autumn and winter, when nature seems to be resting after the harvest, November appears cheerless, dark and cold. The deciduous trees are bare and the fallen leaves have lost their brilliant colours of October. Yet a stroll through woodland on a bleak November day is relieved by knowing that, in their maturity, the trees and birds and many other creatures do need their rest; and for seeds to germinate in beautiful leaves fallen into decay, to make new life out of old, there must be a dark November. It is nature's way.

November is a month of much superstition and tradition. Since ancient times Hallowe'en has been a kind of harvest festival. It was an occasion for feasting on all sorts of food grown during the summer. *Samhain*, meaning 'summer's end', was a Celtic festival held on the first day of November, which marked the beginning of the new year – winter. The new year began on 1 November, not 1 January, and was associated with the opening of the *sídhe*, the 'hollow hills' of the fairies; and it was a time of the dead. At *Samhain*, beasts were brought in to shelter; others were slaughtered for winter store – possibly this was why Anglo-Saxons called November 'the blood month'. And Cailleach Bheara, the blue-faced hag who represented winter and was reborn every *Samhain*, brought cold weather and snow.

Snow still comes in November, but the redwings, fieldfares and wild geese arrive from far colder climes. The snow seldom hides the bareness of the landscape, but the greys and browns of the broad-leaved woodlands are relieved by many colourful fungi. And away from the woodlands, along the shoreline, in rocky inlets, grey seals are born.

THE SEALS

Only two species of seal breed in Ireland: the grey or 'Atlantic' seal and the common or 'harbour' seal. Apart from reasonable numbers in the sea loughs of counties Antrim, Derry and Down, the common seal is not at all common: excepting Strangford Lough, which hosts more common seals than any other sea lough in Ireland – and where the common outnumbers the grey – there are far fewer common seals than greys around the Irish coastline. In this brief introduction, since seals are so important in folklore, I mention both species together.

Bloody Foreland, County Donegal
DERMOT DONOHUE

Always at this time of year I go along Donegal's northwest coast to the townland of Magheraroarty to watch grey seals. The seals, maybe twenty of them, with only heads above the water, stay fairly close to the pier – and beyond them, looking on, stands Tory Island. I go to see these seals for good reason: legend tells that, while being taken from Tory to the mainland, the children of women who were in attendance on the daughter of Balor of the Evil Eye were allowed to fall into the sea, and they immediately turned into seals. Balor was the one-eyed king of the Formorians, the earliest people of Ireland who lived beyond the sea or under it. While spying on Druids who were preparing a draught of wisdom, Balor's eye was splashed by the concoction, and thereafter his glance was baleful to any person he looked upon. The god of darkness, Balor and his followers were associated with every possible evil.

Seals are fascinating creatures: like humans, they have families, they suckle their crying babies, they are vulnerable, inquisitive, and look at us with eyes like our own. They have brought us a great wealth of folklore and, undoubtedly, will bring more. From *The Irish Wildlife Book* one story accounts for their origin by claiming there was no room for some people in Noah's ark, so they were turned into seals to escape drowning. In *The Aquarian Guide to British and Irish Mythology* we read that seals were fallen angels; and there are stories in which they transform from seals to human beings. It was believed that people with webbed hands or feet were descended from seals. In the Scots Gaelic, seals were called *Cuilein Mairi*, or 'Mary's whelps'. Some believed that seals were the children of kings under enchantment, and the marvellous stories of selkies incline towards this tradition.

Selkies are seal-people who have the ability to hide their seal skins and take human shape. Sometimes seal-women are said to be the offspring of ordinary men and selkies, whose skins have been stolen and concealed elsewhere by the mortal who wants her for his wife. Should she find her skin, the selkie is likely to leave her husband and return to the sea.

Legends tell of seals saving fishermen from drowning; this was likely before rivalry grew up between seal and salmon fishers. There are also stories of seal-women who can be heard mourning the loss of their children or, like the Sirens of the *Odyssey*, trying to lure men to their doom. Such marvellous stories were probably inspired by the calls of hungry grey seal pups: pathetic bleats that sound almost like a baby crying, to which the cows reply with mournful howls. Distorted and magnified by echoes from the cliffs along lonely breeding places, these eerie calls could easily stir imaginations to create legend.

Grey seals

RICHARD T. MILLS

Attempting to differentiate the grey and the common – grey seals tend to haul out and lie on rocky ledges or beaches or in caves under cliffs, while common seals prefer sand banks and beaches or inlets in estuaries. When the greys are hauled out, their size will help tell them apart – the adult common seal is smaller than the grey. The adult male grey is distinguishable from the female grey by his longer Roman nose. In theory, the adult grey's coat is black with white spots, and the female's coat is muddy white with black spots. In reality, because of much diffusion of black and white in both sexes – and in both grey seal and common seal – differentiation by colour marking is unreliable.

The common seal has a round head and a cute face with a tilted nose but, sometimes, young greys have these features too. A person needs to get really close to be sure. Play a mouth organ or sing a song and the seals will come close and stare at you. Common seals have V-shaped nostrils. On land they are quiet and tend to stay where the tide leaves them; and they are smaller and less social than greys. The grey seals easily tolerate each other and form close groups; but they are very noisy – barking, farting, hooting, hissing, snarling. The hunting grounds of the two species overlap, but the common and grey seem to co-exist without animosity. Common seals mate in November and pup in June or July. Grey seals pup in November.

Grey seal

RICHARD T. MILLS

GREY SEAL
Halichoerus grypus

The grey seal is our largest carnivorous mammal. The adult male, or bull, can grow to a length of three metres and weigh 363 kg. The cow, slightly more than half the bull's weight, measures up to just over two metres. The grey seal has a noticeable convex outline to the head and a large down-turned Roman nose; the female's muzzle is relatively narrow. This profile is very distinct in bulls and it is the best feature for differentiating the grey seal and the common seal, which has a concave dog-like profile – like the face of a Labrador pup. In quiet parts of sea loughs, where curiosity causes both kinds of seal to come close to look up at a lone person in a boat, or on a rock, or even walking the water's edge, that person can enjoy the seals' company, clearly distinguish one from the other, and be enchanted by their friendly, inquisitive gaze.

The grey seal is seldom grey. The colour varies from dark slaty grey, through brown to silvery – depending on whether the animal is wet or dry, and on its state of moult. On many of them, grey is the ground colour interrupted with irregular blotches or spots of brown. The back is generally darker than the undersides, but about the shoreline of Ireland and its many islands, there are grey seals that are totally brown and others with the markings of dalmations. Look for the nose, see the size of the animal, listen to the voice, and watch the social behaviour and location, in order to identify the seal.

For thousands of years the grey seal has provided skins for humans to wear, and oil for their lamps, and as recently as the turn of the twentieth century the grey seal was almost hunted to extinction. Thanks to legislation, today the grey seal has survived total destruction, but people still want to kill the animal. Because of its habit of eating salmon, herring and cod – an age-old, natural and necessary activity – commercial fishermen persist in seeking licence to control numbers.

On land the seal slumps and slides and moves slowly and clumsily. In the water, hunting flickering, gleaming fish, it is graceful, agile and fast – propelled by hind limbs to speeds of 12–15 m.p.h.; but mostly dallying, it generally feeds on flatfish, fin-fish and crustaceans. In Atlantic waters that would almost instantly freeze a human to death, the seal happily swims, having a 64 mm layer of blubber to keep out the cold. As well as this, the seal – a mammal which must breathe air – can remain at great depths for twenty minutes. By steadying and slowing down its circulation, it can conserve the oxygen stored in its muscles, and while moving down into deep water, it closes its nostrils to prevent water entering its lungs, and can reduce its heart rate tenfold, from about 150 beats to 15 a minute – this reduces the amount of oxygen to the body tissues.

The grey seal is a truly aquatic mammal. Floating upright, it will often fall asleep at sea. Yet its speed and agility, breathing ability, and contendedness in the water are not enough to keep the creature alive and strong. To hunt efficiently, it also needs to smell, see, feel and touch. The seal's nose is therefore very sensitive; its eyes are adapted for night vision and the poor light in murky depths; and its whiskers are hypersensitive to vibration and touch. It is a superior predator.

Although births occur from September to December, about Irish coasts the grey seals bear most of their pups in November. The season starts with adult males and pregnant females congregating on breeding grounds, or rookeries. The larger and dominant bulls, usually over ten years old, occupy the best territories and noisily and fiercely drive the younger bulls away. Eleven months pregnant, the cow quickly delivers her single pup, and sniffs at it carefully. Now knowing its scent, the cow will feed only this pup and chase all other hungry ones away.

At birth the baby seal weighs 14 kg, measures 85 cm, and wears a coat of white fur, which is shed in about three weeks, leaving the fat pup with a dark bluish coat. Meanwhile, feeding on the mother's highly nutritious milk, converted to blubber, the pup doubles its birth weight in ten days. After three weeks, when the suckling is brought to an abrupt end, the pup should weigh about 41 kg. At this time the cow deserts the pup and, soon afterwards, she mates.

The pups spend the next few weeks splashing around in rock pools, learning to swim and feed. If during this period they lack a good reserve of blubber, they will starve to death. Pup mortality is high. Before going to sea, the young feed on shrimps and small fish found in the rock pools.

After the breeding season of some two months, which is a time of fasting for the cows and bulls, the adults return to the sea to feed. In the spring they reappear and haul out on different locations to moult. The females come ashore during later February or beginning March, and the males arrive from late April into May. After moulting, the seals go into the sea to feed again, to build up their reserves for the coming breeding season. Male greys usually live for about twenty years; females may live to be forty years old.

COMMON SEAL
Phoca vitulina

Just as the grey seal is not really grey, the common seal is not really common; and although both species are described as earless seals, they do have ears: the slits behind the animals' eyes are the external openings of the ears.

Mostly seen in small colonies along quiet sandy shores of sea loughs, there is little difference in the size of adult male and female common seals; but, as with the grey seal, there is much variation in colouring. The average length of an adult is about 1.7 metres, and the weight is 85–90 kg. Hidden between the hind limbs is a short tail about 8 cm long. The coat of short hair varies from pale brown with dark mottling to silver, grey, and almost black. Some seals have light-coloured coats spotted with dark markings; other seals have dark-coloured coats showing light markings. The head of the common seal is round and the face is concave, with a short muzzle beneath a steep brow. This profile distinguishes the common seal from the grey, which has a heavy down-turned Roman nose.

RICHARD T. MILLS

Common seal

On land the quiet common seal is even more clumsy and less mobile than the lumbering, heavy, grunting grey. However, in the water the common seal is a most graceful swimmer and it has great speed: using its strong fore limbs and rear limbs to help it catch up with very fast-moving fish; and, like the grey, its thick layer of blubber keeps the seal warm in cold deep water. Searching for bottom-dwelling flatfish, the seal is comfortable in depths of ninety metres or more, where its eyes, adapted for darkness, its sensitive nose with nostrils closed against the water, and its long whiskers, or vibrissae – hypersensitive to vibration and touch – enable it to take prey.

Like the grey, the common seal eats crustaceans, flatfish and fin-fish. It especially likes sea trout, salmon, herring and cod, and because these fish have commercial value, the seal is unpopular with fishermen, who want their numbers controlled, but the animal is protected by law. Fishermen argue that the seals, grey and common, are not only killing the salmon at sea and in the loughs, but that they also take the fish out of the nets – indeed, for their own convenience, the seals even herd the fish into nets, where they kill far more than they can eat, and often damage the nets.

Common seals mate during the autumn, from September into November. Then, after spending the winter and spring feeding at sea, they make their way back to familiar breeding grounds. For the single pup, the gestation is seven and a half months, so the cows arrive to deliver their pups in June or July. The characteristic breeding sites are sand banks near deep water. Born on a sand bank at low tide, the pup often takes to the water on the first tide following its birth. Supervised by its mother, for the next few days the pup rarely comes ashore, floating and then swimming near the bank.

The pup weighs about 10 kg at birth, and quickly gains weight as it feeds on the mother's oil-rich milk, which is converted to blubber. Unlike the grey seal pup, the common does not wear white fur at birth, but it is still very attractive in its dark coat. After taking milk for about a month, the pup begins to catch shrimps for itself, and at six months old it is feeding on crabs, molluscs and fish.

Killer whales are the natural enemies of seals. However, in the autumn of 1988, the common seal populations in Irish waters suffered from a highly virulent disease now known as phocine plague. The disease had already killed up to twelve thousand common seals on the coasts of northwest Europe; and within a fortnight of the epidemic in Britain, victims were found in Strangford Lough. The condition left the infected seals in a pitiful state: the animals could hardly breathe, and their ability to swim and feed deteriorated; finally, before dying, they became paralysed and could only drift with the tide to be attacked by gulls. The epidemic was over by 1990, and a recurrence has not happened. However, careful watches for the return of the condition are continuing.

THE FUNGI

In the popular mind plants have roots, green leaves, attractive flowers with nectar and pollen, and bear fruit such as berries or seeds of some sort. It is difficult to recognise moulds, yeasts, mushrooms, toadstools and other fungal growths as plants. Yet in the scheme of nature, where visible objects are identified as animal, vegetable, or mineral, fungi cannot be seen as animal or mineral. Fungi are plants, but they differ fundamentally from other plants in their method of obtaining food, in their structure, and in their mode of reproduction. All plants are classified according to how they reproduce. With ferns, liverworts, mosses, seaweeds and certain other plants, fungi are members of that division of the vegetable kingdom known as cryptogams, from two Greek words meaning 'hidden marriage'. Because they produce neither flowers nor seeds, and their method of having offspring remains relatively obscure – in fact, something that cannot be seen or understood without microscopical examination – fungi continue to be

Earthballs

RICHARD T. MILLS

RICHARD T. MILLS

Shaggy ink cap

known as cryptogams: plants which reproduce by means of spores, too tiny to be seen with the naked eye.

Confining fungi to those found about woodland in November, and bearing in mind that the mycelium – the main vegetative body of the fungus – is usually underground or, for example, climbing up the inside of a dying tree, the visible toadstool – a popular name for all fleshy, gill-bearing fungi – is the fruiting body, or spore-producing structure of the plant. Since different fungi are sometimes known by identifying the reproductive body, it may prove useful to look at its different parts.

Briefly put, the usual parts of a toadstool are the cap, or pileus, the gills – which are radiating plates on the underside of the cap – and the stem, which rises from the ground to support the cap. The stem is usually central. In some toadstools the observer may find a ring on the stem. Sometimes skirt-like, the ring is usually attached above or near the middle of the stem. There might also be a sheath or cup-like structure at the base of the stem; this additional tissue is known as a volva. On stems of particular species, both ring and volva may be present. On other toadstools, attached sometimes to the edge of the cap, or replacing an obvious ring on a stem, there are frilly, less definite, structures called veils. Together with the colour of the toadstool, its shape and size, its host, and so on, these different parts of the fruiting body can only enable a beginning identification of the species of plant. When it comes to the stage of planning to eat a particular individual, more knowledgeable sources of information should be sought.

The toadstool is just one example of a fruiting body. There are many other types of reproductive body: different species produce and disperse thousands of spores in their own ways. Most toadstools and mushrooms let the ripe spores fall from the gills on the underside of the cap. In the puffballs, the spores are produced inside the ball and, when ripe, they are ejected through a hole in the top of the structure. A disc fungus, such as the orange peel, shoots the spores out into the air.

The vegetative or the main body of a fungus is a mass of hyphae, very fine branching threads which interlace and form the mycelium. Sometimes the threads twist together and become cords or laces – like the long, blackish, shoe-string fibres that can be seen under the bark of trees which are being attacked by the honey fungus. While the visible toadstool or any other reproductive structure is usually short-lived, the mycelium is always present, underground, threading its way through the earth, mulch, and the roots of trees, and always feeding.

Fungi do not feed like other plants: they do not contain chlorophyll, a green-colouring matter which in the presence of light makes carbohydrates such as starch and sugar from carbon dioxide and water – a process of photosynthesis. As they cannot make their own food, they feed by dissolving and absorbing nutrients from dead animal and plant matter such as fallen leaves, twigs, rotting tree trunks and the like. The mycelium secretes enzymes that liquefy organic matter, and the nutritious fluid is absorbed into the body of the fungus.

Fungi convert debris into valuable and readily usable substances – they are recycling agents – although certain species are parasitic and may cause serious damage to plants and animals. In general, however, the role of fungi is very important. By promoting decay and decomposition, breaking down diseased, dead and waste matter into the simple organic forms, which can be used by ground flora, bushes and trees, the lowly fungi are essential to the survival of woodland and other habitats for insects, spiders, birds and mammals.

In November common woodland fungi can be divided into four distinctive groups, according to the shape of the visible fruiting body. The groups are the mushrooms and toadstools with umbrella-shaped bodies, the funnel or cup-shaped types, the ball or pear-shaped fungi, and the bracket-shaped species that are seen growing from the trunk or branch of a tree.

SHAGGY INK-CAP
Coprinus comatus

Umbrella-shaped and growing on the ground to a height of 10–30 cm, this very delicate fungus is common throughout the countryside. Growing in groups on rich soils deep in woodland, about clearings, woodland edges and fields, even roadsides, the shaggy ink-cap is easily recognised. Also called the lawyer's wig, when young the cap is covered in white shaggy scales, the gills are white, and the hollow white stem has a noticeable ring. With age the ring quickly disappears and the white gills turn a pinkish colour, then black, and liquefy into an inky fluid. After a day, the cap becomes a dripping mass of black spores.

RICHARD T. MILLS

Shaggy ink cap

COMMON INK-CAP
Coprinus atramentarius

Umbrella or bell-shaped and growing to a height of 8–25 cm in clusters on ground near rotting tree stumps, this fungus lacks the obvious scales that cover *Coprinus comatus*, the shaggy ink-cap. Up to 5 cm tall, the cap of the common ink-cap is pale grey, ribbed and faintly scaly – especially about the apex where the structure is tinged light brown. When young, the gills are white, and tapering upwards from a slightly swollen base, the stem is up to 20 cm tall and nearly 2 cm thick. With age the margins of the cap become moist as the gills turn into an inky fluid full of black spores.

SHAGGY PHOLIOTA
Pholiota squarrosa

With rounded cap, and growing in clusters to a height of 5–12 cm from the base of the trunk of a wide variety of old broad-leaved trees, this inedible fungus is widespread in woodland. Also called the scaly cluster fungus, the shaggy scales on the cap and stem clearly distinguish the shaggy pholiota from other clustering, yellow or orange-coloured species such as the honey fungus – *Armillaria mellea* – found growing on the trunk or at the bottom of a seemingly healthy tree. Convex at first and then flattening during growth – except for its incurved margins – the cap measures up to 10 cm across. Both cap and stem are yellow, covered with orange-brown scales. Dark brownish-yellow at the base, the tough stem has a torn ring; the stem is smooth above the ring and scaly below; the gills are yellow. With age, the rim of the cap breaks and then turns up, showing the gills becoming rust-coloured. The spores are brown.

WOOD BLEWIT
Lepista nuda

Growing on the ground to a height of 7–13 cm and widespread in all sorts of woods, the violet coloration of the attractive wood blewit's gills and stem is unmistakable. Bluish at first and slightly conical, the cap flattens to measure up to 15 cm across; and the stout violet stem has a slightly bulbous base. The flesh is a deep lilac colour and offers just the hint of a pleasant scent. With age, the cap margins begin to turn upwards, and the gills and stem lose their violet colour.

BLUSHER
Amanita rubescens

Fairly common in broad-leaved woodland throughout the countryside, and 5–15 cm tall, the blusher has a red and pinkish flush in all its features. Emerging from the earth, the new fungus has a domed cap which grows to become pink to reddish-brown, with off-white or creamy-pink to red patches, and flattens to measure 15 cm across. With a swollen base, and a prominent, membranous collar-like ring – typical of the Amanita – the hollow stem has a pinkish hue, especially below the ring; and when cut or bruised the white flesh turns pink. With age, the white gills show reddish spots, and the off-white patches on the cap may turn deep pink or red.

FLY AGARIC
Amanita muscaria

Umbrella-shaped and growing on poor soils, usually under birch trees but often under pines, this attractive and very noticeable fungus grows to 25 cm and is unmistakable. It is very colourful. Usually about 15 cm across, spotted with white pyramid-like portions of skin, the convex cap is bright scarlet. The stem is interesting: often scaly, but firm and white, hollow when old, and up to 20 cm tall, it tapers from below upwards – to where the Amanita collar-ring hangs down. For the younger fly agaric the ring was a means of support. Now tattered and torn, the ring remains as the membrane which attached the edge of the vigorous, upward-moving cap to the stem. The bulbous base of the stem is also interesting: a few wart-like or scaly fragments of the volva remain as irregular rings. The white gills are very crowded, and they reach the stem but do not touch it. The flesh is white, with a yellowish skin; and, with age, the scarlet cap is sometimes reduced to orange. Without doubt this attractive plant is dangerous. Commonly illustrated in children's books, with elves or fairies nearby, the fly agaric is the picture book toadstool. Yet, if not fatal, this fungus is poisonous, causing hallucinations, intoxication, and serious gastric upsets; it even repels flies – hence, its name.

RICHARD T. MILLS

Fly agaric

STINKHORN
Phallus impudicus

With its phallic shape, honeycombed cap, and offensive spore mass, the stinkhorn is easily recognised. Commonly found to a height of 20 cm in rich mulch, the fruiting body first appears as a hard round egg-like structure up to 5 cm across. When ripe, the egg starts to push up a white stem with a cap covered in olive-green spore-producing jelly. The delicate spongy stem lengthens in a few hours and the slimy conical, honeycombed cap produces a very bad smell. The stench attracts different flies, which eat and carry and distribute the spores.

DEAD MAN'S FINGER
Xylaria polymorpha

Growing on an old tree stump, this fungus is usually 5 cm tall and widespread in broad-leaved woodland, and is commonly found on a stump of beech. It presents as a clump of stiff black finger-like growths pointing skywards. About the length of a child's fingers, the structures are irregular, arthritic-looking, or club-shaped; from a very narrow base, the fungus slightly spirals to become swollen, yet each finger has its own peculiar shape. When broken and examined, the flesh is tough and white, and has rows of very tiny sacs on the outer margins where the spores are formed.

Stinkhorn

HONEY FUNGUS
Armillaria mellea

Found everywhere on live and dead wood, this attractive fungus grows to 12 cm tall and is seen as a clump of up to two dozen caps on stumps, dead trunks, even on live and apparently healthy trees, and on the soil at the bottom of a tree – where it is attacking the roots. Measuring 2.5–10 cm across, the rough cap is yellowish to brown, with dark honey-coloured hairy scales. Below the thick and whitish or pale yellow ring, the stem is honey-coloured and has a swollen base. The gills are cream to yellowish-brown, and they run down to the stem. The flesh is white and smelly.

Dead man's finger

Unfortunately this attractive fungus is a very serious pest. Once it takes hold of any tree – dying or healthy – that tree will surely die. The cords of mycelia which live and spread underground can spread for up to ten metres or more; and on reaching a tree, or trees, they coil round the roots and force themselves up between the bark and the heartwood, all the way penetrating the host tissue with fine white feeding threads. The mycelium produces enzymes capable of dissolving the host tissue, and then absorbing the nutritious fluid. This is the function of the feeding threads, and the rotting enzymatic activity of these threads may be seen 'shining' in the dark.

BROWN ROLL-RIM
Paxillus involutus

Particularly common under birch trees and 5–12 cm tall, this funnel-shaped fungus is a yellowish-brown colour. The cap is domed at first and has a noticeable incurved margin – hence the name 'roll-rim'. The margin remains incurved, so when fully grown the cap has a deep central depression. Up to 12 cm across, the downy rust-coloured or olive-brown cap becomes smooth and dark with age; and it gets sticky when wet. Short and slightly paler than the cap, the stem may be off centre. Extending down from the cap to the top of the stem, the gills change from yellowish to brown. When bruised the brown gills stain the fingers; and, when cut, the soft yellow-brown flesh darkens, and is poisonous. The spores are brown.

EARTHBALL
Scleroderma citrinum
Common on bare earth around woods, and sometimes on sandy soil in woodland, earthballs are more or less spherical or pear-shaped structures, 2.5–7.5 cm across, with coarse root-like threads at the base. Fleshy when young, they develop a thick tough yellowish skin with scales and irregular cracks on a grained surface. At maturity, the interior of *Scleroderma citrinum* consists of a blackish spore mass. When fully ripe, the leathery coat splits open and the dry powdery spores are expelled. Earthballs have an acrid smell and taste, and are considered poisonous.

Jew's ear

RICHARD T. MILLS

JEW'S EAR
Auricularia auricula-judae
This bracket fungus is found growing on the elder, and it is widespread and abundant in woodlands throughout the country. It really does have the shape of a human ear, and the name 'Judas ear', corrupted to 'Jew's ear', comes from the belief that Judas Iscariot hanged himself from the branch of an elder tree. Moist and flabby and flesh-like, and facing downwards, the 'ear' bud is about 1.3 cm across. Fully grown, at 2.5–6.5 cm across, with a velvety outer surface, and still facing downwards, the liver-brown bracket is cupped on the underside and has ear-like folds and a translucent flabby flesh. With age, the bracket hardens and turns black.

BEEFSTEAK FUNGUS
Fistulina hepatica

This impressive bracket fungus is found growing on living oaks and on chestnut trees. Taking about a fortnight to reach full size, the bracket is plate-like, and sometimes tongue-shaped, 10–25 cm across. The orange-red upper surface is sticky, hairy and skin-like; the under-surface has fine yellow tubes. Well-named, the flesh of the beefsteak is rich red and meat-like and it produces a bright red juice. The mycelial invasion of the tree turns the tissue a rich brown colour, and this wood was used in cabinet-making.

RAZOR-STROP FUNGUS
Piptoporous betulinus

Called the razor-strop because its fine corky dry flesh was once used for sharpening razors, and called the birch polypore because it lives exclusively on *Betula pendula*, the silver birch, this bracket fungus is very noticeable growing from the bark of a diseased tree – which quickly dies. Fully-grown, the wavy-edged bracket is 10–20 cm across and light brown above and white below. Rubbery at first, then drying to become very hard, the flesh may be 6.5 cm thick. As well as sharpening razors, the dry flesh was sliced and used as cork, and it was made into pin cushions.

RICHARD T. MILLS

Razor-strop fungus on birch

DECEMBER

With December comes the year's shortest day, the end of autumn and the beginning of winter, when the sun appears to have gone as far south as it can go and stands still over the tropic of Capricorn. It is the darkest month of the year, yet the festivities of Christmas keep December bright and cheerful. This time of year always had harvest and religious festivals to keep it bright, and the modern Christmastide has adopted many of the old customs. Always related to nature and its seasons, age-old celebrations were held to thank and make sacrifice to powerful gods, and the darkness and lifelessness of beginning winter were greatly feared. The ancients visualised the sky as a great dome lighted from late evening through the night by a changing moon, and stars, and during the day by the sun, and they believed that these lights were gods to be thanked and pleased, especially during this time.

Among other things, the ancients worshipped trees, particularly trees that were favoured by the gods: trees that could survive dark cold wet winters; and, in ways, their traditions are still practised.

> Holly and ivy, box and bay,
> Put in the church on Christmas Day.

From autumn through winter, when the broad-leaved trees were bare and looked lifeless, people in ancient Scandinavia worshipped the 'living trees' – the evergreens; later the Scandinavians made the evergreens part of their Christian festivals. At the start of winter the Romans exchanged green branches for luck. The English adopted this custom for Christmas, and used the holly tree – 'holy tree'. Druids have sprigs of mistletoe as charms, and the mistletoe was used at religious gatherings. Dating back to pagan times, there are several stories about the origin of the Christmas tree. The custom of 'burning the yule log' came from the Norse and the Anglo-Saxons: they burned a huge oak log to honour Thor, the god of thunder. When the Norse became Christian, the yule log became an important part of their Christmas ceremony.

Apart from festivals, December is still interesting in its own way. Most of this month is usually warmer than the other winter months and much wildlife is about. The feral mink, fox, and both the red and grey squirrel are busy. Feral goats are down from the hilltops to browse on stems of willow and rough grasses. Feral cats are stalking the countryside to catch birds sheltering in low cover. Red deer stags and hinds live in their separate groups, feeding on rough grass and the bark of trees. Hedgehogs are fast asleep. From very cold faraway places, many thousands of wild geese, swans, ducks and wading birds continue to arrive to shelter and feed about the wetlands and mudflats of Irish loughs. Redwings and fieldfares and other migrant dry-land birds become more numerous. Hungry, cold and wet woodland birds are arriving in gardens to seek food and shelter. Holly trees still keep bright berries, and heliotropes begin flowering, and different conifers are challenging to identify. The grey heron stands solitary and motionless along the shore of a lough or down at the river's edge. Pike and roach, and other coarse fish, are in prime condition; and in shallow gravel-bedded streams, salmon can be seen spawning.

RICHARD T. MILLS

Grey heron

THE SALMON
Salmo salar

On Saturday 15 July 1950, alone and fly-fishing Maginness's stream, along the upper middle reaches of the River Faughan, in County Derry, I hooked and lost my first salmon. I grew too excited, froze, and would not let the strong fish run. With line taut, rod buckled, and my heart thumping and my whole body trembling, I refused to give the fish any line and did not attempt to play the animal. I just held the fish in the same place in the stream – but not for long; after a mighty leap, the salmon broke the line in the air and returned to the stream with my fly in its mouth. Pale and shaking, I stared at the upright rod, dangling line, and the quiet stream, then I sat down on a rock and wept in despair.

A fortnight later, two days before my fourteenth birthday, I landed my first salmon, weighing just under 6 lb. On that unforgettable occasion, angling the same stream, I let the fish run – I had learned much from bitter experience. Since then I have caught many salmon and I have lost many, and during the past ten or twelve years, I have returned unharmed female fish, caught ripe with eggs. For me and countless other people, the salmon is a very special animal.

On Irish rivers an eel is called an eel, a trout is called a trout, and other fish are given their expected titles, but a salmon is called a fish. It is the fish of all fishes, and holds a respect that dates back to early times. Eight thousand years ago the first people to settle in Ireland, the Mesolithic people, hunted the Lower River Bann where they could catch the salmon. Ever since, the animal has held a special place in the lives and minds of Irish people. A valuable source of food, the salmon is the most important catch in the fishing industry; a wary and strong fish, it is the most prized specimen in the field of angling; and within mythology it is an interesting character.

In Celtic mythology the salmon is one of the great symbols of wisdom: it is Fintan who survived the Flood and hid in the Well of Segais. As the salmon of all knowledge, Fintan swam in the well and ate the magical hazelnuts which fell into the waters. Living by the River Boyne, Finegas had guarded the salmon for seven years. It was prophesised, however, that to obtain all knowledge the poet Finegas should eat the salmon. And while helping Finegas to roast the salmon, the poet's pupil Demne – who was really Fionn mac Cumhal in disguise – burnt his thumb when turning the fish; and because he sucked his thumb where Fintan's hot juices had scalded him, it was Fionn who gained all of the salmon's knowledge.

The salmon's importance in natural history is due to its superb structure and abilities, and its unusual life cycle. Like the sea trout, the salmon is anadromous – a fish that is born in freshwater and then goes to sea to feed and become physically and sexually mature before returning to breed in its place of birth. Its way of life makes the salmon easily seen and subjects it to more risks than any other species of large fish.

The name 'salmon' is a title of relatively recent times, coined by a visiting Roman. In their wanderings throughout Britain the Romans observed a powerful fish in rivers such as the Thames, the Trent, the Severn, the Avon and the Usk. They saw the fish as it leapt and called it Salmo – the leaper. Two thousand years later, despite all that is known about it today, we are still ignorant of many aspects of the life of a salmon.

A salmon is built for speed and leaping, and anglers fortunate enough to have played one on rod and line can give long accounts of the energy and power of this great fighting fish. A fresh-run salmon is a magnificent-looking animal. The average length of its streamlined body is about 65 cm and it weighs 7 or 8 lb; occasionally 20–30 lb salmon are caught, but these are exceptional fish.

The scale-covered skin is a silvery blue-green on the back, the flanks are silvery and the belly is white. Scattered over the flanks and back are small round black spots. Belonging to the family Salmonidae, which includes *Salmo trutta* – the trout – an Atlantic salmon is known as *Salmo salar*. The flexions of the head and body and power of the tail provide a salmon with movement, the swim bladder enables the fish to stay high or low in water, and the fins offer support and allow adjustments of position and poise. Of all the sensory structures none are more important than the lateral line and the swim bladder – after these comes sight.

Apart from differences in size, all fresh-run salmon look alike in a pool. It is only when you get close enough to examine the lower jaw that the sex of a fish becomes known. On the lower jaw a male salmon has a hook of gristle, termed a kype.

Fresh salmon run Irish rivers throughout the year. From the first day of January they are seen leaping about in tidal stretches, and at the first opportunity they make their way from brackish water to freshwater. The main runs of salmon occur during the summer months, and they arrive at the up-river spawning beds before December, their progress influenced by an adequate flow of water. But a salmon usually takes its time getting to the spawning ford and rests in lies along the way. To shelter from the full force of the current, a salmon will lie behind a submerged tree trunk or a boulder. These lies are found in most pools along a good salmon river. Flat rocky ledges are often used and, at times, salmon seem to prefer to rest in a deep shady part of a pool. If there is enough water in the river, fresh-run salmon will be seen climbing and jumping weirs from the beginning of July onwards – a sight not to be missed.

By the time brown leaves are floating down river, most of the salmon are nearing their spawning fords. There are stragglers, of course, and these salmon can be seen lifting themselves over weirs during later October. For the game angler this is the end of another fishing season; for the salmon it is the beginning of the spawning season. In salmon the amounts of reproductive hormones increase at this time, and cause noticeable changes in the behaviour and appearance of male and female fish. Soon the occasion will come for courtship, nest-making, chasing rivals, egg-laying, and fertilising. Meanwhile, the salmon assume a spawning dress for the occasion.

The beautiful silvery-green of the male's flanks and upperparts changes to a copper and red colour, and the white belly becomes greyish-yellow. His skin becomes hard and tough – but looks spongy – and the scales are almost buried in it; the black spots on his back and flanks become much larger. The snout lengthens and the upturned kype grows considerably longer. Why the kype increases in length and size at this time is not known. It is not used as a weapon: an angry male appears to use his snout to dunt rivals. In fact, the kype looks like a hindrance, because he can neither open nor close his mouth. And it is not used as any kind of tool or pick for dislodging or digging gravel when the nest is being made; the hen fish uses her tail and pelvic fins to construct the nest. Some claim that the cock uses his kype to grab the tail wrist of the hen and drag her about the pool. I have yet to observe this carry-on. The cock salmon's kype almost disappears after spawning has happened.

While the male is assuming his spawning dress, the female is becoming a blackish-blue colour. But, apart from this, and the distension of her belly with ripening eggs, the hen salmon manages to retain her normal appearance and good looks.

These changes in cock and hen salmon happen gradually, and many 'red' fish and 'black' fish are observed moving up river from the end of August onwards. The purpose of the spawning dress is not fully understood; it is clearly an external sign of sexual maturity, but no other general or particular function is ascribed to it. However, since it is sometimes difficult to distinguish fully dressed stationary salmon from other structures on the river bed, the dress possibly allows the salmon some camouflage and protection from enemies.

I have watched salmon spawning in rivers for more than forty years. I always find them about the same places, and very often in exactly the same spots; they can select the site of previous spawners with uncanny accuracy. I accept the belief that salmon return to the place where they were born four or five years before. The laying and fertilising usually occurs in a shallow gravel-bedded stream, running into or out of a quiet smooth-flowing pool which offers a plentiful supply of lies. Until the business of spawning is to be done, the salmon take up residence in the pool. The spawning ford or stream is bedded with pebbles that are heavy enough to firmly remain in position under the full force of winter spates, light enough to be moved out of the river bed by the nest-building hen. The stream must be shallow, but not likely to run dry, and it must be brisk enough to aerate the developing eggs.

Called a redd, the nest is a hollow in the gravel bed. It is easily recognised as a basin-shaped trough, about 60 cm in diameter and 20–25 cm deep. Too heavy to be moved by the hen, large stones occupy the bottom of the redd. Each hen constructs two or three redds for herself; these then sit in readiness. Most salmon lay their eggs from late November through December. When the time for spawning has come, the hen positions herself a few feet upstream of the redd. While she is settling down on the bed, her partner chases other cock salmon away from the location, then lies beside the hen and his body begins to shudder. This seems to make the hen's body convulse, and while extruding

Atlantic salmon

ÉAMON DE BUITLÉAR

some of her eggs, the sideway flexions of her tail cause small pieces of gravel to be displaced. The stream's current carries the eggs, or ova, and the disturbed gravel down into the redd. The male then sheds his milt and this is carried into the redd to quickly fertilise the ova. A hen may use all her redds during spawning. The egg-laying and fertilising actions appear to exhaust both hen and cock fish and they move into the nearby pool for periods of rest, before resuming the process, which takes about three days to complete.

Salmon expend most of their energy and food reserves during spawning; they become very wasted and thin, exhausted and weak. When spawning is completed many spent fish, or kelts, die. Their body weight is almost halved and they suffer a serious loss of co-ordination of movement. Kelts cannot withstand the force of floodwater and many are drowned and swept down-stream; others fall prey to low-grade parasites and die through disease; very few of the more virile soldier fish survive the breeding season. Compared to cocks, the hen kelts have a much higher rate of survival; this is probably due to differences in their spawning and post-spawning activities.

When the hen completes her egg-lay, she moves into the nearby pool to rest in a lie, but the cock fish, already more exhausted than the female, remains in the spawning ford, where he moves from one used redd to another. Why he does this nobody knows. On many occasions I have watched male salmon positioned alongside redds during the last week of January. Some believe that this is a brave and obstinate stance to protect ova. But how cock salmon can protect the eggs is difficult to understand. Another theory suggests that the male salmon is possibly awaiting the arrival of other gravid females. Whatever the reasons for his vigil – long after the business of spawning is done – this stubborn behaviour is the chief cause of the male salmon's death. While his partner is already beginning to recover, the exhausted male is trying to stand firm against the full force of the winter's spates which sweep him away to his death. It is not difficult to understand why, on their second return to spawn, cock salmon are fewer than hens.

When the surviving spawners have gained a little strength and are assuming the lustre of rehabilitating fish, they are better able to withstand the sudden spates of winter. They have recovered some of their balance and poise, and can control the movements so necessary to seek shelter from heavy floodwater. However, it is only when the river settles down that the kelts face the flow of water and drift with the current. Now and again they turn and glide down through the gentle flowing stretches of river. By the end of April these kelts have migrated back to the sea, where they remain – some less than a year, others more than a year – before returning to their spawning river.

The number of eggs laid by a salmon is variable, but the expected number is 650–700 per pound weight of fish. Therefore, from a 7 lb salmon – the average weight of a hen – we can expect some 5,000 eggs; of these 4,998 eggs are not likely to reach the maturity of spawning fish. Many are not fertilised, and many that have been are eaten by resident trout, eels, and other predators. There is also the likelihood of used redds being disturbed by very late spawners, with the *in situ* eggs being destroyed. Eggs can die because some redds are swept away by heavy floods, or sediment of sand or peat smothers some redds, or the stream runs dry. Only 3 per cent of the eggs are likely to survive the first year of life, and between the stages of hatching egg and migrant smolt, hopeful fisheries expect a survival of 0.1 per cent of wild salmon. They hope, therefore, for five fresh spawning adults from a 7 lb hen and her partner; but with seals, porpoises and cormorants in the sea – as well as netting, angling, poaching and diseases – Irish rivers are fortunate to have the hen and her mate replaced. (Salmon development from egg to smolt is almost identical to that of the trout, described on pages 197 to 198.)

Until about thirty years ago the behaviour and feeding habits of salmon in the Atlantic Ocean were not known. The only salmon caught at sea, or near the coast, were those returning to their spawning rivers. The great puzzle was that very few salmon were caught in the deeper waters of the Atlantic – where they went to feed was a mystery. Then in the mid-1960s adult salmon feeders were located in the waters of west Greenland and this led to a commercial fishery which, understandably, caused conservationists a great deal of concern. But the feeding grounds of the smaller species of salmon, known as grilse, have not been exploited. The salmon off Greenland feed on herring, eels and shrimp-like plankton called krill. The pinkish colour of salmon meat is probably due to the pigment of krill. The salmon occupy most of their time at moderate depths and, at night, they probably come nearer to the surface after the upward-moving plankton. Little else can be offered about the sea life of salmon.

Why and how salmon seek and successfully find their own rivers are not yet understood. Apart from a few theories centring on homing instinct and imprinting, not much can be said to explain why salmon return to their parent river. Much speculation, however, surrounds the issue of how they find the rivers and some suggestions are that: the salmon follow the lines of channels and flows of currents; varying levels of salanites or oxygen in the water direct them; the senses of smell and taste detect familiar water; celestial bodies direct them to the source; or possibly all of these factors are used in combination, or separately at different stages of the return journey. We can observe that when salmon have found their rivers, they do their utmost to spawn in the beds of their parents.

Apart from the 'spring' salmon, fresh-running fish which enter a limited number of Irish rivers during winter and early spring, two groups of salmon return to most rivers from late spring onwards. These salmon are simply called first return and second return. After a period at sea for longer than one year – the approximate minimum time before their return – first generation spawners are classified according to the period they have spent in the sea. The classification has nothing to do with the comparative weights of the fish.

The youngest returning fish are grilse, meaning 'silver-greyness'; and since the day they left the river as smolts, they have spent one year and a few months in the Atlantic. Grilse usually come into rivers from mid-May until the end of July. The other first-time spawners, the 'summer' salmon, are senior in sea life to the grilse by one or two years, and usually arrive from June onwards. The average weight of first-return summer salmon is 7 to 8 lb; grilse are usually smaller. The matters of age and differentiation of grilse and other first-return salmon can only be accurately determined by reference to scale readings. Like the number of rings in a tree, the scales of the salmon tell a story: the age of the fish and its years spent in the river and in the sea, but because of erosion the reading of scales can be extremely difficult and untrustworthy.

Some of the second-return salmon come back to the river during the late summer or early autumn of the same year in which they went out to the Atlantic as kelts. These fish were well-mended in the spring following spawning: they fed in the river and in the sea and were restored enough to return to spawn within a year; other kelts stay in the sea for a year and even longer. In short, all the salmon which survive to return to the river for their second spawning do not spend the same period in the sea. Some of them come back after six months, others stay in the sea for a year, and some take a year and a half before returning to the river. The period in the sea must be sufficient to give the salmon enough strength, food reserves, and sexual ability to spawn. The heavier salmon – 15–20 lb – caught in Irish rivers are usually second-return fish. Because there are so few examples of third-return spawning salmon, it is not possible to offer more information than this.

THE PLANTS

Without the distraction of broad-leaved trees, December is the time when a stroll through the countryside, plantation, parkland and open estate allows appreciation of the evergreens, which, of course, include the trees with needle-shaped leaves – the conifers – some of them huge and awesome. Apart from the native yew and the juniper, and the Scots pine from the Highlands, the conifers we see about us were brought from different parts of mainland Europe, Asia, northern Africa and America. The conifers most extensively planted by the Forestry Commission in 1919 were the Scots pine and European larch; and since then Forestry departments have planted the Japanese larch (*Larix leptolepis*), the Corsican pine (*Pinus nigra* var. *maritima*), the lodgepole pine (*Pinus contorta*), the sitka spruce (*Picea sitchensis*), and the Norway spruce (*Picea abies*). Other genera found planted in private estates and gardens include fir (*Abies*), Douglas firs (*Pseudotsuga*), cedars (*Cedrus*), cypresses (*Cupressus* and *Chamaecyparis*), redwood (*Sequoia*), and the monkey-puzzle (*Araucaria*).

But as trees of the month I choose holly, yew and juniper, and also briefly describe Scots pine, sitka spruce – and the Christmas tree.

Yew arils

Holly berries

HOLLY
Ilex aquifolium

As one of Ireland's few native evergreen trees, the holly's leaves and berries were likely used by the Druids for their beginning winter festivals. And still during the fortnight leading up to Christmas Day, female holly trees along laneways, river banks and in woods are pruned for their branches of dark glossy green leaves and clusters of bright red berries to decorate homes and churches.

Each individual tree is either male or female, and can grow twenty metres high. In later spring, usually mid-May, both trees display flowers, lily-white with four petals, but only the female trees produce berries, fertilised by nectar-seeking insects carrying the pollen from tree to tree. Holly berries are drupes – fruit whose seed is contained in a pit or stone – hard and unpalatable to small birds. And attracted by the colour and shape of the fruit, young children who eat about twenty berries may suffer severe vomiting, diarrhoea, and drowsiness.

Holly leaves are watertight and evergreen. Thick, with a waxy surface, the leaves resist water loss and may survive for three years on a tree. Sharp spines on the lower leaves help to protect the tree against browsing animals; the upper leaves on the tree are often spineless. At first glance the prickly leaves seem relatively safe from any form of attack; yet insects feed on the leaves, especially the holly leaf-miner larvae which live inside the leaf tissue. A close look at a leaf will often reveal pale patches or blotches on the glossy upperside. The small and inconspicuous female adult flies appear in June and lay their eggs in the midrib of the leaf. The tiny larvae hatch and mine their way forwards to the centre of the leaf. The larvae grow slowly and their presence is usually detected only when the blotches appear. Often more than half the leaves on a tree are attacked by the larvae, and as mined leaves drop off prematurely, the season of leaf fall is endless: severely affected trees lose leaves all year round. Trees not attacked by larvae usually drop their old leaves in June and July around the time the new leaves are forming. The old leaves sometimes turn a lovely deep shade of yellow. During late December and through winter, the bark – green when young, grey later – is often gnawed by squirrels.

For woodworkers, holly wood is very hard and has an especially fine texture. It is very white, almost ivory-like, and is easily polished and can be readily stained various colours. It is suitable for cabinet-making, veneering and inlaying; and can be turned into many attractive articles. Numerous handles of metal teapots, kettles and other utensils were made of holly wood, which could be stained black to look like ebony. From the bark of the young shoots of holly, birdlime – once used by bird-catchers and gardeners – was primarily obtained by softening the bark through soaking and then grinding it into a very fine powder.

In superstition, branches of the holly tree will defend a house from lightning and any evil. In folklore the holly tree is the symbol of forethought, and the holly berry is the symbol of greeting.

IRISH YEW
Taxus baccata var. *fastigiata*

Very slow growing, hardy and durable, the yew is one of our most interesting trees, found as gnarled and twisted evergreens in churchyards and graveyards, lake islands, cliffs, and rocky places in the north and west of the country. The yew has, however, been planted throughout Ireland for hundreds of years and the native tree is well-known in placenames: the Irish word for 'yew', *iubhar*, pronounced 'yure', features in names such as Terenure, which means the 'land of the yew'; Ballynure – the 'town of the yew'; Newry – originally Iubhair Cinn Tragh – the 'yew tree at the head of the strand'; and so on. Near Oughterard in Galway, Aughnaure – 'field of the yew trees' – still had one of its old trees in 1984.

Why so many church grounds host the yew is not really known. According to tradition, a number of the trees, or their progeny, had churches built around them. One tradition explains that yews often marked the sacred places of the ancient Celtic tribes, and built on such sites, the early Christian churches were more readily accepted by the pagan natives who were being converted to Christianity. Another tradition tells that yew trees sheltered the first Christian missionaries and, thereafter, the trees were planted about churches to symbolise faith and immortality – many churchyards have only two yews. The yew was also the source of the fronds of 'palm' brought into the church on Palm Sunday. Whatever the reason for the tree being so closely associated with Christianity, the Irish yew is also known as the churchyard yew.

In Ireland and Britain two forms of yew are usually found: *Taxus baccata*, the common yew, also called the English yew; and the Irish yew – *Taxus baccata* var. *fastigiata* – which is a variety of the common yew, and all plants of this form derive from one survivor of two found on a hillside in County Fermanagh before 1780. On the common yew the leaves appear flat; on the Irish yew the leaves appear curved. Also, while the branches of the common yew spread almost horizontally from the trunk and give the tree a somewhat triangular outline, the branches of the Irish yew are more erect and the tree appears round and compact. As these differences are insignificant and as the leaves and branches and other features of the two trees are almost identical in every other way, I prefer to simplify the matter by generally speaking of both of them as the yew.

Because the ringed heartwood of the older yew rots away, the real age of a tree is impossible to know. Seldom growing taller than twenty metres, old trees are recognised by the nature and circumference of the trunk. When comparatively young, the tree forms an upright pyramidal or rounded shape, keeping this outline until it becomes very old. Noticeably, a very old tree appears quite flat-headed and not very tall compared to the girth of its trunk, which is a very gnarled and knotty structure, covered with reddish bark that flakes easily. The trunks of very old trees are massive. According to W.S. Coleman, author of *Our Woodlands, Heaths and Hedges*

Irish yew

RICHARD T. MILLS

(1859), in Tisbury churchyard, Dorset, a yew had a trunk nearly eleven metres in circumference, and capable of housing several adult people, its hollow interior was entered by a rustic gate. Also, there was a yew in Perthshire which had a shell of a trunk with a circumference measuring seventeen metres before it caved in.

With its lovely foliage, flowers and fruit, the yew is a handsome tree, much abused by topiary artists who are likely to leave a young tree the shape of a duck, or similar. Some 2–3 cm long, the needle leaves are closely and spirally arranged around the stem. Looked at closely, the needles are uniformly narrow and are a dark shiny green above, lighter below. The tiny flowers are found in the leaf axils, immediately above the attachment of leaf and stem. Almost always borne on separate trees from mid-March through April, the female flowers are pale green; the male flowers are greenish-yellow. In September–October the ripe fruit are noticeable as berry-like female cones. The green seeds develop singly from flowers, and are partially surrounded by a reddish or scarlet fleshy cup; and saplings will grow from the poisonous seeds dropped by birds.

Despite its long-standing presence, the yew is poisonous. Except for the fleshy aril, or casing, of the seed, every other tissue of the yew tree, including the bark, contains toxic chemicals. Even when the yew wilts or its branches are clipped, the leaves and stems retain properties that dangerously affect the heart and greatly upset the digestive system.

The heartwood of the yew is hard, finely grained, and its shades of rich brown and red were always excellent for the cabinet-maker and turner. In folklore the yew symbolises sadness.

COMMON JUNIPER
Juniperus communis

One of a group of evergreens of the cypress family, the common juniper is a native of Ireland, confined mostly to the north and west of the country. It prefers limy or calcium-rich soil and can be found on hillside screes, or growing on heathland and about the shoreline. It is described as local and occasional: scattered or occurring singly or widely apart in a locality. Looking at the juniper in the wild, a ground-spreader or mat-forming bushy plant, usually about 60 cm tall, it might be difficult to see it as a conifer; yet when planted in suitable soil and, without too much shade, offering it a little protection against the rigours of the cold and wind, *Juniperus communis* may grow into a handsome conical tree, some six metres in height.

Juniper berries

Still, shape and height apart, the wild prostrate plant has the bark, leaves, flowers and fruit of a true conifer.

Covered with a flaky red-brown bark, the branches produce spiky, blue-green needle leaves with a linear white band above. In whorls of three and crowded along the branches, each pointed leaf is less than 2.5 cm long. Dioecious, like the yew, the holly, sea buckthorn, and others, the juniper's male and female flowers are found on separate plants. The scaly flowers or cones appear in late spring, May into June. The small yellow male flowers have eight to ten scale-like stamens; the tiny green female flowers contain three ovules, or egg cells, surrounded by scales. After fertilisation, when the ovules become seeds, the surrounding scales swell and fuse together to form a berry-like structure, which encloses the seeds. Green at first, the fleshy swollen scales of the female berry-like fruit may take two seasons to ripen. In September, when they eventually ripen with an attractive bloom, the blue-black berries are well known for flavouring gin. Always the distinctive fragrance of this little plant can produce very pleasant aromatic wood smoke for ham and home-made cheese. And, if I were a woodworker, its beautiful colour and susceptibility to high polish would encourage me to produce works of art – very fine articles of Celtic design.

In folklore the common juniper is the symbol of protection.

SCOTS PINE
Pinus sylvestris

A splendid tall pine from the Highlands of Scotland, the Scots pine was extensively planted in this country in 1919; and since then the tree has planted itself in districts in the north and west. However, because it grows quickly when young but soon slows down, we must wait another century to see a mature planting. The truly mature and magnificent stands of native trees – thirty-six metres tall and two hundred years old – are found only in Scotland. Even there, the Black Wood of Rannock, alongside Lake Rannock in Perthshire, is one of the few relics of pine forest left for anybody to see. Nevertheless, growing alone or in clumps on Irish hills and moorlands, the Scots pine can heighten the beauty of the landscape; and the trees themselves are old enough to show us their pleasant features.

Scots pine

As the tree matures it loses its lower branches and the pyramid-shaped crown becomes rounded. On the lower trunk the bark is red-brown, rough and deeply fissured; higher up the bark is a warm red-orange. Arranged in pairs and usually twisted, the blue-green needles are 3–7 cm long. At the base of the new year's shoot, the clusters of yellow male flowers, or cones, comprise numerous scale-like stamens; at the tip of the shoot, the ovoid crimson female flowers, or cones, consist of numerous scales, each bearing two ovules. The male flowers shed their pollen in May and June, and the female cones grow to about 1 cm by the end of the first season.

New leaf buds appear during winter; and in the spring the leaves grow with the previous year's female cones resuming growth beneath the new leaves. These cones are now green and greatly enlarged, and they become brown and woody by the autumn of their second year. The following spring, the woody female cones 'pop' open and their seeds, with their membranous wings, spin to the ground. In beginning May, a three-year-old stem holds crimson female flowers at the tips of possibly three different shoots, young green cones, open woody cones, and yellow male flowers at the base of the stem.

Known as red deal, the soft wood of the Scots pine can be used for building, poles, paper, and making furniture; it is also a source of turpentine and creosote. In folklore the branch of the Scots pine is the symbol of aspiration.

THE SPRUCES

Spruce is the common name of a genus of cone-bearers in the pine family. Two species of spruce are planted in Ireland: the sitka and the Norway. The sitka spruce is a native of the west coast of North America; the Norway spruce is from the subalpine conifer woods of central and eastern Europe. All spruces have cones that hang down, and the scales remain on the cones. The foliage of the spruce is also different from other cone-bearers: most spruce needles are four-sided and are less than 2.5 cm long; and tiny, woody, peg-like projections appear to hold the needles on the twig. Spruce trees have tall, straight trunks and are pyramid-shaped. In old trees, the lower level or drooping branches sometimes brush the ground.

Spruces are usually planted as timber trees. Known as white deal, the wood has many uses. It has a clean white appearance, with distinct annual rings and numerous small hard knots, which dull cutting tools, otherwise, the wood is soft. It is also light, elastic, and resonant, and can be used as sound boards for musical instruments such as violins and pianos. Nowadays it is widely used for wood pulp in the paper-making industry, also for chipboard and medium density fibreboard. Its tall, straight nature makes it ideal for telegraph poles, and it was once used for masts, spars, and oars. Builders' planks and temporary constructions may be of spruce, and it is used for piles, packing boxes, and similar rough work. Its clean appearance makes it suitable for flooring, skirting, matchboarding, other interior joinery, and for kitchen furniture such as dressers and tables. Resin, tannin, and turpentine are products of spruce bark.

Sitka spruce

SITKA SPRUCE
Picea sitchensis

The sitka spruce is easily found and recognised. Wander through any teenage or young adult conifer planting today, and you will find the sitka. It is the most frequently planted spruce in Ireland, and it thrives in wet upland areas and on poor soils. It is fast growing and yields very good wood. From any distance, the tree is tall, growing to forty-six metres, and conical, with long heavy lower branches. Touching the tree, the greyish-brown bark is likely to peel off in thin plates; and dark green above and blue-green below, the narrow needles have surprisingly sharp points, and often display linear parallel white bands.

Early in the year, on new shoots, the cone-shaped male flowers are pale yellow, and the female flowers, or cones, are an attractive greenish-red. The mature cone is unmistakable: light brown with many crinkly, papery, loosely attached, blunt-tipped scales; and stripped cones on the ground during late autumn and winter may indicate the arrival of a flock of crossbills – those marvellous stocky finches, irregular autumn and winter visitors which sometimes come from coniferous places in mainland Europe and rob the sitka spruce.

Without any doubt, this spruce is a superior and handsome survivor; yet

RICHARD T. MILLS

the best and most successful specimens can be stripped of success by quite lowly parasitic creatures. In dry summers, when attacked by the spruce aphid, the hard-working and usually successful sitka spruce will suffer a severe loss of foliage.

NORWAY SPRUCE
Picea abies
There are several interesting tales about the origin of the Christmas tree – here, I tell my favourite.

This story tells how the first Christmas tree was miraculously shown to an English missionary called Winfred, later named Saint Boniface. One day, about 1,200 years ago, as he was walking through northern Germany, good Winfred came across heathens at a great oak tree – a 'blood tree' – who were preparing to sacrifice the little Prince Asulf to Thor. Winfred stopped the sacrifice and cut down the oak, and as it fell a young fir tree appeared. And Winfred told the heathens that the fir was the tree of life, representing Christ. That fir was the very first Christmas tree. And the people of Germany were probably the first to use the Christmas tree as we know it today; for in 1884 the tree and its custom were brought to Britain by Prince Albert. But the tree Albert popularised was not a fir – it was the Norway spruce.

Less frequently found, compared to the sitka, the Norway spruce earns closer attention. It can grow to a height of forty metres, and from any distance it looks pyramid-shaped, but the higher branches noticeably lift and the lower branches droop. Closer, the bark is warmly red and scaly, and the short leaves are light green and prickly, but not as sharply pointed as the leaves of the sitka. Four-sided and needle-like, the leaves are spirally arranged on the twig. Every three or four years, in May, on the tips of new shoots, the female flowers appear pink and erect. From late May into June the golden yellow male flowers appear. The ripe cone hangs downwards in autumn and releases its seeds in the spring. With scales tightly packed, the shape of a cigar, and rounded at the end, the cone is easily distinguished from the crinkly cone of the sitka; and the seed of the Norway spruce can delay germination for five years or more.

Susceptible to the spruce aphid, with severe loss of leaves, the Norway spruce survives and attracts the crossbill, goldcrest and all the tits. And as well as providing wood for so many uses, this conifer tree offers its arrangement of level branches as supports for bright lights, tinsels, and various decorations, when it becomes the Christmas tree.

Before the colder and damper days of winter set in I enjoy an easy walk during the week after Christmas Day. There is much to see. Out in deep water, not far from the estuary, seals bob about. Swans, many waders, and wildfowl shelter and feed about the estuary. Standing apart, the heron is there too. Into woodland, following the feeding river inland, I watch small trout darting across sand and gravel beds; and the dipper hurries upstream ahead of me. Through the woodland, the resident birds – especially the robins – accompany me to the edge of their territories; and charms of finches fidget and watch me from small sheltered meadows. Along laneways and hedgerows, and in nearby fields, immigrant thrushes ignore me and search for berries on bushes, fallen haws, and seeds below withered weeds. Magpies and crows are everywhere. To visit the spawning beds of salmon and trout in upland streams, I cross rough and

scrubby ground and see snipe and woodcock; and then – back in woodland – I look for squirrel, otter, badger, and easily find prints in the soft ground. Soon, ice and snow will harden and then break up the ground and mercifully kill old and weak wild birds and mammals. For the next few months heavy rains and gales will wash and scour every rock, tree trunk and branch, and remove every dead twig and leaf. And while the ice and snow melt and flow with the rain in spate to refresh the rivers and streams, mighty tides will clean the shorelines. Meanwhile, with the close of December, the days start lengthening again.

Winter landscape
RICHARD T. MILLS

BIBLIOGRAPHY

ALLEN, GWEN and JOAN DENSLOW. *Freshwater Animals,* The Clue Books Series, Oxford University Press, 1979

ARDLEY, NEIL. *Birds: A Kingfisher Guide,* London, Ward Lock, 1978

BAGENAL, T.B. *The Observer's Book of Sea Fishes,* London, Frederick Warne, 1974

BARNES, R. *The Natural History of Britain and Northern Europe: Coasts and Estuaries,* London, Book Club Associates, 1982

BOATMAN, D. *The Natural History of Britain and Northern Europe: Fields and Lowlands,* London, Book Club Associates, 1982

Britain's Wildlife, Plants and Flowers, London, Reader's Digest Association, 1987

BROWN, ROBERT. *Strangford Lough: The Wildlife of an Irish Sea Lough,* The Institute of Irish Studies, The Queen's University of Belfast, 1990

BUXTON, D. (ed.). *The Country Companion,* London, Marshall Cavendish, 1987

CAMPBELL, ANTHONY (ed.). *Natural Health Handbook,* London, New Burlington Books, 1984

CARTER, BERNARD F. *The Floral Birthday Book,* London, Bloomsbury Books, 1990

COLEMAN, PHIL and BOB GIBBONS. *Britain's Natural Heritage,* London, Guild Publishing, 1987

COLEMAN, W.S. *Our Woodlands, Heaths, and Hedges,* London, Routledge, Warnes and Routledge, 1859

COOPER, MARION R. and ANTHONY W. JOHNSON. *Poisonous Plants in Britain and Their Effects on Animal and Man,* London, H.M.S.O., 1984

CRAWFORD, P. *The Living Isles: A Natural History of Britain and Ireland,* London, Guild Publishing, 1986

CULPEPER, NICHOLAS. *Culpeper's Complete Herbal,* London, Bloomsbury Books, 1992

D'ARCY, GORDON. *The Guide to the Birds of Ireland,* Dublin, Irish Wildlife Publications, 1981

DARLINGTON, A. *The Natural History of Britain and Northern Europe: Mountains and Moorlands,* London, Book Club Associates, 1982

DONY, J.G., S.L. JURY and F.H. PERRING. *English Names of Wild Flowers,* London, The Botanical Society of the British Isles, 1986

DOWNER, JOHN. *Supersense: Perception in the Animal World,* London, BBC Books, 1988

DURRELL, GERALD. *The Amateur Naturalist,* London, Book Club Associates, 1982

EVANS, G. *The Observer's Book of Birds' Eggs,* London, Frederick Warne, 1972

GENDERS, ROY. *Natural Beauty: The Practical Guide to Wildlife Cosmetics,* London, Promotional Reprint Company, 1992

GOODERS, J. *The Complete Birdwatcher's Guide,* London, Kingfisher Books, 1988

GOUGH, H. *Coarse Fishing in Ireland,* London, Unwin Hyman, 1989

HAAS, HANS. *The Young Specialist Looks at Fungi,* London, Burke Publishing, 1969

HIGGINS, LIONEL and BRIAN HARGREAVES. *The Butterflies of Britain and Europe*, London, Collins, 1983

HOEHER, SIEGFRIED. *Birds' Eggs and Nesting Habitats,* translated and adapted by Winwood Reade, London, Blandford Press, 1972

JOYCE, P.W. *Irish Place Names,* Belfast, Appletree Press, 1984

KEITH, STUART and JOHN GOODERS. *Collins Bird Guide,* London, Collins, 1980

LORENZ, KONRAD Z. *King Solomon's Ring,* London, Methuen, 1967

McGILLOWAY, OLLY. *Along the Faughanside,* Derry, Dubh Regles Books, 1986

McGILLOWAY, OLLY. *Greyhood: The Year of the Mink,* Belfast, Blackstaff Press, 1988

MEARS, RAYMOND. *The Complete Outdoor Handbook,* London, Rider Books, 1992

MENZIES, W.J.M. *The Salmon: Its Life Story,* Edinburgh, William Blackwood, 1931

MITCHELL, FRANK. *The Irish Landscape,* London, Collins, 1976

O'FARRELL, PADRAIC. *Superstitions of the Irish Country People,* Cork, Mercier Press, 1989

O'GORMAN, F. (ed.). *The Irish Wildlife Book,* Dublin, John Coughlan in co-operation with the Irish Wildlife Federation, An Taisce, and the Irish Wildbird Conservancy, 1980

ORR, R. *Mammals of Britain and Europe,* London, Pelham Books, 1983

PERKINS, B. *Trees,* London, Century Publishing, 1984

PERRY, K.W. *The Irish Dipper,* published by Ken Perry, 1986

PRICHARD, MICHAEL (ed.). *Collins New Encyclopedia of Fishing in Britain and Ireland,* London, Collins, 1990

ROBINSON, E. and G. SUMMERFIELD (eds). *Clare,* Oxford University Press, 1966

SAUNDERS, DAVID. *RSPB Guide to British Birds,* London, Hamlyn, 1982

SBORDONI, V. and S. FORESTIERO. *The World of Butterflies,* London, Guild Publishing, 1985

SCOTT, BOB. *The Atlas of British Birdlife,* London, Guild Publishing, 1987

SOPER, TONY. *The National Trust Guide to the Coast,* London, Guild Publishing, 1984

STREETER, D. and I. GARRARD. *The Wild Flowers of the British Isles,* London, Macmillan, 1983

SUTTERBY, R. and M. GREENHALGH. *The Wild Trout,* London, George Philip, 1989

THOMAS, ERIC and JOHN T. WHITE. *Hedgerow,* London, Dorling Kindersley, 1982

WEBB, D.A. *An Irish Flora,* Dundalk, Dundalgan Press, 1967

WHITTON, B. *The Natural History of Britain and Northern Europe: Rivers, Lakes and Marshes,* London, Book Club Associates, 1982

WILDE, LADY. *Ancient Cures, Charms, and Usages of Ireland,* London, Ward and Downey, 1890

WOOD, NIGEL. *Birds in Your Garden,* London, Hamlyn, 1985

WRANGLES, ALAN (ed.). *Salmon and Sea Trout Fishing,* London, Davis-Poynter, 1979

YOUNG, G. *The Sunday Times Countryside Companion,* London, Guild Publishing, 1985

INDEX

INDEX

237

Fannia canicularis, 148
Faughan, River, 33
Felis catus, 30–2
ferox, 202
field grasshopper, 186
fieldfare, 15
finches, 11–12, 70–1
Fistulina hepatica, 218
flies, 147–9, 165–7
flounder, 92
fluke, 92
fly agaric, 215
Forficula auricularia, 128
four-spotted orb spider, 184
fox, 21–2
Foyle, River, 1
fraochan, 79–80
Fraxinus excelsior, 109–11
Fringilla coelebs, 11–12, 71
frog, 41
froghopper, 165
fulmar, 101–2
Fulmarus glacialis, 101–2
fungi, 212–18

Galanthus nivalis, 26
Galium verum, 152–4
Gallinago gallinago, 75
Gallinula chloropus, 57
gannet, 102
garden spider, 183
garden worm, 167
Gasterosteus aculeatus, 141–2
gean, 82
geese, 18–19
Geometra papilionara, 152
Geranium robertianum, 108
Geum urbanum, 153–4
gillaroo, 201–2
goat, feral, 20–1
godwit, bar-tailed, 19
goldcrest, 73
goldfinch, 119
gorse, 39
Gough, Hugh, 50
grasshoppers, 185–7
great black-backed gull, 100
great reed mace, 133
great tit, 10, 70
grebe, little, 54–5
green plover, 54
green worm, 168
greenbottle, 166–7
greenfinch, 11, 71
greenfly, 104–5
grey heron, 53
grey seal, 209–11
grey squirrel, 179–80
grey wagtail, 73–4
greylag goose, 18
ground beetle, 127
grouse, red, 158–9
gull
  black-headed, 101
  common, 99
  great black-backed, 100
  herring, 100
  lesser black-backed, 100

Haematopota pluvialis, 166
Haematopus ostralegus, 19, 102–3
Halichoerus grypus, 209–11
hare, 45–6
harebell, 78
Harpalus rufipes, 127
hawthorn, 108–9
hazel, common, 170–1
Hedera helix, 205
hedgehog, 47–9
heliotrope, winter, 38
hen harrier, 160–1

herb Robert, 108
heron, grey, 53
herring gull, 100
Hippophae rhamnoides, 203–4
Hirundo rustica, 96–7
holly, 226
honey fungus, 216
honeysuckle, 134–5
hooded crow, 53
horse chestnut, 188–9
house martin, 97
house mouse, 91–2
house sparrow, 53–4
house spider, 184
houseflies, 147–9
hover fly, 166
Huxley, Thomas Henry, 78
Hyacinthoides non-scripta, 78
Hymenoptera, 126

Ilex aquifolium, 226
insects, 162–8
invertebrates, 167–8
Irish yew, 226–8
ivy, 205

jackdaw, 120–2
jew's ear, 217
John of Fornsete, 68
juniper, common, 228–9
Juniperus communis, 228–9

kestrel, 76
kingfisher, 74
kittiwake, 98–9
knot, 19

lady's bedstraw, 152–4
Lagopus lagopus, 158–9
Lampetra fluviatilis, 39–41
lamprey, river, 39–41
lapwing, 54
larch, 204
large emerald, 152
large marsh grasshopper, 187
large white, 125
Larix decidua, 204
Larus argentatus, 100
Larus canus, 99
Larus fuscus, 100
Larus marinus, 100
Larus ridibundus, 101
Lasiommata megera, 125
Lasius niger, 163–5
Lepidoptera, 124–6, 149–52
Lepista nuda, 215
leptospirosis, 34
Lepus capensis, 45–6
Lepus timidus, 45–6
lesser black-backed gull, 100
lesser burdock, 154
lesser celandine, 60–1
lesser trefoil, 63
Limacidae, 103–4
Limosa lapponica, 19
linnet, 71–2
Lithobius forficatus, 202
little grebe, 54–5
loach, stone, 142–3
long-eared owl, 55
long-tailed field mouse, 90–1
long-tailed tit, 55–6
Lonicera periclymenum, 134–5
Lorenz, Konrad, 121
Lotus corniculatus, 129
Lucilia caesar, 166–7
lugworm, 139
Lumbricus terrestris, 167
Lutra lutra, 43–5

Macrosiphum rosae, 104–5
magpie, 36–7, 56

mallard, 56–7
Malus sylvestris, 113
Martes martes, 87–9
martin
  house, 97
  sand, 97–8
meadow buttercup, 107
meadow grasshopper, 186
meadow pipit, 74
medick, black, 63
Meles meles, 27–30
Melolontha melolontha, 128
Menyanthes trifoliata, 130–1
merlin, 123–4
mesh-web spider, 184
millipede, common, 203
mink, feral, 65–7
minnow, 142
mistle thrush, 15–16, 57
money spider, 184
moorhen, 57
Morris, Desmond, 12, 182
Morris, William, 181
Motacilla cinerea, 73–4
moths, 149–51
mottled grasshopper, 187
mouse
  house, 91–2
  wood, 90–1
mullet, 118–19
Mus musculus, 91–2
Musca domestica, 148
Mustela erminea, 34–5
Mustela vison, 65–7
mute swan, 17, 146–7
Myrica gale, 79
Myrmeleotettix masculatus, 187
myxomatosis, 24

Necrophorus humator, 128
Necrophorus vespillo, 128
nettle, stinging, 135
nightshade, woody, 130
Noemacheilus barbatulus, 142–3
Norway spruce, 231
Numenius arquata, 19, 103

oak, 168–70
Oenanthe oenanthe, 75–6
O'Farrell, Padraic, 14
Oiceoptoma thoracicum, 128
Omocestus viridulus, 186
Oniscus asellus, 203
orange-tip, 125
Oryctolagus cuniculus, 22–4
otter, 43–5
owl
  barn, 51
  long-eared, 55
oystercatcher, 19, 102–3

pale-bellied brent goose, 19
Parus ater, 10–11, 70
Parus caeruleus, 10, 70
Parus major, 10, 70
Passer domesticus, 53–4
Paxillus involutus, 216–17
peewit, 54
peregrine, 57–8
Petasites fragrans, 38
Phalacrocorax aristotelis, 58
Phalacrocorax carbo, 37–8, 52
Phallus impudicus, 216
Phasanius colchicus, 69–70
pheasant, 69–70
Philaenus spumarius, 165
Phoca vitulina, 211–12
Pholcus phalangioides, 184
Pholiota squarrosa, 214
Phoxinus phoxinus, 142
Pica pica, 36–7, 56